Thoughts and Memoirs on God and Man's Relationship to Humanity

Spoken by Guy P. Darden, Sr.

God and Man's Relationship to Humanity©
By Guy P. Darden, Sr.

All rights reserved. No part of this publication may be reproduced, stored in a retrieval system, or transmitted in any form or by any means – for example, electronic, photocopy, recording – without prior written permission of the publisher. The only exception is brief quotations in printed reviews.

Copyright 2007 by Guy P. Darden, Sr.

GMRH Publishing
POBox 554
Painesville, OH 44077

ISBN   978-0-6151-4539-6

To
Rising Star Church and its congregation

    The congregation of Rising Star Church is the essence of what this book is about. No one ever has to ask for money, they give it freely because they are a giving congregation. They are dedicated to helping their fellow man. If you need help, they will be there for you.

Rising Star Church
502 Fairlawn Avenue
Painesville, OH 44077

PREFACE

It's about the hopes and dreams of an unplanned life and how it can take you into a fantasy of pretending. It can give you all of the bubble-busting hopes that you might want. Maybe you haven't given yourself the foundation, the love plans that one should have in their lives. It may not be the dreams that you need in your life. I believe that we all have dreams of assault. We need to examine and see if these are the dreams that we need to have in our life or are they something that we just want. I think we need to have priorities; well examined plans. I believe that when we do things in our lives that we feel are going to raise us up to a level of success, and then we need to find out if that is going to help anyone other than ourselves because if it isn't, it may not put us on the level that we need to be on.

We need to know that when we live in a society that no one is successful but me. I'm the only one that's successful. You're not going to have the success that you might think that you would have. You need to be surrounded with the things that all of us need, all of the people in the area which you in. They need to be successful. They need to be thriving on something that they can grow on. If you are living in a society that is not moving, you're not going to move very far. If we don't build up our surrounding, it won't give us the support we need. If you are living in a community and that community is dying and it is fading away, you are either going to have to move out of that community or you are going to have to try to help raise it up. Search for the things that you need in that community and that area and try to produce it. Don't just produce it by yourself but teach those that are in your reach about the things that you are trying to do and the things that we need to do. You need to have a research counsel that can research our communities and our people in our communities and surrounding areas. We need to examine our locations spiritually, mentally, and physically.

This is what this book is about. It is about trying to think about the things that we need to do, not always what we want to do. It is about searching for ideas. It's about believing in Godly principles. It is about searching out people that you believe in, and by their records, that have wisdom and knowledge that they want to share with someone. To lift you up in front of the people in a way that can be successful more than just money but allows our physical beings to work in our society and be example for our society and our nation. We want to do things in our nation that will be an example to other nations. We want to live a life in front of our children that might inspire them to do those things that are positive.

This book is about hopes and dreams for humanity. It is about looking for those things that can prop us up and keep us from falling or failing. It allows us to find weapons against those things that pull us down. It helps us look for those instruments that can fight the things that push us away from God's principles. It is about family unity, finding those members in your family that you haven't seen in a long time, and bringing family love before you and making it the foundation for love. It is about doing a lot of things that I was too ignorant to do. It's about getting an education. When I say getting an education, I truly mean getting an education and not just learning about things but learning how to do things with Godly principles. This book is about pity parties and being a party pooper to break up a lot of welfare victims; and I do mean victims. When you get hooked on things that the state and government hand out to you, they sometimes defeat you and don't allow you to fight for the principles that you truly believe in.

Yes, this book is about most of the things that happen on this earth. It is asking questions that will make you think. It is about challenging your conscience and motivating your ideas and thoughts that will uplift you into a love passion that will make you love your neighbors and love your family in a Christian and Godly way. Yes, this book is about love. It is about the hopes and dreams of all of us. This book is not about Guy Darden but it is about the things that he would like to be. It is about senior citizens that do not believe that they have a value. It is about every imaginable thing that love can produce and tough, tough questions.

I was born outside of Newport News, Virginia, way back in the countryside on a farm. I loved that farm and loved the people on it. But some of my people did not know the essence of love and when you don't know the essence of love you sometimes stumble. Sometimes a fall that you might have today can dig a valley for someone else tomorrow. May God bless you in a mighty way. May your hopes and dreams be successful.

TABLE OF CONTENTS

PREFACE 4
IT IS ABOUT ME AND YOU 11
    THE WEAK AND THE STRONG *15*
GOD AND MAN'S RELATIONSHIP TO HUMANITY 17
THIS WORLD AND THIS NATION HAVE BEEN MY BOOK 25
    A FUTURE TO BELIEVE IN *29*
GODS RULES & REGULATIONS 31
    LIFE *34*
TRADE SCHOOL – MONEY - POWER 35
SELF-DEVALUATION 41
    THE PLAYING FIELD OF LIFE *48*
DO WE KNOW WHO WE ARE? 49
    A WORD FROM PEGGY *53*
WHY HAVE WE STOPPED KNEELING IN THE PRAYER HOUSE 55
IT IS A LIFE 59
    PROFILE OF A SPECIAL CHILD *63*
FOLLOWING ORDERS FROM GRANDPA GEORGE 65
    TRULY HAPPY *71*
GO ALONG TO GET ALONG 73
    HAPPINESS *78*
FARMING 79
PINE TREES 93
HAVE WE DISCOVERED OURSELVES? 95
    NOT ENOUGH TIME *99*
MORE ABOUT THE BOOK 101
WHO AM I? 105
HUMANITY 111
    REFLECTIONS *115*
WEAKNESS 118
GOING BACK TO THAT OLD HOUSE 119
EVALUATION OF A PEOPLE 123
    LIVE FOR GOD *130*
BLAME MAMA 133
I BELIEVE 135
WHO CONTRIBUTED TO ME? 139
WHAT BENEFITS US? 141
GROWING UP 147
    INCREASING OUR CAPACITY FOR GENUINE COMMUNITY *154*
INSIGNIFICANT 157
SEEDS 163
    A CORRECTIONS STORY *164*
GOING BACK TO THAT OLD HOUSE 167

TECHNOLOGY	177
HOW DO WE GET THE JOB DONE?	*181*
GOOD AND BAD	185
THE POWER OF SIN	*188*
SAW SOMETHING I DIDN'T LIKE	191
LEADERSHIP THROUGH FOLLOWING WELL	*197*
IF CHRIST WERE ON EARTH TODAY	201
FOUNDATION	213
WHY WE ARE WEAK?	*219*
FOUNDATION FOR LIFE'S JOURNEY	221
LOVE ONE ANOTHER AS I HAVE LOVED YOU	*231*
MANEUVERS	233
OUR MISSION - Pastor, Elder Larry D. Barclay, Sr.	*240*
LIFESTYLE	243
THE CHRISTIAN HOME	*247*
LIVING AND DYING	251
EDUCATION	*262*
LOVE LIFE	269
MAN'S ESCAPE CLAUSE	281
THE UNITY OF THREE BROTHERS AND SISTERS: Guy, Claude, and Mary	289
INTUITION	*291*
THE BUMPER OF DESTRUCTION	295
GOD IS NOT COMPLICATE	297
LOVE IS AN ANCHOR, THE REVELATION OF HOPE	303
REPENT	305
WHAT IT ALL MEANS TO ME	*308*
SET AN EXAMPLE	311
REPAIR SHOP	313
A FEW MORE THOUGHTS ABOUT…	317
VOLUNTEERS	*317*
MEDICAL COMMUNITY WORKERS	*317*
MY SIS - VERA MITCHELL	*319*
THE SHAW'S	*321*
PHOTOGRAPHS	324
MEN & WOMEN UNITED FOR HUMANITY	327
TAILORING	329

Holy Father, I come before You on this day asking You to give me something to say what will inspire someone. Holy Father, I ask You to remove me from the scene and you be my spokesman. Dear Heavenly Father, amplify your meaning and inspiration. Give me the things to say, Lord, that will make men and women depersonalize themselves and become neutral and bring forth the things that You need people to hear and do. Father, take away all selfishness and personal feelings that keep us from lifting ourselves up to You. Lord, let us amplify those people who are feeling so insignificant. Let's have admiration for You and let's be able to amplify the holiness that You generate. Let it be present with the spirit of God rather than with the spirit of man. Dear Lord, if we are amplified and glorified, let it be the inspiration of You and Your will. Father, this day is glorified because of You. It is an inspiration to man because of You. Let us be a spokesman under the inspiration of You. Almighty God let our platform be built upon You and the holiness that You give us. We ask this in Your name, Father. Amen.

"You can change the stage of hopes and dreams to sadness and misery or you can take sadness and misery and give it life and give it hope. You can take people and show them that you are willing to sacrifice for them, willing to share their lives, willing to share your experience and show them by the way you live your life that you have a giving and loving spirit, and you do this by your actions through your belief and faith in God Almighty. God gives you that strength. He'll light up your heart and give you the things that are important to your survival."

IT IS ABOUT ME AND YOU

I'm going to tell you a little bit about what this book is about. First of all, it's about me and you, it's about humanity, it's about the world and the way I see it today. It's about the things that we don't seem to care about anymore. It's about our survival. It's about the value that you and I as ordinary citizens put in our lives. It's about the way we see life today and the way we saw it yesterday.

I believe that we've lost the part of society that we really don't want to know about. I believe very strongly that the people today, some of our leaders, are trying to erase society's history. They're trying to take the part of history that the young people of today don't know about and are trying to erase it. We don't want the young society today to know about what happened yesterday. The way we began this nation - the way we came by this nation. What happened? How did we get to be Americans? We go around talking about we're the greatest nation on earth. We go around bragging about how great and wonderful we are, and how much freedom we have in America and how democratic it is.

I was born in 1924. I remember when I was born I could not go to any white place in Virginia and sit down at a table beside any other white man and have a meal. It didn't make any difference how hungry I was; that was not allowed. It was against the law in any place in the South I know. I don't know about New York. I remember going to New York in some of the outlying places in the country and finding bars and places that would not serve me or they would serve me and give me - I'd ask for one brand and they'd give me another and then stare me down that I asked for something else in order to antagonize me. But that's small things, very small. I remember that you could get your head blown off for just speaking to a white lady. I remember when you were not allowed to go in a store and try on a hat, go in a store and try on a pair of shoes. I remember that certain stores would not sell you certain merchandise. I remember when you couldn't buy a Coca Cola. I remember when they called RC "nigger beer" because so many black people liked RC cola. You could buy that, but they wouldn't sell you a Coca Cola, that was a white man's drink.

Some of the greatest people I knew where white. Some of the greatest people that did the most for us in the South were individual white people. Sometimes they had to sneak it to us when they would come to our homes and bring food and were very kind to us. They would bring us food but they didn't want anyone else to know about it. I remember that, but that was something very rare. I remember when you could not go into a white church. You would have to go into the basement or stand outside and they'd put a speaker out there. That hasn't been so long ago. That was even in the 60's; that's not very long. How can you justify enslaving a nation of people; the black people, for hundreds of years?

We have problems in this nation. There's nothing that I didn't expect to happen. I don't believe that we or a nation or anyone else can continue to do wrong things and not pay a penalty for it before you leave this earth. I believe the just with the unjust will suffer. You can prove that by the way drugs have taken over our cities - all over this nation. And our government allows a lot of it to be imported in here. I, as a black man, have seen communities torn down by our people. I have seen black people move in a community that was beautiful and wonderful when they came in and they turned it into a skid row. I've seen that happen over and over again. I see our children today condemning our race because they don't want to get their hands dirty. I find that black people are doing it far more than white people are doing it. The next thing I find is that the youth of today, black and white have not had the proper foundation. And some of us, our city ordinances and laws, government and state ordinances and laws are the cause of it. We punish the unjust and the just.

We haven't sat down as a nation of people and come face to face throughout this nation and talked to each other to try to have some type of consensus about what's going on. When you tell me it's free speech for me to call a white man a 'honky' or a 'cracker' or a 'peckerwood', when a black man can talk like that to a white person, or a white person can call a black person a 'nigger' or a 'darkie' or all kinds of names and you tell me it's free speech. All the swearing and cursing and all the bungled scenery on TV and on radio and you tell me that's free speech. One man's morals may be one thing and another man's morals may be another. That is absolutely true, but it doesn't make it right. These and other things are what I'm talking about.

I'm talking about how the farmer's land has been taken away from him and how we are torn apart as a people. Not as a race of people but as a people. No race should stand out over another. No man should stand out to dominate and push other people down. But there should be laws to protect this nation and its people, protect our land and especially the soil, our timberland, that's being destroyed throughout the nation. Our farmlands are being destroyed and condemned one by one so the rich can come in and the poor can go out and be at the mercy of a few rich people. How can we can sit in our communities and allow the drug lords and gangsters to take over our community, and we keep running and running and running? And our ministers and our churches throughout the nation have become mute and they don't give us the kind of teaching and training that we need. We don't put ourselves on the line. We're not bold as speakers of the protection of the people, especially our children. That's what I'm talking about.

I'm speaking about who we are and where we are and what makes us live and what makes us die and what makes us grow. I'm talking about our value system as a people, as a nation, as a youth, and as an elderly people. I'm talking about us as a group of city, government, state, and county officials. We're talking about "we". All of us have a job to do. We have to be activated in a way that will mean something to everybody, that will have a consensus that can work with each one of us so that no group of people can dominate and misuse and abuse another group. I'm talking about masters over the weak, and we're not talking about weak people using their weakness for crutches. We're talking about people that care about each other, that have sensitivity. That's what the book is about.

The next subject that I will speak about I'm guiltier. I'm extremely guilty. We're talking about families being together and building a foundation for our offspring. That has been the responsibility of man ever since the beginning of mankind and I've let them down on all counts. We're talking about men and women, and I don't put the emphasis just on married families. I think marriages should be the most important thing in our land when it comes to families. But that happens to not be the fact. Then I don't see where a single person that has a family should have any less responsibility than any married person. You created a family so you have the same obligation. It doesn't make any difference. If you adopted a child there is no difference. It's the same responsibility. And to not put strong emphasis on that would be a terrible, terrible mistake. May God bless you; I would like you to be a critic and a reader. I would like for you to be kind enough. I ask for that kindness, please, and to forgive me for my errors and mistakes. Thank you.

THE WEAK AND THE STRONG

Why would a man with eleven years of higher education, an annual income greater than one hundred thousand dollars and the respect of his peers and family feel inferior?

My strongest childhood memories are those of rejection and inferiority, mostly from activities common to most school children.

Every sunny school day from my earliest years of elementary school, the boys in my class would retire to the back lot of the playground during recess. There, the biggest and strongest boys would choose up sides for softball, touch football or whatever. Being the youngest and one of the smallest boys, I would always be chosen last or next to last.

Every day, I would go through the anxiety and gut wrenching anticipation of this ritual. After over a decade of this, how could one ever expect to feel worthy or good enough when, every day, you are told by the actions of others, that you're an inferior person and not good enough for them.

This continued into high school where through peer pressure and the insistence of my athletic older brother, I was more or less forced to try out for the football team. I weighed less than one hundred twenty pounds. There was only one other boy my size so we kind of bonded.

Our football uniforms hung from us like sacks and the shoulder and hip pads looked ridiculous. When we ran, everything just rattled around on our bodies. During blocking and tackling drills, I would wait in line for my turn and try to determine which of the big guys in the opposite line I would have to confront. Usually, upon contact, my helmet would go askew and I would feel pain somewhere in my skinny body.

The games were the worst. I would get dressed for the games, knowing that I was never going into the game unless the outcome of the game was decided. Then, I might go in for a couple of plays but, most games; I just sat on the bench.

My parents were always there though. It would have been better if no one from my family had been there because I always thought that they should have been ashamed of me for not being good enough to play.

I remember that when I was a senior, the coach let me start one game. I was torn between pride and shame because I felt that he had done it out of pity for me.

I don't know what life lesson these things serve but, I do know, that I'm not the only one who has been damaged by this system that judges kids by their physical prowess and rewards the strong.

Several times a week, I see in my office arrogant kids who are local sports stars and have been taught at an early age that their athletic prowess has placed them on a higher plane.

They treat not only me but their own parents as mere mortals who have been placed on this planet to worship them. Unfortunately, many of these parents allow their children to feel that they have every right to snarl at the doctor and themselves with no consequences. Heaven help the doctor or therapist who might suggest that the kid needs to lose weight or take a couple of weeks off. They immediately demand that they be referred to a real sports medicine doctor at the Cleveland Clinic. One who takes care of the Cleveland Indians or Browns?

This usually delights me because I know that these physicians are going to read the parents the riot act and give them a dose of reality by not only agreeing with me but by insisting on even more draconian measures. The parents will usually come back to me well chastened and with a more compliant attitude about junior.

Unfortunately, even with the recent anabolic steroid revelations, I see no end in sight for this phenomenon.

Kids are still going to be harmed by their peers, their parents and their coaches. Small kids are still going to be humiliated about their size. Harm is still being done to children who are obese and unathletic. The non-beautiful and the non-athletic will be made to feel inferior at an early age.

I plea that those who read this will seek out a homely or obese or skinny kid and say something uplifting to him. Don't let him go on thinking that he is inferior.

By Gary L Stabler

Dr. Gary Stabler reminds me of Dr. Harris in Franklin, Virginia. He was a cousin of mine. Sometimes you went to his office but he would also come to your house. If you were sick, he wouldn't leave until he saw some change in your medical condition. You may not have had any money, but he would accept your bushel of wheat. He had chemical knowledge. Sometimes he'd mix you up a special tonic. He felt it's not the doctor that heals you—it's the medicine and that patience, love, and care can lift a person up when they're depressed or down.

This doctor I know in middle Ohio is that old-time, caring, loving doctor. He never turns anybody down over payments. He looks at hearts, not just bodies. He puts himself in your position. He has had some hard times and some good times and he doesn't look down on anybody. He's willing to put his arm around you.

Dr. Stabler is an ideal doctor. A lot of hospitals don't want to embrace him because they feel he gives too much love. They are jealous because their pricked consciences tell them they should be doing more. I find Dr. Stabler's whole staff to be caring. Each nurse has Godly patience.

By Guy P. Darden, Sr.

GOD AND MAN'S RELATIONSHIP TO HUMANITY

When you reach a ripe old age and you feel like you've paid your dues and then a phrase like God and Man's Relationship to Humanity attacks you personally. It attacks your integrity. It attacks your spirituality, your religious belief, your vow and contract that you have with God Almighty, Jesus Christ. You signed your name at the foot of the cross that you would accept His word and would do the things that he asked you to do.

This thing messed with me. It tumbled in my mind. It was telling me things that I knew about all of the sudden that I would like to ignore. But I really know in my heart, in my inner being, that I'm not just responsible for myself. I'm responsible for my family. I'm responsible for my neighbor. This thing works together for the good of all and I'm being challenged by it.

I said to myself that I really do understand this somewhat. I do believe that I will be held accountable if I don't do the very best I can do with this thing. I need to talk about it. I need to talk about inside of me; my heart needs to speak to me. I need to examine myself. I need to question me. I need to know my self-value, my self-worth. What goes on inside of me that I don't know about? What kind of spirit moves in me that touches other people? How can I live my life in a way that has value to others? What's going on in me that troubles me about my nation, about my community, about my home? What is it that I'm not doing that could make a difference? What could I say and how can I live my life in a way that people would want to know anything that I know? What could I say that would shake up the world, shake up people, and make people understand that I have a Godly love for the people around me?

Everybody wants to say something spectacular, say something that's exciting, or do something that would shake up the world. I just want to say something that will make you think. I want to say something that would make a person examine someone in my class status. I want that person to say that if this person who never went to school, never learned to read and write, if they know what I think they know, what it sounds like they're talking about, why haven't I examined this?

Ladies and gentlemen, sisters and brothers, people of this nation, I want to tell you something. What I'm talking about is as old as life itself. You know, what we do on this earth is not just our business alone. Everything we do touches the life of somebody. What we say and do does make a difference. Love is the greatest resource we have. The funny thing about it is that it's available to us all. I believe the problem is that we either don't know what love is or we know what love is and don't know how to use it. It seems to me that we have a problem with distributing love, and even receiving it. It seems to me that Christ explained love thoroughly to those of us who are Christian men and women.

I sometimes think that some of you have made the mistake that I made. This biggest mistake I have ever made and the one that I made that I regret more than any other mistake I made, including the sins that I have committed; this mistake has been a tragic error in my life. That is to have not learned how to read and write, or to not be the best that I could be in every area that I have something to do with. I was very angry with my people; with my family for many years.

I was able to give up the anger and assume responsibility for myself. I realized that I had an opportunity. There was a window then that I could do anything that I wanted to do with my life. It doesn't make me forget or excuse the mistakes that were made in the building of my life. In the process of developing my life; my parents had something to do with that. It was their job to prepare me for life, to prepare themselves in the best possible way so they could be the best teachers that I could possibly have. It was their job to prepare my life so I would be able to face this world with a reasonable amount of conditioning.

I think that it troubled me so much until it stifled my growth. I remember every time I would ask my parents why I couldn't go to school that year, they would always say to me – I don't remember them saying anything else – I'm sorry, but you don't have clothes to wear. I had clothes to farm. I had clothes to plow with the mule. But it seemed like their pride was more important than my education was. Oh, my God! How I wished that I could have found out what was in all those books.

I'm a tailor. God saw fit to teach me and train me to be a tailor. I'm pretty good at it. How my work looks depends on the condition of my equipment that I use and how well I keep them in condition. In other words, I have to keep my equipment in good shape in order to do a good job. That is the same way that we have to be as Christian men and women. We need to be well-honed like a well sharpened razor; you can shave really well with it. It doesn't pull hairs and it doesn't bump you, as long as it's honed well. That was a real important word years ago because people always understood. The barber always kept his razor very sharp. In other words, he keeps his tools in condition so when he is ready to work with them they are not a hazard to him. He feels a sense of security. You put a sharp razor on a person's neck or on a person's face; you have to have faith and confidence that you're not going to cut that person. The person sitting in the chair has to feel the same way that when you are shaving him, you're not going to cut him or harm him. He has to believe that your equipment is in good condition and you're in a good mental capacity in order to do the job.

That is the same way that Christian men and women have to prepare themselves and know the right words to say. Know when to say them. Know who to say them to. We have to talk to the Lord and get that wisdom from Him. From time to time, we have to go back to our pastor or maybe to our deacon; the teachers of our church, and get the knowledge and the wisdom and the assistance that we need. So that means that we need men and women in the church that are prepared to teach God's word. That means the church of whatever church he is pastor of, whatever domination it is, that he is capable and qualified to delegate people that can do some of the work that he has set aside to do.

A minister that has a good-sized flock has to have a system. He has to be secure enough in his job that he's not afraid to delegate certain jobs to certain people. He cannot be a type of person who has fears about giving other people a certain amount of power. He has to allow them to be able to demonstrate their talent. Everybody has somewhere in them something that needs to be brought out. A pastor who has the wisdom of God and the capacity to receive it is capable of teaching men and women to be leaders and teachers; to be people who can demonstrate Christ's lifestyle in their community. We need people that when they leave our building called the church, are able to saturate our community with God's word.

We have ministers in our churches today that don't care too much about teaching you about how to teach outside of the church. But our lives, the way we live our lives, the way we carry ourselves, can be a teaching pattern within itself. Just the way in which we live our lives can teach men and women how to live. We need to be taught that boldness and only Christ can teach us that through the wisdom and the knowledge that we get by listening to our minister can we have the capacity to receive these things. Some of us have more gifts than others. Some of us are easier to teach than others.

We need that basic teaching and we need to put a lot of emphasis on that because we are responsible for humanity; because we are the other arms and legs of humanity. We are those missing links that need to plug into the puzzle of humanity that keeps it thriving, keeps it rolling, and keeps the hope of man alive. We are those giving him the inspiration to walk forward and be what God needs him to be in his world. Man was put on this earth to be a leader on this earth. Man is God's little helpers. The structure that is built into our life can brace up humanity; can hold us accountable for our weak spots. The weakness that we show in our lives shows up in the lives of people that are not saved yet. We need to be very sensitive and very much aware of what we do, how we do and when we do.

Our ministers must have the trust of his flock by knowing and seeing that men and women carry God's true message. We need people that we can trust. We need to be aware of where we are at all times and who we are. We have to remember that we represent the highest power on earth. We represent the highest power and the strongest force that is known to mankind. We represent God Almighty. We represent Him in all His holiness. You see, the thing you call faith must be embedded into our spirituality. We must know that if God is leading us and God is with us, the whole world can be against us, but yet we will survive.

We need to be sensitive concerning our fellow man. We need to be sensitive concerning all men, all women and men, all of humanity, because we are part of it. We weren't put on this earth just to be nice to Christian men and women. We were put on this earth to be the "help-mate" of all men and women, regardless whether they are Christians, atheists, or whatever they are. We are God's people and we claim that right at the foot of the cross. We ask God to release that power to us. We must be worthy of that. We must be responsible for that. We must give our all.

Where we have weakness, we must seek strength. Where we have blindness, we must seek the light of God's word. That is the only thing that can shed away the darkness. The only thing that can block out the darkness and give us the light is the holiness of God's word. As I walk through this valley of sadness, trouble on every hand meets all of us. Life is a struggle. It's a lot of things that come before us that will defeat us if we don't walk with Christ. But walking with Christ doesn't make you any better than any other man. It just makes you see a light that shines beneath your feet to point out the dark places, to point out the holes and valleys that wait for us.

You know, the longer I live, the less I depend on me. The more knowledge that I get, the less I depend on me. The more wisdom I get, the less I depend on me. I depend on Jesus Christ. I depend on His word. I depend on the faith that I have through trying to live by His standards. There is only one way that I can see us surviving and that is we must realize that we need each other and that God put us here on this earth to help each other, work with each other, to pull each other up, and to point out the way for each other. He didn't put me on this earth just to work with Christian men and women.

He put me here on this earth to help mankind. Just because the gentleman down the street is a Christian doesn't mean he can't do anything wrong. Just because the man down the street is a sinner doesn't mean he can't do anything right. Just because the man across the street is an atheist doesn't mean he can't do anything right. It doesn't mean that he doesn't want his kid to get a good education. It doesn't mean that he doesn't want his kid to be free of dope. It doesn't mean that he doesn't want his child to survive in this old, wicked world. He just hasn't seen what he needs to see in order to accept Christ. But that's God's job and our job is to do what we're supposed to do as we meet him. As we survive in this wicked world, we need to let people know what we are about and who we are.

We don't lock up our people in the church on Sunday morning and try to keep them so holy that they can't go out and touch the hearts and minds and souls of men and women all over this world and all over this nation. It doesn't mean that they are supposed to be blind to the ugliness that goes on in their community. It doesn't mean that they can't see the dope addicts on the corner selling dope in front of their house. It doesn't mean that have to draw a blind eye to the guy who's breaking into the lady's house next door. It doesn't mean that you walk through this world scared and frightened of everything that is not clean and clear with Jesus Christ in their lives.

It means that you must be aware of what is going on around you. It means that you must show some assistance and that you're willing to help wherever you can help. It means sometimes putting your life on the line. It means sometimes dying. If a man doesn't have anything to live for, he may not have anything to die for. If a man doesn't have anything to die for, he may not have anything to live for. If you are living a bad and ugly life and sin is covering you, you certainly don't have anything to die for. Because all you have is the physical sight and you don't have the spiritual sight that carries you over that mountain and through the valley and over the mountain; anyway you can get over the mountain, you're over as long as God is the supervisor and the leader.

You see, too many church people are being locked up in the church. I don't want to say anything. Someone will break my legs. Someone will kill me. Someone will hurt my child. Someone will set my house on fire. These are the traps that the Devil put in front of us because when we think like that, we think as one. But when we think as humanity, we think as a nation, as a world, as a people. You can't destroy a people if they are working together for the good. No way can you destroy a people. They may kill one of us. They may destroy one of us, but it only ties the knot of relationships tighter. It binds us together as a unit that only God can break up. I can assure you if you tie together with the spirit of God, it will hold.

There is something else that I want to discuss. Maybe you think that you're too holy. Maybe I think I'm too holy to work as a team with people who haven't accepted Christ as their personal Savior, haven't accepted God as their leader. Ladies and gentlemen, all of us are not Christians, all of us are not saved and all of us are not going to Heaven.

But all of us have to live on this earth together until God decides to separate us. It doesn't matter who you are, what you say, you've got to live in this community with me. Isn't it better that we do it together as a people, organizing our hearts and mind? Don't you think you have a better chance to win people over for Christ if you live that kind of life like Christ lived and let people see Christ in you, let people see the love and kindness and the decency and the respect moving in you? Don't you think that you have a better chance to understand and get acquainted with the people who are saved? If you have a relationship with them that you have some kind of forum that you can discuss your way of living, your philosophy of life, your spirituality, and your beliefs, your faith; don't you think that you can get along better talking love rather than putting people down? Don't you think that God will bless you more and better and more often if you show the hopes of God and His hope is that you survive out of all the hazards that you go through?

THIS WORLD AND THIS NATION HAVE BEEN MY BOOK

We sometimes get education mixed up with knowledge; with knowing a lot about a lot of things. I think sometimes we underestimate ourselves. We underestimate what we have in us and what God has given us; all the mechanisms that He has given us naturally. Most of the knowledge, wisdom, and education that I think I have, has come from just observing things around me, listening, talking to friends, listening to brilliant men and women talk over the years, and seeing business men and women - intelligent and bright people in action on this earth. Some of it came from just traveling and drifting all over this nation.

This world and this country, America, have been my book. I've read people and I've tried to read myself. I want those of us that don't feel we are educated to examine what education is. I think if I'm not mistaken and what I want you to know and understand are that some of the things that I see are not just my opinion. They're known facts. Some of us have overlooked our personal and intimate intelligence, knowledge, and wisdom.

Now, not being as educated as some of you may be and I'm sure that you are you can be educated by gaining knowledge. I gained a lot of my knowledge from talking books. I gained a lot of my knowledge from radio, TV, and listening to lectures. I've had 77 years and a few months, as of now. That's a long time thinking, listening, and looking at sinners, atheists, believers, and those that didn't believe quite so much; agnostics.

If I seem ignorant it is because I am ignorant about a lot of things and I recognize that. I think when we know that we don't have the brain capacity that some of our friends have, we recognize it and are better off. I think we are much more capable of thinking for ourselves than those that have the problem and don't know about it. I would say one of the most unfortunate individuals is the one who thinks he has an abundance of knowledge and education, and he doesn't have the capacity to show it or to demonstrate it. He doesn't have the belief, energy, drive or vigor to push himself ahead to share what he has with other people.

What I think the meaning of the word education is that it means to draw out, to withdraw, and be able to manage things, and be able to process and be creative so that you can take something that might not be so much or may not be so valuable and make into something worthwhile. You know how to process knowledge. You know how to reach in yourself and pull the things out that you need; this is if you have love in you.

If you have love in you, you have God in you. To have the capacity to respect other people's opinions, to listen to other people, then I think if you are educated or get an education, that you'll observe everything in your reach. You will listen even though you may think that the person is a fool or you may think he's not too intelligent. There are very few people that I have listened to for any period of time that didn't have something that made a lot of sense. I believe that every human being that lives on this earth was put here for a special purpose.

Do you understand what I am trying to say? I'm trying to make you think about the things that you stumble over every day looking for something bigger than what you see with the naked eye. I happen to be one that believes if you search humanity enough and look at the world as a learning process, understand that you have the capacity to draw from something that it bigger than you, that if you believe in God as a lot of us say we do, than you have to know that He loves you and He cares about you. He cares about your survival. I know that in the Bible it tells you how well He takes care of the sparrow; in other words, a little bird. It tells of how well He colored and decorated this world with the flowers and things on earth. God is quite capable. As a matter of fact, I believe personally that I am a miracle that God placed on this earth. I don't know anyone else that could possible have made me other than God. Man is trying to make people this day and time. God didn't make us well enough; man is trying to do a better job and I can't figure out why on earth, with all the people on this earth; ignorant and brilliant. Stupidity I feel has taken over some of our lives and overwhelmingly we have felt like no one knows anything but those of us who are in the church. We don't feel that a person that doesn't believe in God too much; we don't feel that they have very much to offer us. We don't feel like if a person isn't a believer and he hasn't accepted God in his life or Christ as his leader and his teacher that he has no value whatsoever.

I want to tell you something. I believe if God can take a donkey and teach someone a lesson, He can take an unbeliever and teach us something. We learn something from Him.

As a matter of fact we learn their ways and the way they conduct themselves and we learn enough from God Almighty to be able to live a life in the front of Him that makes them believe that we have something very special in our lives. Those of us, who believe in God, have something to demonstrate before people other than just talking and making pretending that we are holier-than-thou or just going to church and sitting there. We have more to do on this earth outside of teaching Sunday school or preaching the sermon. God made man more valuable than that. He set forth the rules and regulations that they are supposed to follow. He didn't do it with professors, doctors, or lawyers; that's not the way He started off. Now we have decided that those of us that don't have quite as much book-learning, or we haven't graduated from high school, college, or university, that we are almost obsolete.

I can understand why you feel that way because most of us as senior citizens and poor people that don't have very much, have to work for minimum wage, and we can barely make it, we just don't feel like we are important to anybody but ourselves. So what little bit we get, we share it with our personal families, friends, and in ourselves. We can't see very much farther than that because we haven't had experience of sharing. We don't know too much about sharing. We have forgotten about the time when we had 10 and 12 people in the immediate family and they all lived in the same house. They all weren't children, some where grown people. We survived because we cared about each other. We were close enough to be sensitive to each other's needs. Nowadays, we have gotten a little pension; a little check from some city organization that assists us and we slow up on our pace of accomplishing things. Sometimes it slows up our ambitions. It makes us think we're not very valuable.

Those of us who are senior citizens that have retired, we are going to be in trouble in a very short period of time. I don't mean 10 or 15 years from now, but I mean in the next couple of years; happening right now. All our government offices all over this nation are evaluating us. They are trying to find out which one of us is valuable enough to save. I can kind of understand why they don't see very much of what we have to offer because we like to retire and talk about what we used to do and what we used to be and we don't offer very much to society anymore. We sit in our rocking chairs and wither away. We act like we don't know anything and we don't have anything and we can't do anything. No wonder this world looks down on us as a has-been. Ladies and gentlemen, we have value and we need to emphasize it and use it.

A FUTURE TO BELIEVE IN

We need something better than reform or some politician to continue the same old system of things. We need a new worldwide system to make this world a better place—if you will, a paradise for everyone.

Yes, what needs to be changed is the whole system. This is what the Bible promises. Yes, the Bible. The Kingdom of God is a heavenly government that will do much more than just reshape, remodel, reorganize, or reform human society. That government will introduce a completely new way of running man's affairs, uniting all of mankind under its rule.

This government will attend to such matters as education, work, housing, nutrition, health, and the environment.

Psalm 72: 12-14 describes prophetically what that government will do for mankind. It will deliver the poor one crying for help, also the afflicted one and whoever has no helper. From oppression and from violence he will redeem their souls. God's government will replace all governments on Earth and that kingdom government will give individual, personal guidance on how to lead a joyful, purposeful and rewarding life right here on this Earth. Yes, that government is a superior remedy for society's shortcomings. God's kingdom or government will have made all things new. "The former things have passed away," as stated in Revelation 21:4,5.

By Bob Lanning

Maybe I'm a little partial concerning this gentleman and his family. We have been the kind of neighbors God appoints. I don't believe a neighbor is just someone who lives next door. A neighbor is someone you can count on. You know something about his lifestyle and you care about each other. Bob is a good friend of mine, one of the greatest humanitarians I know. My family loves his family really well and we have an extremely high regard for each other because he loves God and he is a man of action, not just talk.

I find this gentleman and his family to be full of integrity and Godliness. I don't believe in denominations because they are stamps. But when someone calls God Jehovah that is who he says he is. Many denominations claim salvation but that wears a label too. I don't believe God puts a label on anybody. I don't put denominations in this book. But I represent what I believe Christ would put his mark on. There are a lot of things my friend and I don't agree on but that does not change our loving friendship.

By Guy P. Darden, Sr

GODS RULES & REGULATIONS

I'm going to mention something right here that is going to be rather controversial. But that is alright. I tell people I am 400 years old. I can say this. When you are 77, it doesn't make any difference how old you are. But if you are as old as I am and haven't accomplished anything, you've made a lot of mistakes on this earth and you've seen a lot of mistakes. If you were reasonably intelligent you've been able to analyze some of them. If you know anything about Christ or know anything about God Almighty and what He put man on this earth for, and if you know anything about Christ's teachings, and if you believe what you say you believe then I don't think you've got a strong argument about what I'm going to be talking about for the next couple of minutes.

Number one; let's get this straight. If you don't agree with me on this, I need you to tell my why. I don't believe God ever called any minister that was stupid, ignorant, or was unable to comprehend if he didn't know when he was called into the ministry, that God put someone in front of him or put someone there to teach him and show him and lead him. God doesn't put people in charge of His word and His people that are ignorant and stupid. God put forth the best He has to teach His people. So if a minister is not teaching what he needs to teach and he's not doing what he is supposed to do, it isn't because God hasn't told him. It isn't because God hasn't taught him. It isn't because he doesn't have the capacity to do it. It is because he chooses not to. We as sinners, Christians, we are men and women that have choices and we make our decision to do what God says to do or we don't. He doesn't put us in prison. We sign our name at the foot of the cross and accept God's responsibility that He gives to us.

If you are a minister or a priest, or whatever you want to call yourself – it doesn't make any difference. I don't care if you're the Pope or bishop or what kind of position you have. Let's get this out of the way first. This is what I believe. God doesn't care any more about you as a bishop, priest, or a pope than He does the gardener. If all of you are men and women are of God and have accepted God in your life as your Savior and He is leading you and you are going by God's rules and regulations – I said God's rules and regulations – I did not say man's rules and regulations. If you are following God's word the way He taught you, not rules and regulations that this or that organization or this or that church might have – you see, all churches, real churches, have the same God. It has the same regulations.

God has the same commandments for a Christian that lives in Mississippi as He does for a Christian that lives in Alabama. He has the same laws and regulations for the preacher who lives in Alabama and He does for the priest who lives in New York City. He has the same rules and regulations, and He's the same God for the Pope as He is for the President of the United States. He has the same laws for the Pope as He does for my mechanic. If he's a Christian, if he has accepted God, if he's a believer and he believes in God and follows God's regulations and rules, not man's regulations and rules, but if he follows God there is no difference in God's love for one man that it is to another. Now that's what Christ taught me.

I'm saying the preacher is subject to the same spiritual living as I am. You don't tell me to follow a man because he is the minister of your church just on that alone. You tell me to follow a man because he's following God and he's teaching me and showing me and helping me to understand the regulations and rules of God – what God is telling him to do. He has to tell me how I can be able to empower someone as you have empowered me. You don't teach people in the church just to sit in the church Sunday after Sunday to listen to you and go back out in the street and do nothing with what you got out of the church. You have to know that the building that we go to sometimes on Sunday and maybe during the week is not the church. It is not the church. The next thing is that it is not a temple. It is not the temple. You're not to treat it like it is a temple. The temple is your body. The essence of God that deals with your soul and the spirit of man, that spirit in you that deals with God personally and intimately; the essence of who you are.

If your preacher and your teacher are not teaching you that, then I've got to say that you're not getting the right teaching. I say that with no apologies. I'm not a Bible student, but I know enough about what you have taught me. Most preachers teach you about what Christ said, about what God said. They teach you what Paul, Matthew, and all the things that writers of the Bible talked about; they teach it. But somehow or another there are millions of different churches all over this nation – I'm exaggerating – that do all kinds of rules and they live by their rules and regulations and you have to live by them too. If you don't follow them and do what they tell you to do then they are not doing the churches business. I thought the minister was supposed to empower the people. I don't think that. I know that.

I've got to stop talking about what I think about. I've got to start talking about what I know about. I've got enough faith in Jesus Christ and God Almighty to believe that they are not liars. They taught us how to live. They said treat your neighbor as yourself. They said if you love your neighbor, you love Me. If you don't love your neighbor and you don't care about him then you don't care about Me. If we are going to church, that building, in order to go to Heaven, it looks like you're trying to fool God. There is more to do on this earth than just go to Heaven and live for going to Heaven. I've heard it Sunday after Sunday; I've got my sights set on Heaven. I'm Heaven bound. My friend, I say this with my strong belief. If you don't do anything on this earth and you don't do what you are supposed to do on this earth, I doubt very seriously that you're going to Heaven. If you're just doing good things to go to Heaven, I don't think you're going to make it. I don't believe that you are going to make it.

LIFE

Life is what you make it. This is a statement that I have heard all my life, but yet I still hear humans blaming each other for one's downfalls. I think of life as a gift, and either you cherish it or you take advantage of this wonderful blessing or you freely give it away to others by allowing the world, and not God take control of your life. Yes, you let man lead you instead of the Lord. By assisting the world, your mind becomes incapable of making wise and compromising decisions that affect our way of living, as God has demanded us to do so. We become independent on a world of chaos and destruction! Therefore in saying all of this, "Life is nothing without our Savior Jesus Christ". Think about it! (?) And if you dare so challenge my theory on life, well good! Get Jesus, go to church, praise, and worship Him because he renews life, and who so ever believe in Him shall never perish.

> *Got Life, Find Christ, Get Jesus!*
> *By Sandra Causey*
> *Guy P. Darden, Sr.'s niece*

This lady is a take-charge person. Her personality challenges mine. Her character is beyond reproach. She says what she means and she means what she says. She follows through with her beliefs. I believe this young lady has God-given principles that a lot of us ought to have. I have the highest regard and respect for my niece because she tells it like it is and she doesn't back down from her beliefs. May God bless her in every way.

> By Guy P. Darden, Sr.

TRADE SCHOOL – MONEY - POWER

I got to thinking about my childhood; that it worried me for a long time. I wondered why, in the early part of my childhood and in my young life, I did rather well compared to a lot of people during that time. When I began to really think about my past and really examine it, I found a lot of answers that I hadn't found in the past. I overlooked a lot of wonderful and exciting times. When people look back there and talk about the "good old days," those days were a lot better than what I had first thought about. People were not as selfish as they are today. I want you to note something. I'm not putting anybody down, I am only stating facts about the opportunities that were there if you really wanted them, if you were really willing to fight for them, and you had the type of training and teaching that did not allow you to be lazy and trifling. Some of you young people will not know what that word means and how to express it because we don't use those words much anymore. We think they're old-time and outdated. A long time ago when I was a boy and now look back over my life and re-examine it as I've done so many times, there are things that I see in many different ways with the experience in my life and the training that God has given me, and that man has given me, and the training that I gave myself. All these different stages in my life have made a difference in my life. In some ways this was very positive and in some ways very negative. I have to say, when I look back over my life, that the early years of my life were the most positive ones even though I had a lot of complaints since then. I suppose, if you want to pick out the worst in life and look at all the bad things, you can find something bad and negative in all of our lives. Looking back at how society saw things when I was a child, I can understand why going to school was not always up front. The elementary stages, I admit, were extremely valuable. Going to grammar school, high school, college, and universities is extremely important; but when I was a boy, most poor people did not have those opportunities. Some didn't even have the opportunities to go to elementary school. They went from the cradle into the fields, or the work shops of this nation. Something, though, went on back there.

Envy, greed, selfishness had rooted out of our society, and not just the people who were blue collar workers. (What I am going to say will be controversial.) When I was a child, people had patience and saw each other as a person who had possibilities of being taught something. Parents who were farmers taught you how to become a farmer, and if your parent was a blacksmith, they would train you and teach you and put you in an apprenticeship to become a blacksmith. If you had a parent that was a mechanic, he would teach you how to do that as well. After you were grown and were out from under his care and supervision, you could do most anything. You were taught along with patience. The reason that I am not some drunk or dope addict, or a person, who has allowed his life to rot away, is because people had patience with me. When I first went away from home, the first job I had was in a fertilizer factory. They taught me how to load a wheelbarrow and how to make it pull itself. I know that doesn't make much sense to the average person, but I was a kid that weighed about 120 pounds when I was seventeen or eighteen years old and was trying to push a wheelbarrow that had 500 pounds in it. They showed me how to tip that wheelbarrow so that the load would help pull itself. I am saying all of these things because I want you to know that people took time to train you in a trade to become whatever they wanted you to do. It didn't matter whether you could read or write. You didn't need a certificate or degree to teach someone a trade either. They needed someone to work – who had a certain talent – that could understand certain training. The labor wages were not as high as it is today or even a few years ago, so they could afford to have a lot of different people. The labor organizations hadn't gotten so greedy that they took over the manufacturers. The unions out-priced the manufacturers over time. (I probably could get bricks thrown at me by talking this way in public.) The labor laws got out of hand. If they didn't do it as a volunteer when you have somebody working for you, then you need to pay them a decent salary. At the same time, you don't need to pay them so much that the manufacturer needs to raise their price so high that ordinary working people can't afford to buy their products. When that happens, you move things into another category; you have a domino effect in society. The financial markets have to change their way of doing things. They started getting so much technology to eliminate high-labor costs, that they got rid of too many people out of the work force. Then when they started going to trade schools the colleges, universities, and unions all over this nation gathered up the trade schools under their control. Before that, a trade school out there was someplace that taught a guy like me to be a mechanic even though I couldn't read or write, but was an excellent mechanic, or a tailor, or a blacksmith - you taught people how to become workers with a technique through trade schools. Too many jobs were being taken from the colleges, and too many students weren't going to college. They were going to trade schools so they could go to work for Joe-blow who had a big automobile manufacturing company and he couldn't even write his name, but was he ever an excellent mechanic! If you had something he needed to read and he couldn't read it, somebody there would read it for him and not look down on him and think he was a fool.

The second job I got after I left the farm was delivering groceries. That was hard because I had to know the names of streets, but if it was printed on a piece of paper and I was told where it was, I would remember anything I saw and could find it with a good sense of direction and a photographic memory. I could remember anything and so people would teach you anything. In Richmond, Virginia, I worked for a funeral home. I embalmed people and learned to do anything that the embalmer could do, but too many people were learning trades.

The Good Old days – they really were. People were willing to train and teach you the trades available back in that time. That was the only way to get training because the schools and organizations were so discriminating at that time. The blacks and liberal whites were glad to teach someone a trade.

"Who's boy are you?" Your last name had a value to it. It determined what you did. If you wanted to be an electrician or something your father would have to have a license in that field and that was a rare situation. Black men had to work under someone who has a license to learn the trade. Usually they said they didn't want to hire blacks but if the black man had a license he would get the job.

Nurse's aides did the bulk of the work in the hospitals like emptying bed pans when they had no toilets in the rooms. Sometimes a nurse's aid was better than a nurse. Back then, a doctor became your family practitioner and he took care of nearly everything that was wrong with you. Now we have specialists who are making more money today but you have less people working now. You don't have the job market that we had when I was a young man.

I don't believe things are better for most people on this earth. I don't see all the technology doing all the things that they claim it does. I remember when a two-story building had to have a fire escape, but now you may have a thirty-story building and it may not have a fire escape. I'm throwing all of these things in here because I want you to understand that money has taken away the power structure of the lower-class working man. The word "labor" now is almost a slave market, because if you can't read and write today, you're in trouble. We train our people. My grandfather was an excellent carpenter and built houses all over in different cities. He was also a basket weaver and made baskets for farmers, and trained almost all of his children to be able to do that.

I'm saying, yes. It was a prejudiced and discriminating place to live in and Jim Crowe was on the rampage, but we found a way to work and to earn a living. A black business man did better during the prejudiced times than he's doing today. Don't get me wrong. There are a few black business men who have better jobs and have raised their status, but you don't have as many in charge of their lives. We have more people who have our government in charge of their lives. You don't have people now who are willing to work – to baby sit – and don't have mothers who are willing to stay home and take care of their children and teach them in a proper way giving them the kind of attention and love that they need. The things that we want that are hanging around our walls and sitting on our floors and in our garages, have demanded that the ladies go outside and work. It's debatable, to live within the cycle of your own means. You see, we raised the houses to where they are, and we raised the prices of clothes to where they are by designer labels, so we're willing to pay for nothing. Some of the things you've got on the market today aren't worth a dime, it is a bunch of junk, yet we pay fantastic prices because it is something we want, not what we need necessarily.

I jump ahead of myself sometimes, and you'll have to excuse me. I need to go back there to laziness and trifling. I know a lot of young people don't know what the meaning of those words is and I need to explain them. I believe laziness is best described as a person who doesn't want to get up in the morning; he's not motivated by anything that is important, and doesn't see any reason to be in a school someplace or have any purpose in mind. Trifling, I believe, is being a person who doesn't particularly care about the things that are around him, and doesn't specifically nail down things and put value on them. He is also not anxious to do things that he doesn't have to do. He just makes out with what he has to do, and doesn't necessarily see life as something that he owes participation to. He doesn't care what happens in any particular place as long as he doesn't have to do anything with work or labor connected to it. He is satisfied to sit down and do the least amount of work, and if it is free, he isn't crazy about how he gets it. This is a person who I believe is lazy and trifling. I think this results from not having been taught responsibility. I think some people have to be taught responsibility, and there are others who seem to have a natural ability to achieve, to accomplish things, and who seem to be born with that type of relationship in life and in the world. They have an attitude of owing people something. Even some who have not accepted Christ in their lives seem to be energetic and motivated by something from within. I think when you are brought up in a family that is motivated by Godly blessings, your life may be a little different; but when we start thinking about just ourselves and ourselves alone, we gave up something, I think, that is very, very important. Today, I think most of us, more than any other time in history, think about things that are special for ourselves, and we feel that all of those people around us are not as important as they used to be.

    We have a lot of lobbyists – every time we turn around we have to have a license for this and a license for that, so that everything we do needs to have a certificate for it. I don't believe that the certificate represents being assured that you are qualified for that particular job as it is about the money. They have a campaign on dog licenses right now and I don't think it is because people love dogs all that much. I think it is because they are trying to collect revenue. Whatever you do, you have to be a specialist and need to have a license for this and a license for that, or you are required to go to school for this and for that. A mechanic who's been a mechanic for thirty years now has to go to someone and get a license; or an electrician who has been an electrician for fifty years now needs a license and a member of your family to also be licensed as an electrician or plumber.

    We've taken away the motivation to make people be what they need to be. We've lost the labor market. Many maids and cleaning services are needed today. They need people to take care of their children when they come home from school, or take care of the yard. This used to be a wide-open market for black people. Today, black people think that is beneath them; they don't want to do that. No. I didn't go to school, but I had someone who cared enough about me to teach me to be a tailor. Ever since I was a young boy, I wanted to learn how to make clothes. There were always two things that I really wanted to do: one was a tailor, and the other was a policeman, but I didn't want it bad enough to go to school to get the training. A gentleman in New Jersey and some in Virginia cared enough about me to teach me trades. The only degree I ever received was in Greenville, South Carolina, when I learned to work on leather. God has blessed me by putting people around me and in front of me that I could ask favors of. Belt Department Store, Mr. Simpson, Greenville, South Carolina, gave me my first management job, a supervising job in the tailoring department. He talked to me and respected me a great deal.

Just So Company, Greenville, South Carolina, gave me my second desk opportunity to be head of the tailoring department. All that they wanted to know was that I was a tailor and that I was good at what I did. I taught them what I knew and they respected me and it seemed that they loved me for it. They showed me love and respect. I was so honored. I've been in business for myself for many years. When you work for yourself, you don't have to worry about being fired because you can't read.

I've listened and looked at so many people throughout this nation, and they've given me so much and done so much for me as a person. I believe the general public gave me my diploma. Many, many thanks.

I'm winding up my journey. May God bless you.

SELF-DEVALUATION

Self-devaluation -the rise and fall of self-devaluation. I've been disappointed in my life. I guess I'm not the only one that has found an area in their lives that they were uncomfortable with. We think of ourselves as individuals. We think of our privacy and we think of our business, our personal business. We even think of our intimate business and lifestyle. Should we consider anyone else in it or should we just think of ourselves and our own individuality?

We have the freedom of action, movement, doing things and creating things. We have it you know. We have those things inside of us that allow us to have the freedom to create on the human instinct. More or less, we have the freedom to do that as a free agent so to speak. We don't call any outside help in. We just do what we think is right on our own and that is right for us in our personal lives. Shouldn't we be thinking about more than just ourselves?

I know when I walk back over my life and try to go back into my childhood, I ask God to try to visualize some of that for me. Now I've grown up into an elderly citizen. I've been through a lot of windmills in my life and through a lot of dark tunnels. At one time I thought I was a pretty good citizen, and if I wasn't what I needed to be, then I needed to go back into my childhood and find out what kind of early start I had. What kind of freedom did I have as a youngster? What kind of parents did I have? Who led me out in the world and tried to straighten out my path for me so I could see ahead and have some idea where I wanted to go? Had someone given me a foundation to build on? I had been a free agent most of my life. I made most of my decisions. Was I inspired by someone to do whatever I had done, good or bad?

When we are trying to find out the substance that we're made of we need to know what path we came up from. What road did we travel on to get to where we are today? I believe that we need to know something about our history. We need to know what was happening in our home when we were growing up. You know, some people will tell you that the past is gone so forget about it and go ahead. But sometimes I believe that we need to know how we made this journey. What inspired us in whatever direction that we went? There was a point in our lives and a time when we were influenced by somebody. There was a time in our lives that we were going by hearsay. We were being guided by the influence of others. What type of influences were they? How did our lives begin?

I say this because it may have something to do with our future from here on out. Let's look at this road clearer and let's try to ask God to open up an airway in our minds and hearts that we can go back over our lives and make a re-evaluation and see if we have made the right decisions up until this point. When we recognize an area in our lives that sent us in the wrong direction and started our ship reeling and rocking, was it our fault? What set us in motion? Good or bad it had an influence on our lives. Not only does it have an influence on our own personal lives - and I want you to put a pin in this - because what we do doesn't just affect our own personal lives. It sometimes has a reflection on someone else other than us. We never know who is watching us and who is following us or who is going down the same road that we are going down because it looks good to them from where they stand, and especially when we look like we are successful.

As I look back over my life, I used to blame my parents for almost every error that I made in life. When I looked back and realized that I was sorry for what I had done, I always said I wouldn't have done that if my Mother would have taught me this or my father had been in my home. I always had somebody else to blame. There comes a time in your life when you have to become responsible for yourself. You have to accept your own responsibility for the decisions that you make. Now, when I say accept them because you make a decision doesn't mean that you have to follow through with it – especially when you find out that you made the wrong decision.

I want us to look back over our lives and not to go back and mope and get hung up back there some place. I want you to look and see if you can find anything there that may give you some data that if you've blown it and you recognize that you goofed or that you messed up back there someplace. Then I want you to be able to put a pin in that – mark it so when you see somebody else going in that direction and there's a door open that you may be able to assist them and give them good advice. You may have some wisdom to talk about. You could talk about experience. You can testify. But if you do like I've done most of my life, things you don't want to remember, you forget. I don't mean just act like you forgot them, but I mean that I was so good at it and wanted to escape reality so much that I truly forgot about it. What I didn't want to remember just disappeared - bad things that happened to me, bad things that happened in my family, and the memories that I just buried and my mental capacity was so corrupted and torn apart that I just didn't remember.

I just started to remember my Mother's funeral. I still can't remember seeing her in the church. I can't remember that the people were there. You have to realize I was a grown man when this happened. I don't remember much about my father. I just remember the good things about him and what he had done for me. Anything that discredited him or made him look bad, I've just forgotten it.

Now, I think that you should forgive people in your life and you should ask God to forgive you for holding any malice against any human being. I think you really, truly, from the deep depths of your heart, bury that in the sea of forgiveness and never remember it again. But not until you go to God and ask Him how to handle these situations. I want you to know that we're devaluating ourselves every day of our lives. Many segments of our society and many segments of our communities are being racially devaluated. Ladies and gentlemen, I realize that this is controversial.

What I do to myself and how I treat myself is just not my business alone. It's not just something that I'm doing to me. If I live on this earth and I'm in this society I have to realize whatever I do doesn't just affect me in a good way when I am doing something good. It doesn't just affect me in a bad way when I'm doing something bad. It affects my race. It affects my family. It puts a dark shadow over my family. It doesn't look good for me as a man. It puts a dark shadow on me as a man. We're supposed to be the leaders of this world. At least that is what God put us here for - to be in charge of this planet. Be an example for those that may not be as strong as some of us, especially those of us who have accepted Christ in our lives and who accepted God as our leader, and as the leader of the universe and ruler of the world. The one who feeds us, who allows us to live on grace sometimes, and sometimes we live by grace almost alone, just grace, because we haven't done anything else to feed ourselves with. We live on the goodness and mercy of God.

We need to remember that we're not just a survivor that is taking care of ourselves and making decisions just for ourselves. Every time we move on this earth we might be shaping somebody else's life. You see, what we do and say is not just our business and our business alone.

Ladies and gentlemen, boys and girls, I believe that at some given time I might have a selfish motive here. I believe that sometimes the reason we are so private and we walk away from our family and go away and we even sometimes go away and get into unlawful activities by our thoughts and socializing that have become too personalized. And if you have a little patience here with me, I'll tell you what I mean. We need to sit down with our family very often and discuss our intentions and some of our plans, our thoughts and ideas, and share them with your family, your children, and your wife. Talk about some of your plans.

Okay, I want you to meditate and concentrate on what I am trying to get out here. Sometimes we have some weird thoughts. Sometimes our thoughts are very negative in some ways but we feel like they are going to come out to a positive end. These are not plans; these are just thoughts that go through all of our minds from time to time. If we do that privately nobody knows what we have on our minds. They don't know how we think. We might be thinking bad thoughts. It might even be criminal thoughts, the thought that a criminal might think in order to, let's say, make money. In most of our plans we think demands a money foundation or a plan that tells us how we are going to make money. What I mean by that is I see the people in the world. Remember, I see church people; people don't believe in the church quite that much, people don't have that much faith in God, or people that have a lot of faith in God and I see them doing things. Some of them are very successful that we call sinners and whether they are sinners or not, we think they are anyway. Most of us are sinners at one time or another. We all definitely have been a sinner. Those thoughts go in all different directions.

If we share these thoughts with friends and family, some of those thoughts may not shine a great light on us. It may not make us look good. So we keep those thoughts private and go out on our own without any advice from anybody else - just our own thoughts. We are certainly not going to go to God and ask Him if it's okay to rob the bank down here. We're not going to go to God and discuss how we should cheat on our taxes. We're not going to go to God and ask Him how to be skillful in hustling people all over this nation for something. Okay, so we take those thoughts and we either go to people who are doing those things and get advice from them or we look at their accomplishments, or what we think are their accomplishments, and we let them lead us into some things. However, if we had to call our family in – because you see we've got good and bad in our families – we've had people who've had bad experiences and done a lot of bad things, got in trouble and they have experience; good and bad. Some of them have experiences that are more bad than good. Some of them have experiences that are more good than bad. So if we discuss things and talk openly with our friends and family, the ones that love us and care about us; if we say something that may not shine a good light on us or shine a good light on our society or may not be a development for our community, it can be anything on this earth that we're discussing and talking about. We have pros and cons in all of these conversations.

You see, we've got so many jewels in this package here and we have a lot of things in there that could cause complete damnation to our lives. We have people in that group that have experienced things and people in there that haven't experienced too many things. So when we start discussing these things we learn a lot from each other. If I have an idea about doing something, perhaps there is somebody in that group that might tell you, if you do this, thus so and so might happen to you. I did this one time or I knew somebody that did so and so, and this is what happened to them. When you get to talking to a group of people, you have so much wisdom, so much knowledge and so much experience, and each one in a group like that will sometimes throw something out there that's very serious that they did but they say it in a joking manner that doesn't make them look so bad.

This is why it is so important to have family counseling, family gathering, and family orientation so that you understand the meaning of love. You understand and see people that maybe didn't go to a university that are still brilliant and intelligent and who have something to offer. In other words, you may reject this or reject that or you may accept this or accept that, or you may not accept any of it, but at least it's available to you. And in families, sometimes we have doctors, lawyers, thieves, robbers and every type of person in our families that's around. Some of them are quiet. Some of them may be in a gang. And something you say there that day may give them some wisdom or knowledge or some understanding about how to pull out of that gang if they want to get out.

In other words, what I am saying is our private thoughts sometimes can destroy us or they can build us up. This is where it is so important not to be so private and not to let everything be alcohol and drugs that mess up your mind so you don't have the possibility to think. In other words, the only fun time is not just drinking and getting drunk. Sometimes you don't drink anything. Some of us may have a drink or a glass of wine. There may be some people in there that overdo it and that may even come up as a discussion about what happens to people when things like that happen in their lives. That's the same thing that goes on at AA meetings or what psychologists and psychiatrists do all over this nation every day of their lives. You see, when you come together as a nation or you come together as a city, a state, or the communities that you live in, you come together with your neighbors. You also come together in the Congress, in the Senate and you discuss things. That's how you weed out a lot of ugliness. You don't want to just be in charge of everything. Sometimes you need to delegate and listen to other people and they listen to you.

This is what life is about. This is what we've lost. We've allowed the TV to dictate to us. We put sports ahead of everything. I've got news for you. Sports for the average individual does not do as much for people that live in what we call "ghettos" who live in what we call "the good neighborhoods." It doesn't help them any. All it does is fill the pockets of the politicians and the racketeers. When I say racketeers I mean people who are trying to hustle you. I mean people who are trying to make money and the money is the guiding force.

Do you understand what I am trying to get at here? I'm trying to throw something up in the air here and let those people that I believe are educated have another line of thought other than just pushing forward down the road and not looking at the neighbors they've passed as they drive down this road that doesn't seem like it has any end. The road to success has trials and tribulations. A sound road to success means examining the road as you go forward while seeing how well this trip was planned before you made the decision to go wherever you think you're going.

God bless you. I hope I have said something that may give your mind that is cultivated with God's spirit and your mind is cultivated with the wisdom and the knowledge that you've gathered up through your life. I hope the education that you've gotten out of the education system will find something here to thrive on. No one has the complete answer. All the knowledge is pieces of a puzzle. All experiences are a part of wisdom. I hope I've touched on something that put a spark on your thinking. It doesn't matter so much that you agree with me or not. All I'm trying to do is to let you know that you are not the only one that thinks about life. There are others who think about it, and they may be thinking about something that you might be interested in. It's going to mean something to somebody else more than just the two of us.

THE PLAYING FIELD OF LIFE

I was born in the South, the state of Alabama, within the heart of loveless people of my color black. I lived on land owned by white folk, being robbed of wages and knowledge. In the midst of all that, there were things given to us by virtue that caused us to acquire a desire to move forward. At that time, I didn't understand what they were. But now I know what it was that I was taught with understanding. There was a saying from Mom and Dad: "Don't mess up my name!" These words had hidden power which I never really explored until later. The word "integrity" carried completeness, fullness, only to allow us to understand that we had help along the way. My parents gave us the assurance that love was in the home; that is and was we were cared for in spite of things we lacked.

We were constantly reminded of responsibility which allowed no place for idleness. Being the youngest of seven-six boys and one girl-I learned not to tarry when carrying water to my dad while we was working in the hot sun. After loosening his belt and swing it on my rear end, never again was there warm water for him!

We were proud folk. Walking in uprightness meant something. Principles were the elements which were used for training for everyday life. Then we had a prayer life that was practiced morning, noon, and night. These practices allowed us to be free in the three states of freedom—physical, moral, and spiritual. God bless!

By Reverend Floyd O'Neal

I've talked to and interviewed people all over this nation. Almost everyone agrees with most of what I am saying. If they truly believe it, why is so little being done? Is it because we're afraid we aren't going to get the gratification that we want? Because I can tell you right now you can work in this field your whole life and not get the gratification you want. Are you working for gratification or are you working see God's word more abundantly?

Pastor O'Neal is one that I respect so highly. I find him to have integrity and truly a God-fearing man. He loves the work and preaches the word. He demonstrates the essence of it.

By Guy P. Darden, Sr.

DO WE KNOW WHO WE ARE?

I've been thinking about what is happening to us as a people. Not as any specific race of people, but we the people – those of us on this Earth. I wonder if we are concerned about ourselves. Do we think that we are going to survive individually and separate or do we feel that we have a unity problem? We have a separation problem. Do we have a problem that we need to be thinking about? Has something happened to those of us that feel that we owe each other something? Do we feel that way? It's the missing pieces in our lives. Has something gone wrong in our society? Has God and man's relationship been disturbed in a radical way? Do we know who we are? As an individual, do I know myself?

My first thought is that most of us say that we know ourselves better than anybody else in the world, and suppose we should. But do we really know who we are? Have we taken a survey of ourselves and come to a conclusion that we are well acquainted with our individuality? When is the last time one of us took a survey of ourselves? I'm concerned about me. I think perhaps I might be taking myself for granted. I know I've done that in the past. Who am I? Do I really know who I am? What are my capabilities? What are my qualifications when it comes to serving me as an individual? Before I can do something for my neighbor, maybe I should find out how well I do it for myself. Am I well equipped to do what I need do for me? You know, if I could have thought like that when I was growing up, then maybe I would be a better person today.

What goals have I set on this Earth? What have my accomplishments been? What have I learned from myself that I did for myself that was successful enough that I could discuss and point out in a way that would help somebody else? Who Am I? Am I sympathetic to my cause and my cause alone; just mine? Am I willing to give somebody the things that I needed and didn't get? Am I able to recognize the things that I needed that I didn't get? Had I gotten them, would they have lifted me up over that pothole on the road of life? What makes me think that I could help somebody on this Earth? What gives me the audacity to think that I have the capability of doing something to help my fellow man over some problem that he might be having today? These and other things are what we need to challenge when we question the condition of humanity.

God and Man's Relationship to Humanity

I see a volcano that is slowly erupting between God and man's relationship to humanity. I feel that something gigantic is happening between man and God. I feel that something is being torn apart between me and you. When people talk about being together, are they talking about groups of wealthy men and women? Are they trying to build a wall between the rich and the poor? Or are they trying to build a relationship that will be productive for all men and women whatever their standard or class might be? Or do the poor have to be the least of all on this Earth? Can't we look around ourselves and see that if we don't come together as a people, that we are going to lose our strength along with our wisdom because we've become too complacent with where we are and feel we can't move any further? Do the senior citizens of this nation feel that they are useless and they don't have anything to contribute to the well-being of human existence? Do they feel that age has taken over their minds, hearts and souls? Or do they feel that the labor they have already given to this country is sufficiently enough, and that they've worked so hard all of their lives and given so much that they don't owe anything else?

Ladies and gentlemen, we can't feel that way and be just. We cannot be just and feel that we've given all we need to give. We can't go to our church houses to serve God and look our neighbors in the eye and say we are holy yet take no action until we come back to church next Sunday. Our lives are dedicated to the purpose of serving God, and you can't serve God without serving man. We have to have an organized heart and soul in order to love each other as we love ourselves. We have to share our resources, but first we must know who we are and where we are. Living and dying on this earth is not the end of life, it's just the beginning of life. You see, growing old does not give you the right to sit down and have a pity-party. Growing old does not give you the right to retire and decide you gave enough. God decides when you've given enough. Our time is not just our own. We use it for the well-being of ourselves and others.

As a child and young boy, I missed the opportunity to give what I needed to give – to prepare myself in the proper manner so that I could be the best I could be. I missed the opportunity because I didn't get the education that I needed to equip myself with the things that would allow me to serve humanity in its best form. What I now have left you can have because God has given me time, wisdom and knowledge. Over the years, He has allowed me to gather up something of value. He's allowed me to live on this Earth in order that I may point out something to somebody that they may not know. The truth is not mine alone. The truth is not hidden down under the sofa some place. Why, you have to search for it to pull it out. The truth is in your heart and it's wrapped up in love and kindness, decency, and mercy. Love is God, in its best form because God is always in His best form.

These streets that we walk on each day of our lives are paved with hatred, with sin, and with disappointment they're paved with all of the ugliness of the world, and only the kindness and love of God can wash them clean. We have to find something within ourselves that is good enough to give to somebody year in and year out, from childhood to old age, whether over-tired and run down by it. If we have a mind that's clear, and a soul that's pure, God will honor us with His presence. We must give of ourselves until the end of our lifetime. We must share and show these young people of this great land in which we live that we haven't always had it easy, that it's not always been perfect, but somehow, someway, we managed to survive. For that reason only and if for no other reason, just living on this earth and allowing God to deal with us by giving us the privilege of sitting in His presence and allowing Him to lead us to something more than just our lusts, is a great privilege. For me, the greatest privilege would be for God to let me to help somebody - to do something for somebody who needs me by sharing my life and my experiences with them; to tell them how I was an alcoholic and became clean and how I was a sinner but I was able to accept Christ in my life. I want to be able to tell people that God does not let people down. Find somebody to talk with and let them share their experience in the life of God. Walk with one sinner for one day and let them hear your relationship with God so that they might have the opportunity to return from their sins and come back into the folds of love, hopes and dreams. That is what we need to make us better. We will never reach perfection, but if we can just get close enough to somebody's heart to show them the holiness that God put in us so that they will know that He can put it in them too if they just ask for it. That's enough to be able to look at humanity and feel that you have something to offer.

I believe that we are separated because we don't feel that we need each other any more. We sometimes put too much value on the little wealth that God has allowed us to have and that he shared with us. We think we can live alone and we think what we do is our own business. Nobody's business is their own business if you live on this earth. Everybody's business is somebody's business. Everything you do touches somebody's life; it interferes in somebody's life when it's not right. It fixes somebody's life when it is right. You cannot walk alone on this earth and expect to be your best. Everybody needs somebody to share their lives with. None of us has the answer. Only God has the answer. He doesn't always give us what we want when we want it, but if we stay close to God and hold His hand, He'll give it to us when we need it.

I want to talk to you about my opinion, and of course, you know that we all have an opinion, right or wrong. This is because I'm so interested in humanity, and I firmly believe that there's a gap that can be filled with our love.

A WORD FROM PEGGY

My name is Peggy. I am the mother of seven living children, two sons and five girls and mother and grandmother to one grandson that I have raised since birth. I have not been happy or lived the way I have desired but God still kept me and my children. I have never been to a jailhouse for my children.

In November of 1994, I was taken ill and was unable to work. While laying flat on my back, I had to wait until someone had the time to wait on me or give me a glass of water. I learned to thank God for the good times and I ask Him for forgiveness of my sins. I wish I could live my life over. I would ask for a better childhood and to be a better mother and wife. I would stay on my knees. I thank my grandmother and grandfather for teaching me to work and stand on my own, hold my head up, and walk proud, love everyone and be thankful for the bad as well as the good. I have learned to look to the hills for which cometh my help. I have learned to lean on Jesus. I love my mother and my grandparents. This may not be well-written but it is from the heart.

By Peggy Garner
Daughter of Guy Darden's wife, Nancy

I am grateful to know that people like Peggy still exist, especially when they enter into my personal family. She showed her love and kindness to her grandmother and grandfather in a strong and dynamic way. I love Peggy for her God-given spirit.

WHY HAVE WE STOPPED KNEELING IN THE PRAYER HOUSE

The peace of God is different from the peace of man. I feel that on this day we have been put on the platform of life to amplify the things that Christ talked about. I think man has become too personalized in his personal belief, not God's personal belief. But I believe man has personalized himself, glorified himself so that he stands out and he looks good. I feel like the time that God has allotted us has become too personalized for us. I think we put ourselves, intimately and personally, too far ahead of God's will. I think, sometimes, we overlook that request that we need to ask the Almighty for.

I don't know, ladies and gentlemen, if you have paid personal attention to our becoming too proud. I want you to notice that when you go to church, how many people you see on their knees before God. It seems that bending down and getting on your knees has gone out of style. I believe we've got to be humble, and not just humble in our feeling in the heart, but I think some of that humbleness has got to be physical before it is regenerated into spirituality. I believe we have to do some action. What I mean by that is that we can't just be humble in our personal and intimate spirit that we need to be humble in the physical and openness. This means that we need to kneel down on our knees before the world and let them know that we respect God not only personally but publicly too. I believe that's the same as coming before God and confessing to the world that you have accepted Jesus Christ as your personal Savior. I believe this is what Christ meant when He said "Every knee shall bow to me."

We stopped getting on our knees. I think sometimes the reason we have so much arthritis problems in our back and knees is because we refuse to get on our knees and honor God Almighty. That's humility. That's obeying God. When did that go out of style? I'm ashamed of myself for not getting on my knees and asking God to forgive me. Nobody else is kneeling down. We're too proud, scared, or afraid we're going to get out clothes dirty. (I do not refer to the handicapped that are unable to do this.) There's something wrong with us when we come to that decision. I think that God has called me to speak out on this. I don't think there is enough knee-bending on this earth. It's not trivial when all the churches all over this nation have gotten so modernized that they won't get down on their knees. Well, they seem to feel that it's "not important." What is important? I think sometimes we forget about what Christ taught us.

We forget (those of us that claim that the name of Jesus is above all names), that we owe Him something special, more than just lip-service. If we are who we say we are, then we must have humility both privately and personally and more. We've got to show it visibly sometimes. We have to let our children, our families, and those who haven't quite accepted Christ in their lives yet, to know that we have to humble ourselves before God. I believe the reason that some of our prayers are not answered is because we're not going down on our knees. I'm sorry about that.

I believe that when I talk about time that I'm saying more to myself than anybody else. I've used it foolishly. I've used it unwisely. The reason that I mention time is because I think it's the essence of life. I think it's all we have to deal with on this earth. I think we are in a cycle and that time covers us. I believe it is a personal and intimate rule that we go into when we wake up in the morning, when we open our eyes that we are in the shell of time. And what we do with it during that day and how we handle it determines our life value. It determines who we are. It determines what we are. It determines our meaning. We have no other cycle to work in. We cannot jump out of it and jump back into it. When we waste it, the only thing that we can do is repent to the Almighty God and ask him to restore us to our value system and give us something that we can use for the up-building of His Kingdom. The Kingdom of God Almighty has already been built by Him, so if we choose to go out of that rim or move out of that circle, I believe that we come away from the Will of God. I believe man deals with holiness. I don't believe that a man becomes fully holy until he has finished the cycle that Christ asked him to complete. I believe that the Christ's cycle is the revealing of Himself and opening Himself up to the generations with goodness and mercy, and I believe the generations are those who are taught under the supervision of God Almighty. I think the only way we can do that is to look back at the knowledge and the wisdom of those men that followed Christ and His teachings, the teachings of John and Paul, and the teachings of other men that God gave authority to. The only way to know that is to get into your Bible.

There is one thing you must know and understand. That God didn't just give men the authority to speak about His guidance and leadership who have long initials behind their names or who stand in the pulpits, but He gave his servants, the people that accepted Him as their personal leader the authority as well. Sometimes these are men come from humble backgrounds. Sometimes those men, in the sight of man, may even be illiterate. They may not know how to read and write. They may be men like me who never learned to read and write but who have been taught by God Almighty Himself through His Word. The spoken word and the written word are available to not only those who stand in the pulpit or who have teaching certificates. That is a great thing, a wonderful thing, a great opportunity and a great privilege. We have to realize that God extended His love to all mankind and all we have to do is reach out for it. Not only did He extend His love, He also extended His peace, His supervision, and His love. He even extended His love to those who hate, and all they have to do is reach out and submit to the Love of God and ask for His understanding.

IT IS A LIFE

For anybody to pass a law, including the Supreme Court, to tell you because you didn't want a child, because you made a mistake, like I have many times, and like we all will again. But you got pregnant and you allowed that child to create in you, you felt its kicks and moves in your body. And for you to feel in your spirit and in your heart that that child is nothing but a thing for you to decide that you want to kill it - I'm not going to use the word abortion - that you're going to murder that child in your body, that's living, that you can hear and see its heartbeat. For you to make that statement and say you have the right is like me deciding that I've got a neighbor living next door to me that throws garbage in my backyard, and he's got a drain that's draining over in my property and its causing my house to decay and since I don't like him, I don't like what he's doing, I go over and shoot him - just murder him because he's creating a problem for me. Or that he's a drunk and he's cursing and swearing in the street in front of my kid, or he's got a kid that uses all kind of language and picks on everybody, and I take my rifle and go out and shoot him if the man don't stop it. That's a crime. It is murder.

Nobody has the right to decide to murder somebody. That is a somebody. That is not a something it's not a thing. If it threatens your life, or may cost you your life, I can understand that because it is self-defense. If it's going to be you or the child, then I would choose you for life. But because you don't want it and you don't feel that you can afford it because it going to keep you from going to college or it's going to keep you from having the things you want or from being as free as you like to be. No. That should not be. No. You should have thought about that before you got that far. You should have thought about that before the sex act occurred. You don't have that right. For our churches throughout this nation, for everyone to keep their mouths closed on a situation like that and to quiet down and to be calm because they're afraid they're going to offend somebody, I'm mighty afraid it's going to be a huge price to pay. I'm afraid we as Christian men and women throughout this nation are going to probably spend some time in Hell for this. When that time is concluded you'll find that it's forever in eternity.

I don't know about what's going to happen to me when I leave this earth. I believe that those of us that don't do what God wants us to do, there's going to be a great penalty to pay. I've paid a big enough penalty's worth on this earth since I've been here. I know I prefer to preserve life in the best way I know how. I believe the reason we don't speak about a lot of things is because we condemn ourselves; because we're so imperfect. I've done so many things wrong myself that there are certain subjects that I hesitate to talk about because I've been so imperfect on them myself. But what gives me a better qualification to talk about something that I did, something that I have been unreasonable about, something that I've been mean about, something that I've been cruel about, or something that I've been trifling about. When I've been derelict of duty on a subject, who better qualified to talk about it than me? Those other men who talk about it are talking about hearsay. I talk about a lot of things because I've had personal experience in it. I've never had an abortion because I'm a man. I do not believe in homosexuals; I don't believe in that. I still hesitate to talk about it because I have members of my family that are homosexual, and they've always treated me beautifully and wonderfully, and I love them tremendously, but that doesn't make it right. That doesn't keep me from talking about it, that doesn't keep me from telling you that it's wrong.

If God is right, if He is right and He has the last say, then it's wrong. If He doesn't, then I don't think it matters what you do too much as long as you make yourself happy, and you do what you want to do, instead of what we ought to do. "As long as I'm not hurting anybody else" - that's a familiar saying in this nation. Whatever I do is my business as long as I'm not hurting anybody else. I don't know many things that can be your business that you do on this earth publicly that doesn't hurt somebody. There are things you do privately that don't hurt anybody. You know, I used to think when my girlfriends and I were going behind the closet and doing what we wanted to do it was our business and it didn't hurt anybody but us. But when you have a child and it doesn't get the proper care, that you don't love me as a lady, or as a man and you feel that we got excited out there and we've got this baby now, and he's already born. You want to take that part of it and want make it a beautiful time of that child growing up because it's more than just your own life. You're affecting other people's lives, too. So what's done behind closed doors is not your business, not your business alone.

After I got into this book, I kept going back into my childhood and finding reasons and excuses why I had never been a success. I was trying to blame illiteracy for my problems and blaming my illiteracy on my parents; the failures in relationship with ladies and my spouse; trying to put everything that happened in my life and shift it over to somebody else. They caused me to do this and they were to blame for it. But, there comes a time in your life that you have to accept responsibility. I mean you've taken on responsibility and you've got to be responsible for the decision that you made. You made the decision to get married to whomever. Whatever decision that you come to, it is now final. And you, as an individual, have to accept this.

How you react to whatever is going wrong in your home with this spouse, you have to assume responsibility for your part of it. And if you happen to be a man, and I believe this with everything I have in my body, that you've got to ride this storm out. I did not know this before, but I believe if there's any leaving done, it would have to be my wife. Because unless you happen to be in her home and it's her property and you moved in, then as far as the marriage is concerned, I think you ought to get a lot of counseling, long before you break up; a lot of counseling, from professional people. I don't think marriages are made to be broken up, as we think today, because you disagree on something. And violence, punching and hitting, I believe is one of the worst things that you could possibly do, especially a man to hit a woman. I've hit two women in my life. I hit one because she hit me and hit another one through anger. I think that the worst mistake that we make is making decisions after you've gotten into a relationship. I think you need to make them before. Allow God to be in your life and lead you through it. I guess that's a pretty hard thing when you haven't been blessed well enough, that both of you are Christians in a home. It's a lot worse when one thinks he's a Christian or she's a Christian and the other one think that you're not; it kind of works against each other. I don't know what to do about that, how to talk about it. Maybe that's a subject we don't need to talk about, maybe we just pray about it.

I would like you to know, personally, that most of the things that you hear me talking about don't do most of the wrongs that is obvious that we all know they're wrong. I broke most of those rules. I've been derelict of duty in most of the things you here me talk about. That's the reason that I'm not talking hearsay. I'm talking about the things that I know. I want you to look down the road of life and see if there are any signs on the way that can allow you to detour and not go the same way I've been. But its one thing that I would not like for you to do and that is to be that person like I was that's always going around trouble. I was a problem 'go- rounder', not a problem-solver. I think we need to experience some of these problems by dealing with them, and then when they come up in our lives later on, we're able to deal with it, on a better level. But not only maybe we didn't deal with when I was wrong; maybe we had a great penalty to pay. But we have the opportunity now to change somebody else's life, to give them a direction, to point out the pothole on the road of life. I'm sorry; I'm not going to duck that responsibility. You see you hear people say get the plank out of your own eye before you try to get the mote out of somebody else's eye. But put it this way, maybe I haven't gotten all of the trash out of my own eye, but I don't have a plank in my eye now. I still have some trash in there but, I'll tell you what, I can recognize the problem zone and I'm not going to hide behind my own faults in order to, not to try to help you see that stumbling block in the road. I'm going to point out some potholes down the road for you, because I don't want you going down the same road that I went down. I got some trash in my eye now, but maybe it's not as large as it used to be. But it's not going to stop me from talking about the things that I know about.

PROFILE OF A SPECIAL CHILD

Stephen Grant Carter was born March 22, 1991. Stephen's birth was planned before he entered the world. His name was chosen from the Bible. It means "crowned one." His life truly expresses that meaning. He is an outgoing, eager young man who's full of life.

At the age of 3 and 1/2, he suffered three major strokes and by the age of five, he suffered two minor ones. Most of his physical movement had to be regained, but tremendous progress has been made. Since 1994, he has been receiving IV treatments every three weeks in the hospital.

He is so grateful to God to be alive. He is expecting Jesus to give him a miracle to "walk independent of others to assist."

By Donna Carter
About her son who is Guy P. Darden, Sr.'s great-grandson

FOLLOWING ORDERS FROM GRANDPA GEORGE

When I go back to that place it still feels like me; my beginning. I came upon some rough and tough mountains to climb, especially for a child; but when I think about those times, I have to think about the good times as well as the bad. Some of those good times were when Grandpa George used to read the Bible to me. He used to talk about integrity and how much respect and how much credit that he gave Almighty God.

Everybody else's farms looked like they had a drought with the crop parching up with the sun. People used to come by when all the farms were brown and the corn and peanuts were in a drought. His corn would be green. It looked like almost a black green. The peanut vines would be so high. Everything he had was always so great and wonderful. It looked like it grew so beautiful. I never saw anything look like it wanted to die around that place. People used to come by and say, "Uncle George, what on earth did you do to make your peanuts grow like that?" He said, "I didn't have nothing to do with it. I just talked to the Lord and He's taking care of all of it. I'm just following orders." I really believed that. I really believed that my grandfather had something going on between him and the Almighty.

I remembered he was not a guy who told you a lot of things to do. He told you one time. He trained you how to do a job and he expected you to do it. He didn't expect to have to go over and over, telling you what to do and how to do it once you learned it. He was not one who would come calling you early in the morning to get you out of bed. He would say, "It's time to get up", and he said that loud enough for everybody in the house to hear and expected you to get up. If I didn't get up, he would send my Mother up to get me, and when she came up, she came up with a strap or a whip, and you didn't have to take a second thought the next time, you got up when you heard Grandpa moving around. He expected you, every once and while, to surprise somebody. He expected to get up one morning and find the fireplace going. He assumed that from his training and his teaching and from him reading the Bible that you got enough foundation from there to know what to do.

I could be a crybaby and go around feeling sorry for myself because I never remember Grandpa telling me I could be anything I wanted to be in those terms. But now that I think about it, if I lived up to the standards that he was teaching in those days, I would have known what to do in tough times and what to do in good times. If you found his God-like instructions, you would know what life had for you. I have to admit, I did not go through life wondering what I ought to do. I just did what I wanted to do in most cases. One of the things that I felt that I should do was when I left Grandpa that nobody, including my mother, was going to do very much for me other than me. And if I wanted whatever, I was going to have to try to make some kind of effort towards that. Every time I asked my mother for anything, it just wasn't available; the money wasn't there. My mother expected other people to give her the things that she needed. She left home too early to get the basic foundation training that you need to face life with. So she had to struggle in life to do whatever man told her that was in her life to do, or have a rough way to go. She didn't have too much wisdom and too much knowledge to give me. Every time I would say something about going to school, she would tell me that I had no clothes. She saw clothes as being something that was needed in society, especially pour people. I saw that if I wanted any clothes, I was going to have to make them or get them. I didn't have money to buy them and so I was going to have to make them myself. I was going to have to try to learn how to do that somehow, so I started tearing clothes apart and putting them back together and started trying to make a living for myself.

I was hired out when I was eight years old. I thought it was wonderful because I was working and I was having something to give my Mother and something to do for myself. I was proud. I was always complimented on the work that I did. I learned everything the best way I knew how and tried to do it better than anybody. One thing my Dad and Mom told me and everybody that I knew, was that whatever I did on this Earth, I had to do it twice as good as the white man in order to get half as far as he would. Now, that is one thing they did teach me and they taught me that well. Whatever I decided to do and it didn't make any difference what it was, I had to do it better much better than any white man. That was goal: To do it better than the best white person could do anything. It helped me a lot. I'm not going to tell you today that I would teach my kids like that but I would say do whatever you can do the best you know how and try to do it better than anybody. Yes. I would say that. Do the best you know how and then try to learn something from somebody else.

I don't think I have been lucky on this Earth. I believe I have been blessed to be born and raised under the circumstances that I was, and to get where I am at today without a world of crime. I think I'm blessed. I believe that if you believe in working and in doing the best you can for yourself, and seek to understand and help other people. I just don't believe that you can go through life helping your brother with the same kind of thing that you have and not be successful in some way. I believe that you can learn how to live on this Earth and teach others to live, and you can learn how to help other people do things and share your life with other people. You get an understanding of what hard work is. You understand that the world doesn't owe you anything but you are able to work for it. If you give God the thanks for living on this Earth and you let Him know how much you appreciate it by following his leadership I believe you will be successful. I just don't believe that you can live on this Earth, give and share, and do the things that you need to do, and not always the things that you want to do and not come out with some kind of motivation in your heart. You may be hungry sometimes and you may struggle sometimes. I think sometimes we need to do some heavy lifting to strengthen our muscles. I believe sometimes we need to go through some trials and tribulations to reassure ourselves that we can do it, and that we can go through tough time like we can go through the easy times.

I don't think that we can take this time that we have here on Earth that God lends to us and use it wastefully. I believe time has a value system built in it. You need to activate that in your lifestyle. I don't believe that we need to keep going around using that phrase, 'we don't have time', because whether you know it or not, you really are telling the truth. You don't have time. God has time and He leases it to you to be used for wise and good purposes and not just for yourself, but for other people too. You need to learn how to use it. Because I believe time is one of the most valuable assets that we are allowed to use. I've wasted a tremendous amount of the time that God has allotted to me. Each one of us has a certain amount of time allotted to us, for a certain period of time. It is not ours to use and do with as we want to. We're supposed to use it for what we need to use it for, for God's purpose and for humanity's purpose. You see, when we help other people, we help ourselves if we help them in a positive manner. You just can't "take the children's bread and cast it to the dogs" just because you have it and just because they ask for it. You need to know something about their needs. You need to know something about their lives. You need to know something about your purpose. You need to know who is leading you and teaching you. You need to know a little bit about self-motivation. I believe self-motivation comes in when you allow yourself to accept Godly principles in your life. I believe that will motivate and activate the love in your heart. I believe that develops strength, encouragement, and energy. I believe that you will have all the vigor that you need to push on forward. I believe the purposes that God laid out in that Holy Bible will give you the connection to humanity that you need.

I had known my Grand Daddy to walk 3 or 4 miles to tell a man that he didn't have the quarter he borrowed but he brought it back to him next week.

I don't know how many times my mother was married. I know I had many last names; as many as 5 last names when I was a child. I know that after I had searched my Mother's life and history and my grandfather's life (Lewis Holland), I learned that he wasn't a very poor person. He had some rough times but he owned land and he was a basket weaver, a carpenter, a shoe maker, and he could build almost any house he wanted to. He dipped in and out of real estate. He was a liaison of sorts. In other words, he would bring whites and blacks together and assure the blacks that this white person that he was dealing with was a good person. He had many children, and back in those days, if you owned a farm and had a large family, you did rather well as far as farming was concerned because you didn't have to hire anybody since everyone in the family usually helped. When I came along, all his children had left Grandpa Lewis except my Mother. I would say this, my Mother did not want to live by my grandfather's rules and regulations, because when I came along, she had already been married several times and my mother died when she was 36 and I was 18. Now, when I say she was married, I don't know anybody that my mother married except that everyone tells me that she did marry my brother's father (Mathey). I never saw my brother but one time. His name was Anderson Ricks. I saw him inside of the car and he would not let him roll the glass down where I could see him good or talk to him. She said she was married, I suppose, to his father. I would say that my Mother was a child that didn't want to follow Dad's rule and regulations, and perhaps that's how she got started in a bad direction. I know that she had to take my brother back to her husband. I don't know if she had to take him back to him, but she did take him back and left him on the doorstep in a basket when her husband was out in the field chopping cotton. She told me that she regretted that and I know she did because I saw her shed many tears behind it.

I didn't have a Mom that taught me and showed me the road of life. But those Bible readings and seeing my grandpa and how he got along with the community and his family and the Bible readings stuck with me. It stuck with me so strong that by the time I was twelve, I joined the church. I joined the church because I felt that was where good people went. I did the things I saw good people do because I saw them get recognition when they did. I worked hard because that's what I was taught to do. I felt good working. I was able to compete and socialize with the best of people during that time because, for some reason, I always knew how to make money; the legal way and the honest way. I just didn't know how to keep it or I didn't care to keep it. I enjoyed spending it and giving it away, and for a period of time, that's what I did. Whatever I made, I gave most of it to somebody else. I shared it with my friends; if they needed it, I gave it to them until someone misused me awful bad and I froze up for ten years and didn't give anybody anything. I found out that you close yourself off from other people and find yourself being the most important person in your life when it comes to receiving things. You always want to be on the receiving end and never on the giving end, and usually in the end; you don't come out that well. I truly believe that if you give, you will receive. That means the organization, a nation, and a people. It means the churches cannot continue to receive in the community and not give it anything back. It is a responsibility of the church to do that. I don't think or believe that a congregation can endure; this is my personal belief. You hear people saying, "Don't say anything to those people. Get the plank out of your own eyes before you try to get the speck out of somebody else. In other words, take care of yourself first. Find out how well you're doing first before you start pointing your finger at other people. I'm not saying, "Go around pointing your fingers at other people," but what I'm saying is, "You don't have to be perfect in order to tell somebody else about the road that you came down and that you've messed up." At least try to get an open door where you can walk in, so you can keep people from going down the same road that you went down, making the same mistakes; just because you made a mistake and you messed up doesn't mean that you can't tell me not to do what you did. If I do it, this is what's going to happen. That's your obligation. That's your responsibility as a Christian person. You're supposed to do that if you know how to do it. If you know how to reach that or if you're going to tear the person down and you don't know how to get into the person, then maybe it is best that you leave it alone. That doesn't mean that I'm going to just close my eyes to what you're doing and allow you to continue to do that without me telling you. Yes, I'm going to pray about it and I'm going to pray about it long before I come to you with it. You've got to put yourself in an embarrassing situation, but we have a habit and we use it as a crutch to keep from telling people because we messed up at one time and we can't tell other people about it. No, you can't make them do what you say, but when you know people are doing things out of ignorance, you can pull their coattail and you can let them know. It is your job to do that. It is not our job to go to other people and talk about them, but to go to them in God, and before long, before you go to them, you go to God and talk to Him about it and ask Him. He'll put you in their lives in a right and proper manner. You don't do anything just on the spur of the moment unless God first tells you and you'll know and you'll feel it.

TRULY HAPPY

I often wonder about how my life would have turned out if things were different. Would I be some corporate big shot that traveled the world meeting the rich and famous, dining at the finest restaurants and sleeping in five star hotels? Or perhaps a judge sitting on the bench passing judgment on the guilty or whom I thought were guilty, or being married to a rich powerful man.

Could money and power make me the woman I am today? No matter how I picture my life as being, I always come back to that burning question in my mind, would I be happy?

I feel as though happiness is the key to understanding not only ourselves, but others too. When we are genuinely happy, all our troubles seem to disappear. Life doesn't seem so unfair. The job isn't that bad. The kids, well, they are just being kids.

If I could change one thing in the world, it would be the way we as humans treat one another. We are so busy judging one another without getting to know the person, as a whole. A person's outward appearance doesn't tell the whole story. You can't know a person's heart by looking at him

I have met a lot of good-looking people on the outside but inside they were rotten to the core. No matter what social class we come from or end up in, we all start off with the same dreams. To be happy and some how obtain that "American Dream" one needs a good job, nice home, and a family that loves us. Not to be judged by the color of our skin, gender, social or education status.

I believe that all things are possible when you have God in your life. There is nothing that you can't overcome. Take my life for example; to be a single mother of three small children; working at a place many believe is no place for a woman at all. Striving each and everyday to teach the children good moral Bible-based values, and being both mother and father while trying to maintain my sanity in an insane world, but through the love and mercy of God, he has given me the strength and courage to overcome the daily battles I face. He has helped me to reach the dreams we all hope to achieve.

I have a family that loves me, a good job, and a nice home, but most of all I have happiness. I am truly happy with my life. I am rich with the treasures of three beautiful children and a spiritual family.

By Priscilla Fitzgerald

I had the opportunity to meet this lady through her volunteer help with some of the transcribing of my tapes for this book. I believe I got to know the essence of what was in her heart. It seemed like she, as a parent, that strove to contribute not only for her well-being but for the building for a better understand and cooperation between parents and the youth of today.

She also is one of the hard working people in our workforce. She seemed to be a dedicated and enthusiastic worker. Sometimes we seem to forget about the people who work in the lower echelon of our city and state government. If it wasn't for people like Ms. Fitzgerald we wouldn't have any city and state government at all. We sometimes forget that these people are the backbone, hard core working force of our nation. Don't you think they deserve the same recognition as our high officials? I do, even if you don't!

I have a great deal of respect for this lady and may God bless her in many ways.

By Guy P. Darden, Sr.

GO ALONG TO GET ALONG

I think sometimes the reason we don't understand our religious leaders, Christian leaders, or our men that teach us is that you're trying to go along in order to get along. Make it plain for us all. I think we've gotten so much book-learning that it's taken us away from what we claim we're trying to teach. I think we make God so complicated that the average man hasn't really gotten acquainted with God in a personal and intimate way; he doesn't know what we're talking about half the time. Someone who has never really had God explained to him as a young person, perhaps he hasn't finished school, gets away from the basic foundation that we are talking about when we talk about God.

When we're talking about God, we're only talking about two things: what is right and what is wrong. We're talking about being the best we can with the leadership of God. We're talking about that basic foundation that makes us all what we need to be. We are talking about common sense, common knowledge, and something that we've all been talking about since the beginning of the world. We're talking about the leadership that our ministers and pastors have taught us over the years. We're talking about what takes a man from stumbling around in the dark, those things that put a light in his path and the things that keeps us safe from slipping when we walk. We're talking about the things that stand in our way that keep us from doing what we need to do instead of always doing what we want to do. We're talking about the foundation that we need to teach our children to make them what they need to be.

Those of us who go to church, stand inside the church walls and listen to our pastors teach us about God, he's not just teaching us but he's teaching himself what he learns. Not what he learned in some educational school somewhere but what he has sought from God to teach him, what he has asked God for. "Many are called but few are chosen." We're talking about the foundation that makes a man know that he has been chosen to lead God's people. We're not talking about the things that we think, we're talking about the things that we are positive God gave us the inspiration for and gave us the wisdom and knowledge to do these things. There is one way that you always know when you're right it is when you allow God to teach you and deal with your problems before you teach somebody what to do. That's plain old common sense. When I was boy they called it "horse sense."

We're talking about the language that anybody in the street could understand; especially you educated people that claim that you have all the book-learning and all the intelligence so you can understand what a fool is talking about. There is no excuse for you to not understand what God's word means when you read it from the pages. Because if you say God is leading you, He's not going to lead you down a path that's going in the wrong direction.

I will tell you what I think has happened. You made up your mind that you want to go along that path that makes everybody happy. You want to go down that path that doesn't ruffle anyone's feathers. You want to walk down that path that makes everybody feel so comfortable and relaxed. You don't want to mess with anybody's conscience. You don't want to make anybody upset so you want to go along in order to get along even though you claim that you love me. You are trying to do everything that I need to carry me over this burden that I'm going through but at the same time you want to make me happy. Yet you know for a fact that this is not what God told you to tell me and you keep stumbling around in the dark and doing things your own way. They haven't worked in the last forty or fifty years for you then what makes you think they're going to work for me. They've lead you down the wrong path all of your life and now all of the sudden you're going to lead me down the same road in order to get along with me and to make me happy. Who are you going to make happy, me or God?

We have a generation of young people out here that need God's wisdom, not yours. We need people that are going to help us get over the mountain where we can build a foundation for our children so they won't be stumbling. But a young child that has an environment built around them that have been carrying them around can teach other children. You don't need someone in your community that destroys the fabric of it because what I see going on in that community has some impression on me.

Let's get it straight, that's a place that you go to congregate and be able to serve God and seek out wisdom and knowledge. That's not a church anyway. The church is found in your heart and it's not a temple. The temple is your body. It's what God has set up for Him to live in and to dwell in, to be able to be your leader and to work with your leadership through your wisdom that He gives you to give to your fellow man. It's not something that you take over in order to inspire you or to give you an inspiration to do what you want to do, but something that gives you an inspiration to do what God wants you to do. When you do that, you get a satisfaction that man can't possibly give you because you get the real, genuine resources from the natural forces that God put on this earth. If you're trying to find some fandangled thing that is going to excite people and is going to make them jump around and holler and scream and that's not what God has for you perhaps. God has something for you that can help your fellow man that can lead people in a way that He wants them to go.

But if we're setting up things as an enterprise to make money in order to feed my family just because I happen to be a minister that you love and care for, and that thing that you call love and knowing that it's going to just satisfy me and my family, is questionable about whether you love me or not. It's questionable whether giving me things makes you love me. If you can't give me what God tells you to give me, I question whether you love me or not. When you love me, you love me from your heart. You don't love me from that affection method that you get out there in the street. You love me for what God has put in your heart from the day you were born. When He created man, he put love inside of them.

Now if you don't want to try to activate the pure and unadulterated love that works into your heart that showed you to be who God is and amplified God through you, I doubt very seriously whether you love me or not. I doubt very seriously whether you love the people on this earth if you just want to satisfy yourself and you just want to make wealth that is going to satisfy you and your congregation, or you and your family, or you and yours. If you're not looking to help humanity and fight for the rights of people to be free of the hang-ups that they have on this earth, then I'm not so sure you're excited about God. If you're going to get excited because you smell a little liquor sometimes, or because somebody hurts your feelings sometimes, or you're going to get upset because somebody humiliates you sometime, and you find out that your church is only filling up with sinners instead of people that are holy, I'd like to know what you think the church was built for – that building you call the church? That's a repair shop where people go to get their broken pieces put together. If you don't understand that I doubt very seriously if you are under the commandments of God Almighty.

I love you as a people. I'm not out to hurt anybody intentionally. But, if your feelings get hurt in order to save your soul and give you a foundation that may help you over this hump that you've been fighting with for years, if that happens and you curse me out or possibly give me a black eye, I'll take that as a reward. I'll accept that. I'll give you an example. I went to a local police station not far from where I live and I began to tell them what I was looking for and that I was trying to get a book together about *God and Man's Relationship to Humanity*, and they said, "What's that got to do with the police department? What's that got to do with us?"

When you talk about humanity, you're talking about everything on the face of God's green earth. There is nothing on this earth that doesn't fit into that puzzle somewhere. It's just a matter of finding out where you fit in it. When you are talking about human beings that means we are all included. It means that I've got to love the police family and be concerned about how his family is being treated the same as I have about my own family. It means that I have to care about the mayor's family and I have to care about how he lives his life because he governs us.

You know, I feel like the reason that some of us don't get along and don't accomplish the things that we need to is because we go out alone on our own and do what we think is popular to the masses instead of doing what we feel is God's wishes, God's will. We decide to go running out on our own. I think a lot of our government officials and our city officials and state officials do what they feel to make the masses happy. As a matter of fact, they may not even know what makes us happy because what makes one man happy may make another one sad. But sometimes the happy part is not what we need. So we need to examine our conscience and examine the conditions of out nation before we make those decisions.

When the President took over he said he didn't care about anybody. He was going to do what he thought he needed to do. He didn't take advice from God Almighty. He did what *he* needed to do. He didn't ask God or talk to God and get the information from God and ask God how to lead this nation to its best form. He decided that he needed to do what he needed to do and if you need to get along you will have to follow me because I am the governing force of this nation. That should never be allowed to happen. But when we pull ourselves out and withdraw into our own personal and intimate family and forget about the rest of the world, that's what happens on this earth. We're part of this earth and when one person is taken out of his position he takes the link of life and distorts it. It doesn't fit together the way it's supposed to fit. The puzzle doesn't work the same way. We are part of a chain reaction of things. These are either going the wrong way or the right way.

When we are talking to people about God or when we are talking to people about the leadership of things, better yet when we are leaders and we are trying to direct a people, especially our young generation, we need to know that we are giving them something that will propel them through life in an excellent and constructive way. We need to know that we are giving them a foundation that will sustain them when they are having problems in life. We don't want them to do what I've done throughout my whole life: learning the system of going around my problems instead of facing them and trying to work them out with the leadership of God's wisdom.

Now we don't always have wisdom. Sometimes we just have knowledge and so we struggle. That's the reason it is so important that we have someone in our life that can teach us about God's value system. Sometimes we get so excited about the financial world, the money value until we lose the moral and integrity value. It doesn't give us the strength to fight the battles that we come in contact with in our life. There is a value system for every man on this earth even though you haven't quite accepted Christ as your leader or accepted Christ as your value system, as your drawing pool. But you need to get in touch with people that you see are leading a good life and they are living with integrity and honesty. Honesty is integrity. You'll find hopes and dreams built on a principle that stands for something. You'll be able to find something that has a value that means more than just the value system of the financial world. It will teach you what to do with a dollar when you get it.

HAPPINESS

Happiness is a state of well-being that is characterized by relative permanence, by emotion ranging from mere contentment to deep and intense joy in living, and by a natural desire for it to continue. It thus differs from mere pleasure, which may come about simply through chance contact and stimulation.

The Hebrew word for "happy" is e'sher (Ps 40:4), while the related verb 'a-shar' means "pronounce happy." (Ge 30:13) These Hebrew terms are used with reference to humans. They often denote the result of positive action, such as acting with consideration toward the lowly one or being in fear of Jehovah (Ps 41:1; 112:1) The Greek word rendered "happy" is ma ka'rious is translated "happy" in KJ at Acts 26:2 and Romans 14:22.

The happinesses described in the Psalms and Proverbs, and particularly those spoken of by Jesus Christ in his Sermon on the Mount, are often termed "beatitudes" or blessednesses" However, "happiness" is a more exact rendering of the Bible terms used, for both Hebrew and Greek have distinct words for "bless" (Heb., ba rakh: Gr., eu-lo-ge'o. Furthermore, "blessed" carries the thought of the action of blessing, while "happy" brings to mind the state or condition that results from the blessing of God. Many modern versions render 'a-shar' and ma-ka'ri-os as "happy," "happiness." (CK, JB, Ph, Ro, Tev, Yg, NW and other versions) Ma-karios is translated "happy" in KJ at Acts 26:2 and Romans 14:22.

All happiness promised in the Bible are contingent upon a right relationship with God; all of them are realized on the basis of love of God.

Happiness–n. 1. the condition of being happy; gladness. (Life is one long search for happiness) 2. good luck, good fortune 3. aptness, appropriateness. (The happiness of the companion caught your attention) syn. fitness, suitability, syn. Happiness, felicity, bliss means a feeling of satisfaction and pleasure. Happiness is the common and general word. (His promotion brought him happiness.) Felicity means great or joyous happiness. (I wish you felicity in your marriage.) Bliss implies the highest degree of happiness. (They are in a state of bliss now that they are engaged.)

Researched and written

By Cornelius C. Braxton

I believe happiness is when you feel content and your mind is at peace concerning your obligation to mankind. And you have stood up for the Godly principles and completed your obligation to humanity. I believe when you have completed that and when you feel at peace with God.

You can describe happiness in many ways and this is what I feel happiness is.

By Guy P. Darden, Sr.

FARMING

I am going to talk about something now that is the closest to my heart. I'm going to discuss a group of people that I feel are the most magnificent group of people on this earth. I don't believe that there is any other community that has contributed as much. I don't believe any other group of people on this earth have contributed any more than what our farming community has contributed to this country, and appreciated the least. I do not believe that we as a people in this nation and in this world have appreciated the farming community in the right. I don't believe that we have thought about or taken the time out to really realize how much value that the farming community has in the world; and its people.

Any nation that controls the food controls the nation. Any people, any individual that controls the food in any nation on earth controls the nation. Anybody that gets over to your food supply is owed to your muscle, your strength. Armies will cease to move; cease to fight, without food. Countries will disappear and people will die by the thousands and thousands if they can't get food.

It looks like the farmer, ever since I've been on the earth, has been the one that has been put on the back burner. I believe that his independence to move and not to beg, and to not allow people to buy up his land many years ago. A family farm; you wouldn't be able to buy it. It was not a money thing. It was an honor. It was a moral value hung up there. It was a matter of integrity. It was a family tradition and honor that was at stake when you owned a farm; one that your father owned and his father and his father, as far back as the generation goes. Sometimes a farm had been in the same family for over 100 years; it had not changed hands.

Another thing was that you just couldn't go up and buy a farmer's property. He had practically everything he needed. He wasn't a person that was greedy and he didn't go around flashing this and flashing that. The city did not excite him. The glitter didn't excite him. He wasn't hung up on this kind of garment or that kind of designer label, or this type of automobile; no, he wasn't hung up on that. He had pride in his work and realized the value of his work. He knew himself what he was contributing to.

My grandfather talked about the ground like it was almost a part of God's family. He honored it and he realized the value of it. He would pick up a handful of soil and shift it through fingers feeling very proud. He would not allow you to misuse the land. You had to treat the land in a proper manner. He said if you were good to the soil, it will be good to you. We put horse manure, chicken manure, and take vines and things and plow it underground. We kept the weeds and bushes and things from growing up and crowding out the ground. When we planted our crops we weeded it properly and we always fed the soil with the nutrients that it needed. We didn't strip our land. We didn't go in the woods and cut down everything that we saw in sight. We didn't cut down little, tiny trees and take them and sell them off because of the money. We saw a great value in our land. Nobody had to tell us how important we were. We knew and we appreciated it. We were grateful.

A handshake was as good as any contract signed by the biggest ball team in the country. You shook a man's hand and gave him your word; that was it. He didn't want any more. My grand daddy walked down to the bank or someplace and put his hand in somebody's hand or walked to a neighbor; he knew he meant what he said. I had know my grand daddy to walk 3 or 4 miles to tell a man that he didn't have the quarter, but he would bring it back to him next week. He promised he was going to pay him and he would go tell him he was sorry that he didn't have it and I'll see you next week and pay you then. He was going to pay him or he was going to show up there. That was the kind of integrity that the farming community had. That's what they believed in and when someone told them something, they took their word for it.

They allowed technology and greed to invade them. They allowed the lust of the world to invade them. Technology invaded and took the farms over. You see, we don't have technology, technology has us. When you hear people tell you that the farmers produce too much or they over-produced, that's not true. That is not true. What the farmer's were doing was using their land the way they wanted to use it and not the way the government or the market wanted them to do it. That was not good for the big time ranchers and the big time farmers. They wanted the little man to sell less and they would sell more. They wanted to hold back just enough to drive the price up. If that happened then the little farmer would have to stop selling so much because they only wanted so much to be out there. They wanted to be the ones to put that out there so they would be getting the money at a higher price. That's what happened. That's what is happening now. That's what happened to the oil. That's what happens to anything when you allow a company to monopolize. That is what the wealthy have done to the poor.

Well, you hear people tell you how great the stock market is doing, remember something. If the stock market is doing so great and their really whaling, you know where the money is coming from? It means whatever merchandise that you're buying is higher. The stock market is not going to go up. In other words, when oil prices go up, you will find that the stock market will go up. When the price of oil falls down, that's when the stock market falls down. In other words, it costs the farmer, let's say, 70 cents a pound to raise cotton. If it costs in 70 cents a pound to raise cotton and the market only give him 35% or 40%, how do you think he can continue to go on that way?

When I speak of stock, I'm talking about if the oil goes up, more than likely your oil stock is going to go up, and the price is going to go up at the pump. If OPEC is selling their oil for $30 a barrel this week and last week they were selling it for $20 a barrel, it's going to go up at the pump. You and I are going to pay the price. Because whoever, way up there on the blind, those people are not going to pay any more money. They are going to pass is down to us. When the price goes up at the pump, the guy who buys it from the wholesaler is not going say to the retailer, "Well, yes, gas went up 20 cents a gallon this week but I'm going to let you have it for the same price". No, he isn't going to say that. He may let it slide for a couple days in order to beat his competitor but it isn't going to be very long before he's going to raise his price. He has to. He doesn't have any choice. When you hear people talking about how great that they're doing on Wall Street; if they're doing great on Wall Street and stock prices are booming, somebody, somewhere is paying some high prices.

I'm a tailor. If I have been buying a spool of thread to make your suit and I have been paying a month ago 20 cents a spool and now it has gone up to $1 a spool, I'm more than likely going to raise my price some too. Because I can't continue to do like that unless I happen to be one of those people that feel like I can cut back on my profit a little bit. It's just not fair for me to do that. I cut down on my profit as much as I can in order to make a decent living. Every man deserves a decent living for his labor. Just because somebody is price-gouging you, that is no reason for you to price-gouge someone else unless it's cutting into your profit to where you can't make a decent living. Then that would be the sensible thing to do; is to raise your prices a little, the least amount that you can in order to still make a profit and make sure that your customers are happy.

It works many ways. Your customers see that you have integrity and that you are working with them. When you go up on the price, be kind and decent enough to let them know why. Let them have some insight on what you're doing and you'll find that things will change a little.

I went through that stock market issue to try to let you know that those prices are set. Price fixing and that kind of thing is kind of set through the stock market. The market system is set up for the farmers. Those people who are setting it up, they don't really know what the farmer has gone through. They don't know the problems that he's having on his specific crop this year – what he's going through. But yet they tell him what they will give him. He cannot tell them what he is going to sell it to them for. They make him a price and most of the time he can't go anywhere else and get a better deal. The market is so fixed that he has to accept what they give him that is if you're a small farmer. If you're not, then you more than likely are hooked into the system so you know pretty much about what is going on. What has happened today, the small farmers are unable to compete with the wealthy people that supplement – the small farmers are not getting that supplement. The supplement that has any value is going to the Fortune 500 companies. The big guys are getting it.

I have traveled all over this nation talking to small farmers. This nation has allowed the farming community to become one of the most misused group of people on this plant. I believe they still have a lot of strength if it wasn't for all these communities coming up on the farms. You see, they want those farms to fail. They want that land that they have. The cities are getting too crowded. There is too much crime in a lot of cities. There is too much going on. They want to build housing developments and factories. These farms are going to be used like the oil well fields were used years ago. Farms are going to produce fuel for this nation. This plan just didn't just start yesterday.

Some of them are realizing that their land is valuable. But you see the wealthy have a way of waiting you out. They have a way of going into certain communities; buying up the property around you and leaving you in a position that if you don't sell then they'll freeze you out. When you finally decide after everybody else has sold out around you, they give you what they want for your land. In other words, they might fix it so that the environment that they build around you, you may not be happy with it. They might have a factory over here and something going up over here and you don't want that. You don't want to live there. But your neighbors are all sold out. That's happening across Georgia. I saw it all over this country in different cities like Alabama where in these small town that don't have enterprises the county is buying out city properties. It's no longer in the city any more. It's a county. Whoever buys that will not have to go by those city laws anymore. But they start to pass laws and condemn your property a lot of times if you don't sell out to them. They'll buy your neighbors house if he's ready to sell or an elderly person lived in it and they're now deceased and the children don't want to live in it so they'll sell it. You've got 2 or 3 more neighbors that live around there and they decide they'll sell out. They'll offer you, at first, pretty good money. The first 2 or 3 people that sell will get good money for their property. But as it goes on, the last one to sell is not going to get very much because he tries to hold out. By then, they don't care whether you sell or not because they're going to build what they need to build there. You're going to have to certain rules and regulations to go by. The laws will get you because there will be certain ordinances and then they'll change the ordinances. They'll build something there that you don't want to live by or they will have a housing development going up there that has to have certain regulations. If you sell that house, the ordinance will change the day you sell it. The next guy that lives there is going to have to pay higher taxes. They'll be different rules and regulations. It may be city property. It may be a shopping center going up in there – anything.

They are taking over communities all over this nation like that. I hate to see that happen. Chicken farms and pig farms are going up where peanuts, cotton, and corn used grow. For me to go by a place where they raise hogs and see hundreds and hundreds of them squeezing so tight together they can hardly move instead of seeing them running lose on a farm across the fields and through the woods. I've seen thousands and thousands of chickens in one house. That's a hurting thing to someone who loves the land and loves fowl. You see, we didn't just love our animals for food and to sell for commercial market, we actually fell in love with those farm animals. We treated them nice. We took care of them. Some of them were pets. Some of them we didn't become too close to them because we knew that we were going to have to kill that animal and we intentionally didn't get too close it.

What I am saying to you is that it was love, integrity, and respect for the land and for the animals. But now, it's dog-eat-dog through those beautiful and wonderful country lands that we used to live in. I want to salute all of the farmers in America because all of the rich and wealthy farmers are not greedy people. Some of them are working hard and some of them want to do everything they can to keep the prices in the right place, and be honest and have integrity.

All of any segment of our society is not bad. There are good wealthy people. There are good rich people, and there are bad ones. But it doesn't take too many bad apples in a basket to contaminate the whole basket. We need to hold out hope. And if we need our farming communities, our cities, roads, villages, country communities; if we want to keep them we better maintain them. We better try to become more acquainted with what is going on instead of looking at easy fixing; all of the push-button lifestyles. It's not working. It is not working. It's not even working for the manufacturers. I have to admit I realize in order for some of the manufacturers in this nation to make a decent living. We do have to organize our states and communities and come together with some kind of consensus that labor and management, manufacturers and people who survive in this nation in order to be enterprises need to have some type of consensus that means something to somebody outside of just personalizing everything.

I realized many years ago that something was happening too fast on the farm land. People were getting too greedy and too lazy. Those things are contaminating the human dignity and human integrity and human survival. Love and compassion and fairness, no, we're dog-eat-dog. Who ever has the best skills; well that is who will win. In other words, the only way we can survive is to fight each other. That's not the American way. It has become that way. We have decided to allow it to be that way. We got too greedy in the labor areas many times. We allowed the unions at one time to control and rule and dominate manufacturing because the mafia was controlling them at one time. They were hustling businesses and they were hustling the union workers. When you start doing that then everything gets out of order.

You see what is happening today with the manufacturers, they're running to another country. As a matter of fact, it looks like we're supposed to try and get a whole generation of people moved in here. They're people that have a different philosophy, who have a lower standard – that's what we're trying to bring in. They're people that can't fight for their rights and don't have citizenship and it looks like we're trying to move foreign labor in where they don't have the rights to fight for their rights.

We are trying to get another labor force from the prison system. We're walking in and holding up our hands and walking in the prisons with a white flag in our hand. We're surrendering to the drug lords and the criminals of this nation. Our young people are joining a completely new society. They're falling right into the hands of devil's trap – money. How can you make money? How can you call it making money by committing crimes and going to jail? That's what you do, commit crimes and go to jail. Commit crimes and go to jail. Commit crimes and go to jail. In other words, what our forefathers died for, especially black people, slavery – all those thousands of people that died, white and black, have died for the nation to make it free. That's starting all over again. We are actually going to have another slave market. The only thing is this slave market the young people are surrendering to it. But listen, I know you're not going to like what I'm saying but that's alright. It needs to be said. You're going to have to give up some of your credit cards if you want what you say you want. You're going to have to give up some of those designer labels. You're going to have to give up some of your SUVs.

You're going to have to start paying for stuff when you buy it. You're going to have to start trying to find prices that meet your income. But what has happened, when you keep buying these designer labels and just looking for labels instead of looking for quality, you're raising the prices on yourself. You're lowering your labor prices and raising the market prices of goods and services. When you decide that you are going to commit crimes in order to buy the big, pretty, shiny, glittery stuff out there, or you decide that you're not going to work for $5, $6, $7, or $8 an hour because your friends might see you working down there.

I want to tell you something, if you use all that brilliant intelligence at least I would hope that you would have - I would like for you to have – then you'll be out here looking for something to serve the people with. You'll be trying to find something that the people want that they don't have and that you can give to them. You'll be trying to build your character up. You'll be trying to reestablish your priorities. Instead of trying to spend everything you've got, you should be trying to save everything you've got in order to raise the type of family. You cannot have your cake and eat it too. If you've blown it and have that baby, you're going to have to try to take care of it. You're going to have to set new priorities. If you made a mistake back there somewhere, you're going to have to try somehow to change your lifestyle.

I've blown it all my life. It took me a lifetime to change my lifestyle. I don't want the young people of this nation to do that. If your child is into this cycle, it can go a complete generation. It will have a domino effect in your lifestyle, in your family's lifestyle. If you don't give your child a foundation to build on, he's not going to do any better than you've done. As a matter of fact, it's going to get lower and lower and lower. Instead of building up your standard of life it's going to be going down. That is what is happening now to this nation. It's not going up, it's going down.

Young men were being called 'hicks' and all of the names and labels that we get put on us from being kind of quiet or not really "hip", as the people used to say, to what was going on out there in the world. He was kind of satisfied with what he had at home. The banker couldn't even get control of him because he didn't need a lot of money. Whatever he needed he took it to town and sold it on the local market. If he needed some extra money for something like to pay tax on the land, he was able to go to the saw mill down the road and make a deal with them to cut 2,000 to 3,000 feet of timber. Whatever amount of money he wanted, he could raise it by cutting some timber in the wintertime or the fall and take it to the saw mill and sell it. He either took it on a log wagon with some teams or he had a truck to come out and pick it up and haul it. The saw mill may have had a truck and they would come out and get so much and they would pay him so much money for it. They racked the lumber on the lot. He got a reasonable price for it. He didn't try to rob the people. When the end of the year would come he would sell as much of his crop as he needed to sell for survival. The rest of it, he would put it in his barn. There would be whole-salesmen coming from farm to farm, speculating and bidding on crops. He didn't try to rip anybody off when he sold his crop. He was the only person that he couldn't get under control because he had his own survival kit.

But then the banker started lending money and the farmer started buying modern equipment, equipment he couldn't afford but needed because he, himself, was tired and the young people were taking over and he wanted to make them as comfortable as he could. All of a sudden he began to get in debt. The loan sharks and the bankers in the commercial world began to see that they could get control over the farmer if they got control of the land. And the only way to get control of his land was to lend him money where he could become involved. They knew that the farmer would not be able to pay. A little small farmer would never be able to pay back on a $100,000 piece of equipment, no way, even for a $50,000 piece of equipment. So the farmer wound up overspending himself.

Then this bright idea of these men realized that the farmers of this country had too much control over this country. They had control of the food. They had control of the land that produced the food. They went from north to south and they found so much land that had been laid-by (meaning you were not producing anything on the land). Farmland was growing up in bushes and this nation wanted that to happen. The government and the money people of this nation wanted that to happen because that meant the land was not producing and when the land was not producing it was presenting opportunities for the greedy, money-grabbing people of this nation.

Now somebody will say, "Explain that." Well you see, most of the land in Georgia, Alabama, and Mississippi, when it doesn't produce the crop land such as peanuts, cotton, corn, or the other vegetation, then they take that land and they plant pine trees. Pine trees have the monopoly over all trees in America. They crowd out all the other vegetation, bushes and undergrowth. They get it out of the way by putting pine trees in. They don't allow those trees to get up large and big like we used to get our lumber so a man could go out and cut ten, twelve, or fifteen trees and build a house with it. Now, if a tree gets up to ten to fifteen inches around, you've got a pretty good size tree. They cut it down for pulp wood. They cut it down for all kinds of things that they use it for. They grind some of it up and make into pulp. I don't know all the things they do with it but it is a big industry of trees growing all over this nation and ninety-nine percent of them are pine trees.

The land that used to produce is not producing now. They say if the land doesn't produce so much that they take it out of the farming section and you'll find that that land becomes a place where they put pulp wood for paper or whatever they use it for. But they don't allow it to reach its full growth. They speed up the growth of it. I used to be able to go up to a tree and be able to count the rings and tell you how many years old it was. Now, you get two, three, or something to make a year and you would not be able to do that anymore.

  They ran the farmers out of business by lending them money that they could not pay back. Men bought up the farms from the banks. Now the manufacturers are running the farms. The land that you see growing is mostly not owned by the farmers themselves. Most of the land is rented because that farming land that we once had is now in the control of manufacturers. The cities are getting too overcrowded and too full and man's plan now is to move the cities to the farms, to bring up new development, housing developments, manufacturing, instead of having them in the city. They are going to move them to the farm lands and into the open spaces and build new housing developments around those areas. That's what is putting the farmer out of business. He can't compete.

  They said the farmers have over-produced and that's causing the price to be driven up. Not so. The little farmers have never over-produced. Who is over-producing are the big farmers that have a lot of land that they bought up. They want to produce as much as they can because they want to make as much money as they can. But they want to control the food so they can set the price where they want it. They want to process the food, or change and alter it, and they want to control the producing of it where they are in a position to produce.

  A farmer cannot go and plant his farm then use the seeds from it to plant back the next year. He wouldn't have to buy the seed and he could plant as much as he wanted to. I cannot move to a farm and buy 5 acres of wasteland, so to speak, out there and cultivate and bring it back into service and raise my own food, my own hogs, and my own cows. It would be awfully hard to do that. You have to be a very wealthy person to do that now. You used to be able to do that. If prices were too high in the city and you were having too much of a struggle, you could move to the farm land. Now they are getting to see that this would happen.

This whole country was controlled almost by the farming community which the farmer himself didn't realize. Now the cities are getting over crowded. The wealthy people are moving to the farm and they want that land, but the manufacturers are going to control it; the big shots, the money people, the Capitalist system where people will buy up this land and sell it back to the consumer for a tremendous price. Farming communities are going out completely because they are buying them up and putting developments in them. It's going to happen all over this nation.

That's what has happened to our farms. That's why the farmers cannot produce. The government has been giving money to the manufacturers to buy these big farms and produce. They have been giving them supplements to get them to take over this space where they can generate taxes and this money. God knows where it goes - to this place and that place. Everybody dipping into the pot, but don't think it's not well planned and controlled. That's what happened to the farmer. He's been taken over by big business. He had too much control. He was the only group of people on the earth that could not be controlled by the money-grabbing people. So they had to put him in debt where they would have the opportunity to control him. They want to take over the food, now they've taken over the food that the farmer has. The farmer has no control over himself. The small farmer is on welfare, so to speak. That's a dirty word to some people, but to the manufacturers of this nation, it's not a dirty word.

On one hand they say the government doesn't need to be in our lives but they got the government in their lives. The government supports them. This was a well kept secret up until a few years ago. Nobody knew about it. We had to fight and go to the Supreme Court to make them release this information. These Fortune 500 companies were squeezing out the little farmer out intentionally, not accidentally. Now it costs him $ .70 to produce something that he gets thirty-five percent for when he sells it in the market because they don't want him in business anymore. They want the big companies that produce the food where they can go in there and put the price anywhere they want to. They can charge what they want to charge because the food has been processed, re-processed and re-shipped.

You see, the producers of food today, if they went back many years ago involving the farmers, the food was no different from Mr. Jones farm than it was from Mr. Smith's farm. Food is food. Apples are apples. That is the way it used to be. That's not the way it is now. Now when they get through dressing it up so pretty, the apples so red, and all the processing that they do to make the food look beautiful, you would think it was just picked off the farm; however, it doesn't have the nutrition that it used to have many years ago.

The people today, the young people under age 35 years, certainly don't even know how food is supposed to taste. They think you're supposed to put the seasoning in it and that's what makes the food taste good. I remember a time when you could pick up a tomato or an apple and when you tasted it, it tasted like a tomato or an apple. Oh, my God. How much change happened due to the chemicals and the processing that they go through? You're not getting a better tasting food; you're getting a better looking food altered by technology. We don't have technology, technology has us. That's what I was trying to say when I was talking about the woman.

They used to say that a man chases a woman until she catches him. We've chased technology until it has caught us and it has trapped us. It has taken it us wherever they want to take us to. We don't have very much to say about it because we gave up all our strength. Now, if we start complaining they say we're "old fogies "and that we don't know anything and people like me who can't read or write, imagine what kind of argument they would have against what I'm saying.

Some time back; a long ways back, over 20 years ago, I began to think about writing a book. So I started at it. I did a lot of writing, and I guess the way I write, most people don't call it writing because I talk on tape most of the time. I've been inspired about humanity; about what it was and how do we relate to it. Do we really recognize it? Does it mean something to us? What part are we playing in it? Do we feel like we are a link in the chain of life, and if we are what part are you and I playing? Can we separate ourselves and point out what this one might be doing or that one might be doing? Or can we personalize on it and think about what I'm doing, and what is it about humanity that shakes me up when I think about it? I don't know. It might shake you up too.

I believe when Christ is in our lives in the fullest potential, that He inspires us and shows us how to do things. I don't think we always have to have all those degrees behind our name either. I don't even think you have to know how to read for God to talk to you.

I know something about life. I'm old enough to know a little about it. I'm a Senior Citizen now. I've come from way back there in the 20's; 1924 was when I was born. I've had a long time to ponder lives trials and tribulations and take out and put in ideas and thoughts. But I've been like most people, I just kind of flowed with the flow; going along with the crowd. Sometimes feeling sorry for myself and sometimes feeling very proud. But life is more than just feelings. We have to find something on this earth that is important enough to us to get our attention; the center of our attention to draw us out of ourselves and make us want to be something and do something.

I was brought up on a farm and I was very proud of that because it was something that I could be a part of. From the very earliest moment of my life, people on the farm, I thought, found themselves useful and they were proud men and women. And the reason I think that the people on the farms felt so proud was because they realized their importance to the world. They thought about more than just money. They felt that they were contributing to the welfare of other people. They knew about their importance to the up-building of their community. They knew the importance of food; decent food and they took pride it what they did. They knew the important part that they played to humanity. I wondered for a while what humanity was but then I realized that my grandfather knew what humanity was; he knew what the word meant. He knew how valuable it was for another man to be assisting and helping someone else. He knew what it meant to be a cog in the wheel and the circle of helping fellow man exist. He knew what it meant to be hungry. He knew what it meant to be a part of sharing with humanity. He knew the meaning of the words friend, neighbor, partner, togetherness and Godliness.

The farming people of this nation were the backbone of this nation. The most important link in history of any nation is the farming community. You can't do anything without the proper diet, the proper food to eat. Ever since the beginning, from the caveman to this day, food is still the most valuable resources that we own on earth. Our armies cannot function, our government cannot function; a nation would be dead without the food that the farmers produce. But we, as a people, and I say this strongly; we as a people have forgotten the farmer. We've neglected him and looked him as being some little small person; as though he hasn't quite got it or he has never had it. We've always looked at the farming community as someone that is not quite so important. Now, if we haven't seen it that way, we certainly have acted that way because we saw the farmer go from thriving and being successful to being the less successful group of men and women in this nation other than a few wealthy, rich people in whom the government has seen fit in the nation, to supplement. We're not talking about poor farmers that need this supplement in order to survive or that we are sending people out to the farms to assist farmers and show them how to raise better crops to produce something better and better tasting food; that that gives us more energy and that is better for our bodies. We're not looking at a nation of people that are trying to assist the farmers and give them something to work with that will make them better at their job that that are doing. We don't look at them as being a strong resource. We think more of the grocery stores and the wholesale stores that produce food than we do the farmers that do the real work of it.

The rich and wealthy people of this nation have taken our farmlands away from the farmers. They taken it and made it manufacturing, so to speak. It's a production plant. In my opinion, it has not happened accidentally. We know; at least I know and most of my friends know that I've talked to, when you control the food of any nation on earth, you control the nation. The farmers had too much control for this nation; for the money and greedy people of this nation. The people who are in our government that are greedy and hungry for control, well they had to take some of this control from the farmers. The farmer controlled all the land in America. When I say all, I don't mean absolute all, but they controlled the biggest portion of the land. And they weren't selling that easy. You couldn't buy it so you had to take it away from them by getting them in debt and the debt was unforeseen because they lost the sight on 'out there'. That there were not people honest and hardworking people; there were people that were greedy and wanted to be in control of the power structure of this country, and they are in control - in control of the food.

I just don't understand how people can tell me that I'm so ignorant because I don't know how to read and write and they can't read the writing on the wall and they cannot understand and see what is happening to this nation. It is happening in the farmlands of this nation. It started there because we didn't have control of the farmers. The power structure needed to be in control of the farmers, needed to be in control of the land so they could do what they wanted to do with it. But they still needed the farmers' ideas. You have to be a college graduate almost now to be a farmer. You have to at least know how to read and write.

The farmlands of this nation were the only hope for a person, practically, that didn't know how to read and write. Somehow people get the impression if you don't know how to read and write that you are dumb. The farmers of this nation didn't bother, many years ago, to send a lot of their children to college because they felt like they were going to be on the farm and what they needed to know, they would teach them. Elementary and high school were probably as far as they needed to go. A lot of them didn't even bother to go. Nobody pushed them off to college. I'm not saying that's a good thing. I know that was a mistake with some people. But you don't have to sit back because you don't know how to read and write and be a total fool and nincompoop because I don't even know what that word means. Somebody said it and I just keep repeating it; and that's what we do in life. We repeat and follow; just keep following people because they say they're going somewhere that's going to make us great and we don't even know their destination. That's what has happened in this nation today in the name of technology. What technology does in certain communities and with certain people is take them completely out of control of their lives and they control your life and they take you were they want you to go.

Have you ever heard this story that a man chasing a lady until she catches him – well that's what has happened. We have chased technology until it has caught us. Now we are totally out of control. We are going for that pot of gold at the end of the rainbow in the middle of the sky some place. If technology came together with this nation and said, "What can we do to make this country a better place? What can we do to help our people?" If we had town meeting where we sit down with each other and debated and talked and questioned and had people going from door to door and people communicating with each other. If we had our churches coming together and being concerned about our nation and our community and our people instead of being concerned about themselves personally and intimately, this nation would be what it was meant to be in the first place.

PINE TREES

Pine trees have monopolized the farm lands that grew vegetables, corn and all the things that farmers planted for eating purposes. Now it is just pine trees. They are cutting down and clearing the large trees, at the same time driving out all the animals. They are not huge trees like long ago. They are little ones. Evidently pine trees make more money for big business than any other tree. They are used for building construction, piling and for ship's masts and spars, fuel, railroad ties, mine props, and making charcoal.

But when I was boy, you couldn't get our arms around them because they were so big. They were used for lumber and turpentine. Years and years ago you could build a whole house with a few trees. Now with our "microwave" society, trees aren't allowed to grow very large.

Oxygen is leaving the atmosphere because of all the trees and vegetation being cut down. Animals are losing their habitat due to man's invasion of our environment. Animals fertilized the soil and the trees were always green. Human beings have a responsibility for animals as well as human because they are part of the cycle of life.

HAVE WE DISCOVERED OURSELVES?

All of the sudden I think we as Americans have discovered ourselves. I think we've truly looked inside of ourselves and found out who we are. We don't even want to admit who we are. We need to examine ourselves as a nation of people and take back our country from the politicians and run it with hope and dreams for all of us, not just for a few.

We have overlooked the misuse of the farming workers of America and the farm owners of America. It has snuffed out almost all of the power structure of the poor people of this country, about how a nation of people that could have been great; a nation of people who could have joined in with the Indian nation of this country. They probably could have taught us something about nature, about life.

But we separate ourselves because of our races and we make that the border line. Certain communities and certain areas and certain segments of society are finding out that it's not so much of a race, but of a class. We segment out this nation and section it into classes. The money level of your checkbook will decide where you eat, where you live, what you do, where you go, and who you socialize with.

You see, we have lost the value of what morals, integrity, love, and being neighborly mean. I doubt very seriously if we know the true meaning of being a neighbor. I doubt very seriously if we know the true meaning of what a neighbor is or if we know the true meaning of what real love is; real love, real integrity, honesty. Do we know the structure that builds honesty, the structure that builds integrity, the meaning of togetherness, the meaning of foundation, structure value of building a foundation? Do we know the essence of what we're supposed to be to each other, as a farming community, as a nation of people?

We don't realize that when we speak about the farming community that we speak about the earth, the foundation of all of us, other than God, nothing could be more structure based than the farmlands of this nation. It produces our food. God produced it and He produces us. Until we realize the real moral and spiritual value that God has in our lives, we're going to always run out there somewhere on our so-called education and our technology and we forget about the essence of moral standards. We forget about who we are as a people and what we were meant to be. We forget about our seed, the fertilizer that makes us grow. I feel like that's the essence of spiritual value and that can only come from God. I believe that when it comes from any other sources that it's useless. It doesn't have the value that it needs to lift us up over certain things.

Just to bounce away from this for a second. When we speak about terrorist groups, we talk about other shores, people in other nations and other places. The terrorist groups that are here come from a foreign place. We don't think about the Ku Klux Klan that killed and murdered in the swamplands of the South, and some places in the North. They are full of the bodies of black people that were killed by the Ku Klux Klan. They still exist in this nation. I don't see us trying to storm out and bomb out their strongholds.

I look and see men who fought for the civil rights of this nation and some of those people look like they have stuck their head in the sand and walked away from this earth. You don't ever hear from them except if it's something that can give them the publicity to make money.

Something has happened to us as a people; as a black people, as Americans, as a nation of people that think about themselves and only 'themselves' is never going to be successful. I don't care how much money they have. The Spanish nation of people that are in this nation, the Port Ricans and the Mexicans; the Spanish speaking people, they want to separate themselves from the black people. The black people want to separate themselves from the Spanish people. The Spanish people don't want to get too close to the black people, the African people. They don't want to be mistaken for a black person. I can understand why, because you'd be treated differently.

The black people say the Spanish people, the Mexicans and the Port Ricans are taking the jobs in this nation from them. That's not totally true. They've given up the jobs because they don't want to do those jobs anymore. A lot of us don't want to do the domestic jobs, cleaning houses and cleaning toilets or dig ditches with a shovel and the spade. We think we've gotten past that and don't need to go back there anymore. I remember when the bus stops on the corner were full with 10, 15, or 20 ladies going to somebody's house to clean it. Those days are gone now. The rich and the wealthy people, a lot of them have to clean their own houses.

They are saying, in the politics and behind the closed doors of this nation that ought not to be. They are going to get a labor force. The labor force they're going to get, if we're not careful, is going to be the same source as they had it before, only it's going to come from a different root. If we are committing crimes in this country, the poor black, Spanish and whites keep robbing and stealing. All will put their selves in a slave market. Their reputation and integrity will not pass in the labor market. The only place they're ever going to have to work is going to be in the prison system.

The prison system is going to teach them how to do technology; how to operate computers. But they are going to be operating the computers from inside the prison. That's going to be the labor force of tomorrow if you're not careful. You're going to find corporations and manufacturers shipping their work to the prison system to be done for them and they are going to have real qualified people there to do it. Because those people in the prison that come out with a trade are not going to be able to find jobs and they are going to start committing crimes all over again. Then they'll go back to the prison to be there for life. They're not going to lay up under the air conditioning and be exercising in the exercise room. They are going to be out here on the farms and places working for rich and wealthy people and they are going to be farmed out on contract and they are going to have guns standing over them and all of the things that used to be automatic slavery, it's going to be forced slavery.

You see before if you were black, you were automatically a slave. Now, if you were once a prisoner, you going to be automatically a slave, so to speak. You're going to be doing the enterprise work that is dirty and the rotten dirt that nobody else wants to do; you're going to be doing it - so much for that.

I'll tell you something. I may not have been to college and may not be able to read, but I'm telling you something that is going to happen, and it's going to happen in America if America stands that long. If anybody on earth is here that long. What we used to think will be by-and-by; finally, I believe personally, that by-and-by is just around the corner.

I want you to know that you can touch something and make it move. I want you to understand that I don't care how many churches or how many preachers that tell you that the only way you're going to know anything about the Bible is to learn to read it. You don't have to read the Bible to get the message. They have talking Bibles of every type all over this nation. They even have talking Bible histories. If you have a mind that will function and think, you can search out things yourself. Yes, it's a handicap in some ways. Yes, it's hard work. Yes, you have to think a lot. Yes, you have to remember a lot.

The reason I am saying so much now is because when my memory was good and excellent, I didn't do anything with it. Now God is trying to tell me something and I want to tell you something. I don't have to know how to read the Bible in order to talk about things that God has planned for us. God talks to me the same as He talks to anybody else. God does talk to us. He talks to us in our spirit. He talks to us in action. He talks to us by looking out in the streets in the morning when you get up, when we go out and see the trees and greenery, He's talking to us. When we see the landscape, He's talking to us. When we see the people, He's talking to us. We are being educated every time we look around us if we seek it and allow it to soak in.

You're not a fool because you were born to be a fool. If we are a fool and I'm a fool, I've allowed myself to become that way. I want you to know that you have something of value that you can share with this world even though it doesn't see anything but money and wealth and the excitement of having our own things. Nobody wants to do anything that is going to rub against the feathers. God is simple and plain. He's not a complicated God to those of us who don't have the education and the college degrees. He explains things well simply. He explains to us, step by step, what He means and what He has for us to do. He doesn't have a man on earth that He wants to just go somewhere and sit down unless He tells him to do that. He'll tell you what to do.

NOT ENOUGH TIME

When Guy Darden was a young boy, he had desires to read, but because of pride, through the years, he put a hold on his desires. The most important desire was to learn how to read. Another desire that he expressed was (with laughter) to become an FBI Agent. Remembering and sharing his mother's vivid words, on why his desires were to wait. Today, the memories and words of his mother were what led to his accomplishments and achievements. He is a professional tailor, by trade. He had been trained by some of our finest in history. Mr. Darden has been a tailor for sixty-one years and in business for himself for forty-two years. He tailored for different celebrities. He was an instrument boy, for different professions, in New York City.

In Mr. Darden's book about Time, he shares with his readers the importance of time. He believes, in the core of his heart, that time has so much value and essence. Time has a quality we should not ignore. Our first obligation is to our Lord and Savior the Father, through his Son Jesus Christ. In Psalms 31:15, "My times are in your hands." Our second obligation is to take our knowledge, and add it in the right perspectives. As members of society, we should pour out our morals and standards, into the empty vessels of our children. Our environments are lacking the substances these young vessels need to survive our tomorrows. The young vessels are thirsting and hungering for our love, compassion and knowledge from this generation and generations to come. The way we conduct ourselves has more of an impact than the words we speak. We have an old cliché, "Do as I say and not as I do ", and another cliché, "Actions speak louder than words." The society has a duty to these younger people of today, of our environments. We need to become more concerned with the whole person. The "whole person has many components, such as psychological, social, physical, financial and vocational, that comprise the total individual". (Introduction to Human Services, Page 157.)

If our children continue to do what we do in our homes, churches, schools and in our environment, it will exempt us out of the equations, as parents, ministers of God, teachers and most of all, motivators.

Mr. Guy Darden is also convinced that we have become unconcerned with the value and importance of the segments of time. He expresses the essence and values we could place on the time. In Ecc. 9:11, "I have seen something else under the sun:

The race is not given to the swift
Or the battle to the strong Nor does food come to the brilliant
Or favor to the learned; But time and chance happen
To them all.

Moreover, no man knows when his Hour will come.
The seconds, the minutes, the hours do not belong to us. Our priorities are critical, with the significance of the present. He also mentions how he was held down in his abilities to learn to read. Pride stopped his levels of aptitude in an education. When you process your knowledge, you need to put it in the right perspectives, in the right times and in the right ways. Process your knowledge sincerely and wisely, you'll have more intellectual insight on your values and the essence of time.

By Marilyn Smith

MORE ABOUT THE BOOK

There is a lot about <u>God and Man's Relationship to Humanity</u> that's not going to be like the average book because <u>God and Man's Relationship to Humanity</u> and <u>Time - The Most Valuable Asset</u> – well, I hope they compliment each other a little bit. Sometimes they kind of jump all over the place. I would consider this an inspirational book. Some people like to call me an evangelist and I **do** have a certificate that says I'm an evangelist. But I'm not a Bible student. I've never been to school for more than a couple of months in the last 15 years or so; maybe 20. The schoolhouse and a lot of records had burned up when I went down there. They say that they don't have any school records of me. But I thought I went maybe 3 semesters. Let me put it this way, I didn't learn how to read when I went and my English doesn't compliment Webster at all. As a matter of fact, Webster doesn't compliment me either, because my English is lousy. But those of you who are educated and those of you who are not quite so educated, and those of you who have plain old horse sense like I think I have, maybe will understand what I mean even if you don't understand what I say; at least I hope so.

I get criticized because I don't quote a lot of scripture. This book is not a book just about godly people. This book is not just a book talking about the Bible; it's talking about everything that happened that I know about. This book is about people, it's about humanity. This is not a book that should necessarily be put on a religious shelf. It is a book to be put on any shelf in the United States regardless if its religion or any other place. It's a book about inspiration to people. It is a book about people on this earth; Godly deeds, sinful deeds, about human beings. This book is about Godly principles. It is about the principles that man demonstrates on the earth, both good and bad.

So I don't particularly quote scripture. When I have the opportunity, I say it and do it, but I don't make it a point to just quote scripture during the book. I try to talk about the lifestyle that I believe that we lived and the lifestyle that Jesus lived and the lifestyle that he represented. I talk about some of the things I do that are Godly and some of the things I do that are not so godly. I just try to talk about the things that I know about, and some of the things that I feel that might give some of us a new outlook on life or recycle ourselves a little bit more; maybe activate something in us that is important.

God and Man's Relationship to Humanity

I believe in God. I love God. He has a great deal to do with my life. I've been out in the world most of my life. I've lived a rugged and exciting life and a pleasant life in many ways. God has blessed me all of my life. I am grateful and I'm honored to live in a country where I have a right to speak my mind. When I talk, I'm talking about what I believe. I think people that I totally disagreed completely with have as much right to speak as I do. I believe we have a right to live in this world and express ourselves as long as we don't destroy the foundation under our young people on this earth.

I want to say this and I'm going to leave you alone for a while. I believe that our young people are our greatest resources. No one man owns his or her family. No one man owns his or her nation. No one man owns his or her race. We do not own our race, and no one man owns his generation. So we need to be careful about what we say and how we say it. Whatever I do on this earth as a black African man, whatever I do, I need to be aware of the rest of the black people on this earth; anyplace, anywhere, especially here in the United States where I live.

My grandmother, which was my mother's mother, was full-blooded Navaho. I know what discrimination and prejudice and Jim Crowe and terror and terrorists; I know what the words mean. I know from the Indian side and I know it from the black side. I know the phrase Jim Crowe; what it stands for. I know what prejudice is. I know what discrimination is. I want you to know that I know exactly the meaning of those words. I know the meaning of slavery and slavery comes in many forms; physically, spiritually and mentally. These are words that I don't have to ask anybody about, I know them firsthand.

I was born in Isle of Wight County, Virginia May 16, 1924 to a farming family on a farm. My grandfather was a carpenter and a basket weaver. I think he owned a little over 40 acres of land which we lived on. He was a well known and high respected person in the community. I don't know much about Lewis Holland's background. I know the ladies and the community respected him greatly. He was kind of a liaison between the blacks and whites; a king of go-between.

That was my real biological grandfather and his wife was Navaho. But my step-grandfather was George Darden. He had the most effect on my life. I met him when I was about 7 or 8 years old. He became my mentor for a while. The greatest man I have ever known in my lifetime - any where, any place. He gave me the greatest foundation that I ever got from anyone. Then I laid it down for awhile. I noticed that I needed to go back and rebuild on that same foundation the best I knew how.

But there have been a lot of wonderful people in my life such as my first wife, Doris, the mother of my children. Now the lovely lady I am with now. Yes, Nancy is one of the strongest supportive people that I have known. She sure has supported me. Without her, none of this would be possible at all. Through all of my weakness she pulled in so much strength and lifted me up from my weak sides. May God bless her along with all the members of her family; and may God bless you.

Guy P. Darden, Sr.'s
Grandmother and Grandfather

WHO AM I?

Who am I? What is my agenda? Where do I challenge myself, and why am I so troubled about this title? The Lord has shown me many things that he hasn't shown a lot of people that I talk with and sit with and love so much. Some people that I have met feel like if you don't know how to read, that you are ignorant beyond comprehension. In other words, you can't function in this society. You don't have anything to say that has a value to it. Your life experience doesn't count in the struggle of life where others are concerned. Am I self-centered? Who am I? Where do my alliances begin? What struggle have I related to the existence of mankind? Why do I feel like that phrase is attacking me? Why do I feel so intimidated? What makes that phrase keep stabbing at me? Maybe I need to go back in my life (reflect) and find out where am I at this time. I'm not going over my life. I'm going into my life – a reflection into my life. What is the meaning of my concern? What motive do I have that makes me want to write a book? What makes me think I can? Why has God put that task before me at this time? I've got to think about that.

I've got to go back in the area of my life that I don't want to go back to. I don't want to go there. I thought it was better to forget about the past and look towards the future. Skip over the places that I was uncomfortable with. Find myself a comfortable zone and relax there, and think about what I want to be and where I want to go. That's what I though I ought to do, but it seems like I'm not comfortable there either. I wonder what happened in my life as a youngster. I wonder how far I could go back in my life. I wonder would God open up that part of my life and allow me to see the foundation on which my life was built. It looks like I'm going to have to go there and find out what the struggle was. Yeah, I think that's what I'm going to have to do.

The part that I remember most vigorously is when I used to stand by the ironing board and see my mother ironing clothes. She would be standing there humming and the tears would be falling from her cheeks. I would ask her, "Momma, what's the matter? Why are you crying?" and she would say to me, "Nothing, Baby. Momma just has a lot on her mind and she was wondering how are you are going to be able to make it on this Earth. Will you have it good or bad? I am just wondering. You know, Momma is very sick and grandpa, he's not doing too well either. It looks like I'm bogged down with trouble and I don't know which way to turn. You know, boy, I sure got myself into something, but you know Momma loves you, and she ain't never going to let you down like some people have let me down. Maybe son, I let myself down. Maybe somewhere down the line...maybe something I did that God is punishing me for." I said, "Momma, why would he punish you?" She said, "I don't know son; maybe he's not. I'm so confused I don't know what to do." I stood there by the ironing board and I held onto it. I was just a little boy. I must have been very young because I remember she was ironing and she would say, "Get back, son. I don't want to burn you." I wonder why so many years ago that this happened. But when I talk about it, the tears still come in my eyes as I saw the tears drop from my mother's cheek and she reached up and she wiped it. She would throw her hair back out of the way of the iron board – my mother had long hair. At about that time, Grandpa would come in the room and he would say, "What's wrong with you gal? You thinkin' about that boy again?"

My mother took my brother back to her ex-husband because Grandpa wouldn't let her keep him in the home. She and her father had some words about that. You see, my Momma was married before. She said her husband beat her and she left him and came back home with my brother, Anderson. Granddaddy told us that "you can stay here but that youngin' has got to go back. We don't have no room for no youngin'. I didn't even let my own youngins stay here and he can't stay here either. Take him back to his Daddy". So my Momma said she packed him in a basket and put his clothes in it. Grandpa took her back in the buggy and she said Mr. Mathew Ricks that she married was in the field chopping cotton and she left him on the doorstep. She said that was the hardest thing she had ever done.

I wondered why my mother had to go through so much. I never could understand why my brother couldn't be with us. Can you understand why I don't want to look my mother in the eye? I said, "Momma, what does my brother look like?" She said, "I don't know son. I haven't seen him since he was a little baby." She said, "I know they're talking about me behind my back. I know they're talking about me but, son, that's all I could do. I didn't have no place to stay. I was so young. My husband, he let me down. My father let me down too." She said, "Life is a struggle, boy, but you know, I'm never going to let you down son." After that day, at that ironing board listening to my Mom, I didn't want anyone to come see my Momma. I didn't want any man in my mother's life. People would come to my house and they would pick up my Mom and they would take her away. You know, I never knew whether she was coming back again or not. I didn't know. I would run behind the car and try to catch it. I would run so hard I would fall down in the sand. Grandpa would come out there and say, "Boy, you come here and don't let me see you do that no more!" I would go in my room and get in the closet and I would sit there; just sit there, hoping that I could never see anybody else on Earth, because this was a mean world. That was one way I had hiding from things. I could go in that closet and I couldn't hear anything. Late at night my Mom would come back, and I'd hear them talking. I would open the door real easy and I'd peek and I'd see them kissing my Mom. I thought they were taking my mom away from me. I said, "When is she going to go away again?" I don't know what happened to children when they see things like this.

After a tragedy of losing my brother, I wondered when she was going to take me somewhere and leave me because I knew I was in the way. She would take me some place and leave me with somebody, and as soon as my mother got out of the room they would start talking about her. I would be sitting at the table and they would talk about her and they would say, "Where did she get this little yellow boy from? You think he might be white? Who do you think his dad was?" They would have a debate about me and I was right there. Then when my Momma came back they would laugh and smile and hug her and embrace her and act like they love her. I found out that people were two-faced. They weren't real. I knew one thing, when I got up to be a big boy, I was never going to trust any grown people.

I saw honesty and integrity being made a mockery of. I saw integrity just being destroyed in my family. I saw ugliness magnified through the eyes of a child. What seemed small to a grown person is big and gigantic to a little child. What hurts a grown person a little; a child, in his mind, when you rob him of the love and attention that he needs to make him grow mentally and spiritually, you see it taken away. I feel that when something is magnified by the trauma of confusion it's being distorted; the trust being messed over. I believe that child hangs on to it more than if it's just an ordinary playtime. I believe when something ugly and distorted happens to a child that his mind will hang on to it. It's blown up. I think something in my mother's life must have happened. She didn't have the foundation that a young lady needed to develop into the type of person that she needed to develop into.

I want to bring up some of the things that I feel that helps us grow. The roots that we have – the foundation – are what make us all grow and a solid foundation is the basis of building on something; the basic needs of mankind. How do we first begin? What is the first thing that we think about when we realize that we are alive? I don't suppose that we can ever cover that ground. Each individual has his own segments of thoughts. But it has to be a foundation under all of us. We have to have something to draw from; something to believe in. I personally believe that there is a seed in all of us that has a beginning. I guess you would say that's obvious. I mean there is something there that is more important than just what you see on the surface. I believe that God, himself, places something in us that activates our beginning. You're not just born with nature of doing the things that are right. I believe that the essence of man is God's seed. I believe that a man has to look at more than just what he sees, just what's visible. The physical visibility is not strong enough to give man what he needs. Sometimes it gives him what he wants; at least what he thinks he wants. I tried to go back and think about when was the first time that I really saw something and remembered something that gave me a feeling of mental activation, or that I felt a hurt or I felt something that felt good, or felt something that excited me, I felt a motivation, other than what I could touch with the physical being. When did I have something moving in me that was a mystery, that I couldn't quite put my finger on it? There had to be a starting point. We all had that point and it has gone through life generation after generation.

I think I want to know what regenerated me. What lit up something in me that I could recognize? When did I see my first spark of hope? When did I see a light or a symbol that demonstrated love? When did I see result of love or a genuine feeling of tenderness? When did I recognize hope? When did I recognize the desire to have a dream? When did I recognize my childhood? When did I come to an awakening that I needed something from somebody else? When did I recognize that needed advice, that I needed teaching? I needed something to motivate me. When was my arising? When did I wake up and feel that I had hope? When did I recognize God's feelings? Did someone teach it to me or did He make

Himself known within me? Did I feel something that was lifting me up and inspiring me in some way?

Is that the only inspiration that a child gets; does it just have to come from his parents. Is there hope somewhere, wandering around, that lands on you when you're born and you become a human being? What do we find to make us feel alive as far as accomplishing and creating something, and being a part of something that has a great meaning? When do we realize that we are alive and we are human and want something that's important? Do you understand what I am trying to do? I'm trying to make you think. I'm trying to ask for feelings. I'm trying to give you more than just hearsay. I'm trying to give you a feeling of research. I'm trying to let you know that you have a value. I'm trying to let you know that there is something in you that means something; that you have something to do with humanity. You have something to do with somebody other than just yourself. I want you to recognize the greatness that's in you. I want you to understand and feel the greatness and the tenderness that's available on this Earth.

HUMANITY

I want to talk to you about humanity - God and man's relationship to humanity. I would like to know how much emphasis we put on talking about and acting on for humanity. Do we know what humanity is? Do you know what it means? Well, I didn't know. I think that perhaps you had to have been a part of doing something for humanity in order to know about it.

I thought when people spoke about doing something for humanity that they were speaking about someone that went to India or Africa to work as a humanitarian. I thought that you were a person who went away like a hermit, more or less, and stayed in the jungle and in the hills of Tennessee somewhere giving your time for free for someone who needed you very badly. Well I found out that that is part of it. I couldn't figure out what it had to do with me.

Why on earth do I keep getting this word about humanity in my spirit? I said to myself that I need to think about this because this is going down a road that, looks like to me, that's going to change my mind about writing this book. If you think about it, I really didn't want to know that much about humanity. I certainly wasn't as interested in writing this book as I thought I was in the beginning. I started talking to people and asking them about humanity; God and man's relationship to humanity. I wasn't getting satisfactory answers. It didn't seem to me like there were very many people doing anything for humanity. It seemed to mean as if the train had gotten stalled on the track somewhere, if it was what I was thinking about. I needed to investigate it a lot more than what I had. I needed to know more about myself.

I want to talk about the Senior Citizens of this nation. I want to talk about our youth; the children. I want to talk about the church; what part is it playing in our lives. What part has it played in the past? Where is it going today in relationship to humanity; God and man's relationship to humanity? What part is the church playing? What part should it play? How close are we to our families? What do we know about each other as a people? What is our relationship to each other as neighbors? What do we know about our spouses that we live with every day in our homes? Where are our children at this moment? How well do we know them? When is the last time or what morning did you have prayer with your child? When did you last sit at the dinner table and have a marvelous meal with all the family present? When did you check on your neighbor last? Who am I? Who am I in relation to my family? Who am I? Am I a leader or am I a follower? If I'm following someone in my home, who am I following? Am I the type of person in my home that someone would want to follow? Do I have a sound, excellent leadership? What makes me want to do things for my family? What motivates me to be the kind of person that I need to be for my family? When have all of us been in the same room, at the same time, talking about things that not only concern us but things that concern our community where we live? Who asked "Who am I"? What do I know about myself? Where is love at in our life? What motivates us to get up and go to work in the morning; is it our mortgage payment, our car payment, the kid's college fund? What makes us want to be the kind of parent that would be able to discipline a child? Is it because the child annoys us all the time that would make me want to discipline them or is it because he's always asking a lot of questions? What makes my family a family? What makes me be a leader in my family? What do I think about my community? Why should I think about it at all? What is going on in my community? What do I need to happen in this community in which we live? How often do we discuss the things that are happening in our nation? How much do we talk about charity in our homes? How much love are we sharing with each other? How well do I know my husband? Who am I to be honest? Who do I honor; my family, my God, my job, my car? What's in my life that disturbs me that I need to do that I'm not doing? Am I concerned about getting a guilt-trip? Does it bother me when people discuss things that don't praise me? Am I looking for gratification for the things that I do? Let's talk about these things and others in relationship with God and man to humanity.

  I want to talk to you about my anger. I want to let you know that I'm angry. I don't have mean type of anger, the kind that I want to damage somebody or hurt somebody. I'm angry with myself because I wasted so much of my life that I could have used more positively. I have hurt other people and I have hurt myself. I've taken away the human resources, the members of my family and my friends and my nation. I think when you see what I'm talking about that you will realize that you have done the same thing. I think sometimes we need to rehash what we've done and reevaluate our lives. You know, I never learned to read and write; that was negligence.

I believe in God and the churches that say that they are serving God and talk to us about God. I want to talk to you about some of the things that I feel that would have disturbed Jesus Christ and would have disturbed God Almighty. I'm not a Bible student. I want you to know that. But I know some things about Jesus. Now you may not believe in Jesus, you may just feel that Jesus Christ and God Almighty are separate when it comes to being God. That's alright; if that's what you believe. But I want you to know that I believe in God Almighty and I believe in His son, Jesus Christ. I believe that I know something about His lifestyle and the way He lived His life on this earth. If a man did not believe that Jesus Christ was God, he would have to at least realize that Jesus Christ was a good role model if He said He was who He said He was. If God is who He says He is, at least we know that God had something to do with Jesus Christ's life. You couldn't possibly believe in God and feel that Jesus was not part of the things that God believed in. You would have to believe that at least He was a good role model; if you know anything about His lifestyle.

I want to talk about our faith. I personally want to talk about mine. I traveled all over this nation. I have examined myself in comparison to other people. I find that I have been so negligent that I know about what negligent is. I know what sin is. I know about spirituality. I'll be extending my opinions. I'll be talking about what I believe in. I will be talking about the things that I've learned over a period of 20 years of talking to people all over this nation; doctors, lawyers, preachers, priests, prostitutes, gangsters, gang leaders, and all kinds of different types of people who have given their lives. Some of them were Satan worshipers and taxicab drivers who have met all kinds of people on this earth; people that were willing to open themselves up to me.

I've had the type of observations that I believe that I can speak from more than just thinking. I believe that I can say there are certain things that I know and I know about them. I've learned a lot through these years about life. When I make a statement I'm not just stumbling. I want you to know that I'm trying to make you think. That is why I have so many bits and pieces.

It's been my opinion – and as people will tell you, everybody has an opinion. Most people convey it. I want you to look at what I talk about and see if it makes any sense. I don't think I'll say many things that you don't already know about. That's why I want to put so much emphasis on the things that you and I know about. That's what I want to talk about. In doing so, I want to talk to your spirit and I want to talk to your conscience. I want to mess your mind up to where you want to go back and challenge your lifestyle and wonder if you have done it right. If you had the opportunity to do it over again, would you do it? These are the things that I want to talk about. I want to talk about people like myself who don't know how to read or write. I want to discuss that. Most of all, I want to talk about the things and how we feel about God. What end of the spectrum do we put Him on? What kind of priority does He have in our lives?

These are the things that I want to talk about. I shall proceed in my own way. I hope that you'll be able to overlook the negative part of this, the bad English. Some of the words may not be correct. I may say things that I mean to say that you don't understand. I hope you'll understand my motives and that you'll see something in here that prods you enough so that you'll at least have some idea of what I'm trying to do. I hope that I can make a difference in somebody's life. I hope you'll help me do that. I don't apologize for saying all these things, I only apologize for anything that I might say that might insult you. I hope that you'll overlook my ignorance and build up your life with the wisdom that I might be able to share with you. May you have God's speed as I go through this in the best way I know how.

REFLECTIONS

When I look back on the summers of my life, the summer of 2006 will certainly stand out. My dream of working on a book finally came true and now I have a new grandpa in its author Guy Powell Darden. He has given me a new lease on life and made me realize how fortunate I am. I am loved!

I am a lifelong resident of the state of Virginia. I was born in Charlottesville in 1963 and grew up in the Hampton and Newport News areas not far from where Mr. Darden spent his youth. I was blessed with the most awesome family-loving, long-married parents who take care of everybody but especially each other, a playful younger sister who shared my sense of humor, love of books, music, and old movies, a maternal biological grandmother who could not read or write but who taught me patience, gratitude, and unconditional love, two generous maternal foster grandparents who always gave of themselves and cheered me on, a paternal grandfather who passed down his love of music and Bible-reading, and of course, many aunts, uncles, and beloved cousins. I even had a fluffy dog who wagged her tail endlessly and only growled if she saw a stranger or if you messed with her during dinner. Hey, mealtime is sacred for animals too!

From an early age, I loved books and knowledge because Mom and Dad read me stories, took me to museums and libraries, and emphasized doing your very best because your best makes Jehovah proud. Mom and Dad never had to go to school to answer complaints about my sister Lynette or my behavior. We were taught to respect authority because such respect is a positive reflection on Jehovah. I had many teachers who returned my respect and taught me things I have kept down through the years. I even remember little songs I learned in grade school that stay with me. School is great when parents, teacher, administrators, and students care, collaborate, and cooperate.

I finished high school with honors but it took me seven and a half years to finish college. From the age of seven, I have suffered from a depressive disorder. I appear to have been born with it. It was nobody's fault. Logic said I should have been happy but the further I got into late adolescence and my twenties, the more I was consumed with negative, self-destructive thoughts. I was unable to find or keep a job. I have been hospitalized seven times for psychiatric reasons. Like many people with mental health issues, I didn't really want to die. I wanted to stop feeling bad.

My family and I both suffered from my severe mood swings. We all felt helpless. Medication and therapy could only do but so much. So at 24, I entered a residential program that taught coping and independent living skills to handicapped adults with mental illness. Some of the residents were deaf. I was drawn to a girl there who was both deaf and legally blind. I was her roommate along with another deaf girl for five months. I did a lot of growing up in those three years at the residential program. I finally finished college in 1989 with a degree in Journalism and I learned to be brave and strong, not to be an infantile whiner but to be there for others. Keeping in touch with family and friends has always been one of my favorite pastimes. I get outside of myself and my own issues when I think of others.

I have been blessed with many good friendships lasting from grade school to adulthood. I met Guy Darden a year ago and now we live in each others hearts forever. Thanks to Jehovah, the God I rediscovered in the throes of my illness, I have had many happy moments since I got my first apartment in 1991. I was Lynette's maid of honor when she married the neatest, most caring Christian brother in 1994. I have stood in front of city and state legislators to speak on behalf of funding for mental health programs. I have received certificates for volunteering at a local library. I've been published as a writer in three college anthologies, two national magazines, and one Charlottesville-based collection of poetry. And I have had the privilege of attending a nine-month-long program of courses in peer counseling that assisted me with the three years I served as a peer counselor in a structured weekday program for adult mental patients.

Since 2003, I have been unemployed for health reasons but I am still involved in a volunteer ministry and civic work by volunteering for the library and a local performing arts theater. Working on this book was just the shot in the arm I needed to teach me that I can achieve just about anything I put my mind to as long as I'm doing it for God's glory. He is my Best Friend. And I thank him for Mom, Dad, family, friends, and my new buddy, Mr. Guy Darden.

By Ann Catherine Braxton
Newport News, Virginia

THE PROMISE

There aren't that many stars tonight
"What do I wish upon?", you ask.
Who can blame creation for shrinking
At the malignancy of war
With its shadows, echoes, and screams of anguish?

But the Keeper of the Stars stands firm
He has granted the innocent refuge
So if you are afraid
Remember that wherever you are
He holds you in His infinite palm

He offers an immortal love
A love that does not bandage hearts
But heals them completely
And whether you belong to heaven or earth
Trust Him to lead you safely home!

By Ann Catherine Braxton

This young lady was one who helped me a tremendous amount throughout this book. I went from Ohio to my hometown in Virginia for her to assist me because she is a writer herself. She offered to assist me. I had the opportunity to meet her while I was at dinner with my sister. Ann and her father were there at the same time. At the restaurant I was speaking to two women. I embarrassed myself more than any other time I can remember. I was laughing and some food flew out of my mouth and landed right on to the lady's face. She had a god-like personality and she laughed with me.

Mr. Braxton, at the next table, heard me talking to them about <u>Time – The Most Value Asset</u> which I had written. His daughter, Ann asked me about it. She asked me if I was in author. I told her I was a frustrated one; but I want an author. I later mailed her a copy of the book and we became friends through the mail.

She is strong and God-believing person whose parents have given her the right foundation. I have now adopted her as my Christ-loving granddaughter. She is only in her 40's and what a dynamic and fantastic personality she has; just like her parents. Her father wrote the article called Happiness. He has a strong and God-loving personality. I truly respect this family in the highest regard.

By Guy P. Darden, Sr.

WEAKNESS

There is no excuse for a man or a woman not to know Jesus Christ in the parting of their sins. Romans 3:23 says, "…for all have sinned and fall short of the Glory of God." This does not give you the latitude to decide that you have a time frame to give your life to God. Some people think, like I used to think, that I will ask God later on to forgive me. When you do that you are taking your weakness to build up your strength instead of your strength to build up your weakness.

GOING BACK TO THAT OLD HOUSE

Hello, Sis. I want to talk. You know my sis; she always teased me about going back to the old home place. I don't think she knew how important that place was to me and still is, and even though only a chimney now stands there, to me home is a special place. I think it's more than just where you stay at. I think it has something to do with being planted. It has something to do with your environment and especially that first place that you remember. It has feelings of all types. Most people have good feelings and some bad feelings and, perhaps, some spiritual feelings.

Feelings consist of many things. I think it is important that we examine our feelings and pick those feelings out that are positive and of lasting value. I think some of the things that we remember and don't like to deal with are sometimes, just maybe, the most important things in our lives. Home was not any place, but the only place on earth that I felt independent. I had some irresponsible times there. I had some tragic things happen to me there. I had some sad and tragic moments there that changed my thinking in life. I had some moments when I felt defeated and mistreated. I had moments when I felt loved and cared for. I had moments that made me feel that the whole world had walked away from me.

I have examined all of the things that have happened to me through my lifetime and I believe each one of those things has strengthened me in many ways. I believe some of them weakened me from my childhood, yet they gave me wisdom and understanding of life's trials and tribulations. I learned about sin in that house and I learned about God's safety valve. My grandfather taught me what God meant.

The only thing I didn't learn in that house was the persistence of a mother and a father's love for their child. I believe the reason that I did not learn was because they had not had it in their lives. They didn't know the strength and they didn't know the meaning of love because they didn't have it in their early lives. No one showed them or gave them the meaning of love and the purpose of love or how love is born into your life. You can't do those things that you don't know about.

Yes. We have a few people on this earth that have stumbled upon great fortunes. They have, through God's grace, been blessed without a mother or a father or a sister or a brother who was there to teach them. God has placed people in homes with other people or in other places where only He could give them the things that they need for survival. When I was on the farm, I found hope. I found ways to survive. I found strength from poor people more than any other place on earth. I found more power structure in the farming community. I found more love in giving love to a neighbor than any other place that I have ever lived on this earth. I found it on the farm. I saw life itself being developed. I saw the creation of things being developed on the farm.

I learned about that place in the Bible where Christ speaks of sowing good seeds on hard ground and have them lay there in the sun and dry out and not develop. I've seen seeds sown in good ground where the ground was soft and fertile and saw them grow up and develop into wonderful and exciting crops. Then I've seen other seeds grow up in good and fertile ground and the people allowed the thorns, the briars, and the weeds to eat up the crop and wither away. I've seen all of these things happen. I've seen seed planted on ground that was even rocky. I've seen the rocks taken out, the ground being dug up and cultivated, the stumps and roots being taken out, and it would start to develop. Then I would see the people who did all that hard work walk away from it and see that same crop die and wither away.

I've seen a sow have seven and eight pigs. I've seen some so fat and beautiful and so healthy. Then I've seen them grow up on a farm where the farmers didn't care about their livestock. They didn't feed them. The farmers were drifting and floating around in the city getting drunk and not taking care of their livestock. Then those beautiful pigs and that sow would just be poor and no one would buy them. Sometimes they even had cholera and died. Then I've seen a runt, a little bitty withered pig that looked awful and they wanted to kill him, so I took him myself. I fed those same pigs and they followed me all over the place. They would be fat and beautiful. They were the largest pigs on the farm.

The Old Place

You can change the stage of hopes and dreams to sadness and misery or you can take sadness and misery and give it life and give it hope. You can take people and show them that you are willing to sacrifice for them, willing to share their lives, willing to share your experience and show them by the way you live your life that you have a giving and loving spirit, and you do this by your actions through your belief and faith in God Almighty. God gives you that strength. He'll light up your heart and give you the things that are important to your survival.

Yes, I go back to that old place because I find roots there. I find hope there. Through all of the agony that I had there I remember one old man that taught me about God Almighty. I walked on this earth, year in and year out, ignoring what he told me and what he taught me and the things that he told me would happen if I didn't hold on to God's hand happened exactly like he said. Yes. He told me and taught me about living and dying. On that place right there I remembered my dead brother dying in my arms. I remember that same man who taught me about God, about integrity, about hopes and dreams and about love. I remember my mother walking away from me and my sick brother. They stayed away long beyond the time that they said they would be back. They were irresponsible. When they got back, my brother had died in my arms.

You can't get through life without going through trials and tribulations. The Devil is going to tempt you and he doesn't care how great you are, how spiritual you are, how religious you are or how godly you are. The Devil is going to tempt you and he's going to put his stumbling block in front of you. I'm telling you ladies and gentleman, boys and girls, that you've got to be grounded in God's spirit. You've got to allow God to deal with your life, each day of your life; you have to surrender your life to God and repent day in and day out as you ask God to forgive you. You're going to have to confess to Him and ask Him to teach you. The Devil is always going to have some kind of thing around you all the time. You're going to have to be alert. You're going to have to be aware. So when I go back to that old house, I remember all of the goodness, all of the mercy, all of the ugly things that went on there. It changes my spirit about all life's things in this world. It tells me that no one is perfect. This loving Grandfather that had so many hopes and dreams for me, he blew it along with my Mother. I believe today that he's sitting in glory with Jesus Christ. I believe that. Yet, he made me one of the saddest men for a long while on earth. I saw my dead brother laying in my arms and I couldn't bring him back to life, and I didn't have a grown person there to guide me, to teach me, and to show me what to do.

EVALUATION OF A PEOPLE

We as a people have devaluated ourselves. We've taken away our muscle. We have taken our personal freedom too personal. We've taken our privacy and our personal business and made it too selfish. These are things that I want to talk about in this book. I want to talk about myself as a person. But this book is not just about me, it's about "we the people." I want you to put special emphasis on this. When I say "people," I don't mean all people, I mean people like us, like me. I've been that way. Maybe you haven't but too many of us are too selfish and we personalize ourselves a little too much. I don't mean this in a negative way. I just want you to be able to think about this and if you have been that way, to re-evaluate it. Re-evaluate yourself. Look at yourself as I've looked at myself. I've been so irresponsible in this area, but it doesn't mean that you have to be. It means that I want you to look at your lifestyle, look at your living, look at your path and see if we are that way. And if we are, it is important to change our direction?

On this earth, especially in the United States, the people that I'm acquainted with, as a black man, are about our culture as a people. I have a personal stake in it. I also have a personal stake in the United States of America because this is where I live. This is the only nation that I know anything about. This is where I was born and raised. My grandmother was a full-blooded Navaho. I learned a lot from her. She didn't do much talking but when she talked you listened because she said a lot of things. The Indians and the black people had a lot in common – racial prejudice. I'm talking about human loyalty. I'm not just talking about Christian men and women. I'm not just talking about people who have a religious background. I'm talking about "we the people." I'm talking about people who have not decided to accept God in their life as the Controller of their lives. They haven't accepted Christ as their Savior and they have not accepted God as their Savior. They did like most of us have done in our lives. We have had a personal, intimate feeling concerning ourselves and some of us; I would say that most of us think our business is our business alone. I think that what we do in our personal lives is just personal to us, period. That's not totally true. I found out those things the hard way.

We have an obligation to each other as a people because the one thing that we have in common is that we live on this earth together. We're all here at the same time and we have to find a way to tolerate each other. We need to find a way to love and care for each other. Personally, and I speak for myself on this, I do not believe that you can truly love fully, absolutely and completely, or love your fellow man until you have loved God and have accepted Him into your life as your guiding force and have allowed Him to lead you. It took me many, many years to learn what I haven't known that for a long time. I feel that we have an unknown personal obligation to each other that we haven't fully recognized and that is going into Godliness and dealing with it as a people. I think survival is getting along and trying to understand each other's needs and it will be extremely hard. Just because you haven't accepted Christ in your life or that you happen to not to be a believer in God Almighty doesn't mean that you don't owe this society in which we live your allegiance. You owe this nation and its people your loyalty. You owe them the right to live without us cluttering up their lives. We continue to do things that damage each other.

    I remember as a boy Grandpa George having a person that lived in the community that was doing a lot of things that was making it hard for all of us. It seemed that this fellow came from the North and he came down South. He was kind of loose-mouthed as we called it back then. He did a lot of swearing and cursing. He used a lot of vulgar language. He was very outgoing when it came to his lifestyle; and he had no problem making passes at some of the white women in that area. He was making life very uncomfortable for our families in the community. He didn't understand the Southern way of life. He didn't understand the problems that he could create by living that type of life in that community. My grandfather went to him and told him, he said, "Listen. I need to talk with you. I don't think you understand the kind of life that we live down here. We have worked all our lives in this community and we have established a reputation for ourselves here and the white people around here respect us and we respect them. We get along rather well in this area. Maybe you don't understand the Jim Crowe laws. I don't like them myself and we don't approve of them but we've learned to live with them and if you keep doing this thing that you're doing; you're going to get some of us killed or yourself killed and cause chaos for a lot black people in this area. (At that time we didn't call them "black people," we said a lot of "Negroes.") And we Negroes are not going to be putting up with this kind of thing. If you're going do these things, you're going to have to do it some place else because you're not going to disrupt all we've built up here in this community. We are respected and we are left alone by the Ku Klux Klan. They don't bother us and we don't bother them. You can't do the things that you're doing and continue to stay here because you're not just messing with your own life, you're going to get yourself killed and get us killed too or some of us hurt and we can't allow that to go on."

Now some of you that are much younger than I am probably can't relate to that. You're probably thinking that this was that man's business and his business alone. What he did, and if he got into trouble, that was his business. No, it wasn't his business; no more that it's your business today or my business today to do things in your community that damage the area in which you live. When any person today ever comes into your community and destroys the fabric of that community and disturbs and creates a disruptive lifestyle in that community, white or black; it doesn't make any difference what race he is, he's upsetting everything in that community. But when a black person does that, he has more to lose than the average white man. Because we've come through hundreds of years of re-direction in our lifestyle and in what is going on in our lives where we have someone in almost every branch of government in this nation, so any time that something bad happens, it takes us back through history; it destroys our credibility and I take it as a personal attack on me. It's the same thing as if you have someone in your family that destroys your family fabric. It is no different.

They are the controlling people of this nation. We fought for hundreds of years to go this distance to where we are today. This place where we are today, this standard of life and the jobs that we have today took us hundreds of years to make this journey. We are not going to stand here and let a few bad eggs put us back into slavery again. I think that's wrong and I think that it would be a bad mistake, and I'm not going to sit and be quiet and say that the white man is just taking on the black person because he's black. I'm saying that we owe it to every black person on this earth and in this nation to our lives as a respectable and descent people. We do whatever we can to hold up the moral standard of the black people of this nation. Every time a black person does something in this nation or any place on earth, it is publicized much more than when a white person does something.

As you go to the large cities of this nation you will find people that don't have the degrees that some of us have. I'm not just speaking to one specific race of people. I happen to be an African-American with a Mother who was part Navajo and my grandmother was a full-blooded Navajo. We know from both sides of our backgrounds what the word slavery is. We know what they mean when they say "Jim Crowe." When you hear me mention the word discrimination, I'm not talking about somebody eating at a restaurant or somebody that doesn't want you to marry into their race. I'm talking about complete white domination. I'm talking about killing and murder. I'm talking about hanging. I'm talking about parts of the body being removed. I'm talking about Ku Klux Klan killing and raiding and burning down buildings. I'm talking about how I have been able to live through all of that. I'm talking about how I survived it, how my family survived it, and how many black people all over this nation survived it including in the African nations themselves. We represent more than just our selfish motives; we represent a nation of people, and not just in the United States but we represent people all over this world. I know personally what it means to see people die and see people destroyed, and see little children being beaten and dogs being set on people, real people, not in a movie. I was frightened then but there is one thing that my Grandpa George and Presley Darden told me, "If you've got to die, don't die running. Die fighting, physically, spiritually, mentally, any way that you can fight. Don't ever be a coward."

I know what it means to be hungry. I know what it means to be without a father. I know what prejudice and discrimination are. The swamplands of the South, and all over this nation, are full of bodies of black people. We represent them and I don't want them to have died in vain. I don't want the Reverend Dr. Martin Luther King, Jr., to have died in vain. We represent a nation of people and we represent the United States of America that I love dearly. But the black people in this nation have more to lose than the white people do.

We have a foundation to build for our young people. We Senior Citizens have got to stop sticking our head in the sand and blaming young people for everything that happens. There are older people in this nation that are doing a marvelous job; they are doing great things. But there are not enough Senior Citizens who will stand up and speak their minds.

I don't ask you to agree with me on everything I say. I know I have some strong views and some of them are my personal opinion and I'm not trying to brainwash anybody, but I am trying to let you know that when you commit crimes like murder, or stealing and robbing, you're headed for volunteer slavery in another form. This includes when you buy things that you know that you can't afford to pay for. When your salary doesn't meet the budget and you build your life on credit cards, every dollar bill, every one-hundred dollar bill that you hold in your hand is a promissory note. It's not real money. That furniture that you own in your house is a promissory note - an IOU. If you buy things that you don't have to buy or buy the things that you want rather than what you need, you're not living on your level. Get some economics training and don't allow your life to float around trying to impress people. I have clothes now that I don't need because I wanted to make a big show, a big splash. What counts is not what you have on you; it's what you have in you.

I'm emotional about this because I want you to have a better life. It isn't all in education. Education is a marvelous thing if you're really being educated about the things around you. Don't look so far out before you find out what is motivating you. Have real hard rock security; God's basic standard. Stop trying to go around things and go through something. Fight the battle that is in front of you. I don't care how many mountains you go around or how many valleys you've shunned, sooner or later you're going to find yourself in some valley and you're going to have to learn how to deal with it. You are going to have to have an example to show the sinners what it is to change their lives and show them what direction to go in.

You see we had this world long before these young people got here. Whatever they are receiving, we put it here. We allowed it to be here. If there's a dope addict standing on the corner two blocks from your door, or at your door, it is because we allowed him to be there. If your city is being corrupted by the crime of rape, we allowed it to happen. If our police department is struggling and it doesn't have the support that it needs from "we the people," we allowed that to happen.

We have to realize that there is more freedom at stake than just a physical freedom. I believe personally that a mental freedom has a stronger hold on us than a physical one. When you are captured in your mind and you're struggling because you can't think properly, you're struggling because you've been handicapped from within. Ask God to reclaim that type of freedom. Through God's Spirit and Jesus Christ's leadership, you can find your way back to being a whole and loving person. I believe that you have to love yourself enough that you don't want just principles and characters and integrity stained with so much anger and so much ugliness of this world. Your character of goodness and mercy means more to you than worldly goods. Because I personally believe that if you maintain a God-loving spirit and you allow it to lead you to search from within yourself for what you know personally is right for you, you will not be reaching out for so much lust. There is more lust out there than just the lust for sexuality. It's more lust than that. It is a money lust. It is a popularity lust. It is a go-along-with-the-crowd lust. It is that plain old "I want" lust. I want for myself and you forget about everything else around you. When you do that, you're tearing down all the lifelines that God put here for us. They're survival kits; love and respect and honor. It's not the kind of honor that someone pins on you. It's not the pedestal that people take and put under you. It's the kind that gives you a satisfaction inside of you that tells you that you are who you need to be. Love of God: imprint that in your heart.

When you start the lust for popularity contests, you want to win; you want to satisfy everybody in your congregation, in your community and even in your country, so you start saying things like this: that will make me look good going through life. By ducking the hard questions and saying the things that make you shine, you soon find out life hasn't done you very much good because you get real good at ducking problems, going around troubles and going around the mountains. When you keep going around the mountain, you never get the muscle for pulling hard going over. When you go over the mountain, you get muscle. That builds up your muscle. You know a little more about that mountain the next time.

Sometimes this all looks complicated. I don't care how much oratory an individual has or how beautiful his English is and how well he speaks, or how many people he impresses. If he's not speaking truth, Godly truth, and he's not talking about the things that Christ stood for, that He put His life on the line for, he may not be talking about the things that are going to repel him to an area of his life. He is going to need the foundation to stand on that will impress people in their heart and soul. He may not be able to make connections with peoples' Godly spirit. He may be dealing with the human spirit instead of the Godly spirit. He may be dealing with the human needs instead of the Godly needs. He may have principles that can be challenged by God Almighty at a later time.

LIVE FOR GOD

My name is Tracy Vest and let me start by saying what an honor it is to be apart of this book. I'm not a high ranking public official nor have I done anything that will ever be in a history book. Nevertheless, as I am closely approaching thirty I have chosen not to let life just pass me by. I can't say that I've made this decision on my own, nor have I received the determination to get up and do something with my life on my own. It was only five years ago that I was a stay at home mom, with no aspirations to be anything but a stay at home mom. Not that staying home with my kids hasn't been a blessing, but their not going to be little forever. It was also at this time that I truly gave my life to Christ. I don't just mean saying I believe and calling myself Christian, but allowing God to change me from the inside out. When you allow God to take control of every area of your life, pretty soon the things you used to do just ain't good enough. For me this included staying at home.

I believe this is the role of God with humanity. Not only does He want to bring order into each of our lives, but He is a personal God that desires to stir us up to become more than we can even imagine or think. At least that's what He has done for me, and God is not a respecter of persons. So what He has done for me, He can do for anybody.

Soon after committing myself to Christ, I began to seek God's will and purpose for my life. I felt lead to return to school and study in the area of Physical Therapy. Now for me this was a huge step of faith. I was 25 at the time and never had taken a college course; in fact, my grades had gotten so bad in high school that I was thankful just to have graduated. And now I was about to pursue a Masters degree while taking on courses like Physics and Chemistry which I failed in high school. When I stepped out and did what I felt called to do, God was there the whole time. Not only did I take Chemistry, but I aced Chemistry. I made the Dean's List after just about every semester and remained an honor student. This showed me that God knew me better than I knew myself. He knows what we're capable of, and if we're obedient, we can become what we're capable of.

After a few years, I had to take a break from school because my husband and I were having our third child. However, during my pregnancy the Lord was leading me to start a business. Now six years ago this would have sounds crazy to me. Being pregnant is hard enough, but developing and opening a retail store at the same time is just nuts. But I know the God I serve and I know He's faithful. Through Christ alone I Can do All things. Within this nine month period, not only did I complete my last semester of school, but I developed the idea for my business Kingdom Kidz, wrote a business plan, received financing, found a location, remodeled the store (with help) by hand, opened for business, and then had a baby. Please don't think I'm bragging on myself, but I'm bragging on God. He is so good and deserves all the glory. If it were not for Him, I would probably still be on that couch in front of the TV all day long. But God had a better plan for my life, just as He does for all of humanity.

This is just a preview of what my walk has been like with the Lord. I don't know exactly where He's taking me next, but I do know I'm more than willing to follow Him. God desires a personal relationship with us, one where we as humanity begin to seek Him daily. Until then, we will remain in our lives of mediocrity. However, if we step out and begin to live for God, He will take us to places we never thought possible.

By Tracy L. Vest

I don't have too much to comment because she said it so well. I believe she is the type of person that thinks along these lines and has examined them and is truly motivated. She has joined the ideas and thoughts that give humanity a foothold. Maybe some of our large businesses and manufacturers should think along these lines. Maybe it wouldn't be a bad idea for the government to pick up a few of those nuggets too.

By Guy P. Darden, Sr.

BLAME MAMA

If there was so much of my life that my Mother hadn't taken care of, and let's say right then I knew about it yet had all those complaints and was upset for many years blaming my Mother for every ill that came in my life. Every time I went for a job and couldn't qualify because I couldn't read or write, or if I could see all the mistakes that my Mother had made with raising me, then why didn't I take more accountability for my family and myself?

When I look back over my life, I made it my business to hang around with intelligent people and people that had strong moral views. The early part of my life, people used to brag to me and tell me how unlike I was from the youth of my day. They would tell me how responsible I was and how reliable I was. So what happened from back there to now? When did I decided that I could have a free run of my life and walk away from the responsibility of straightening out my life and giving myself some of the things that my Mother and Father didn't give me? Why didn't I do something about it after I found out about it? After I found out about my needs, why didn't I find a way? Why didn't I do more in lining up my life with those people that I was entertaining?

For most of my life I socialized with brilliant men and women who had lots of wisdom. But did I just allow it to float away? I had enough complaints about all the ills that were going on around me, and evidently I had an opportunity to not only change my life and put my life on a higher level, but to rebuild a foundation that I had learned about over the years with the experience I had gotten. You know, it doesn't do you very much good to get wisdom if you don't do anything with it. If you're just living in a fantasy world and being an actor, making pretend, you're just like a pre-fab house that you build. When a storm comes along it falls apart it's like taking an old building and putting new siding on it when the termites have already eaten it up from beneath.

Wisdom that is not used is the same thing as a man going to college and getting a Ph.D., then feels that he's an intelligent and educated intellectual, but he doesn't use it. I don't think he's much better off than the man that doesn't have it. Should I find my ability to complain and point fingers at my Mother and point fingers at those that were around me; I find to be irresponsible?

Now don't get me wrong. A Mother and Father are responsible for their children as long as they have them under their wings, but when they get out from under those wings, at some point in life when they feel that they're intelligent enough to go out in the world and take their resources and waste them on foolishness and irresponsible things, you can't blame your mother and father for that. Maybe you could blame them for those early years before you got that wisdom, but now you've got it, you're supposed to do something with it.

I BELIEVE

I believe in God completely.

I believe there is hope for this world and hope for our young people of today.

I believe that God can and will reclaim us even in our bad states. I believe totally that God will forgive us when we do wrong and go wrong. I believe that God can move us out of the situation that this world is in.

I believe that God can restore our moral destruction that we willingly accept and for the most part have created.

We cannot deny it. We have seen it coming long before it came but we did nothing to stop it from corrupting us all because we wanted the small part of it for our very own amusement.

We figured that just a little sex on TV wouldn't be harmful but just enough to satisfy our curiosity. Just a little vulgarity wouldn't hurt just as long as it was only enough to laugh at and not enough to be offensive. Just a little of a woman's body flashed across the screen wouldn't hurt us but satisfy our need to indulge our immorality. But then the little became more and we still sat there and watched and listened and subsequently our children began to watch it with us and we allowed it. We watched with them and along with their enthusiasm we too were excited about it.

Does the woman who dresses seductively cause me to look at her not once but several more times? In my mind I would continue to look at her until I began to commit a sin by just desiring her in my mind all the while expecting God to help me control my mind.

It is so apparent to me that some of the things we do we convince ourselves that we can't help doing because we enjoy and we like doing them. Many people use the excuse that "God said that no man is perfect" for doing any and all things that are evil, immoral and wrong. To merely justify that because of their imperfection it is alright to be the way they are. But Jesus said "No man is good but the Father." We have to realize and know that our meaning of perfect is very different from God's perfect. God instructs us to be perfect for He is perfect. To explain the difference first we must understand that does not mean we don't sin. It means that we are perfect in what we do. For example, if I never lie for any reason to anyone than I am perfect in that although I may be abusive to my wife or stole something, I am perfect in the area where I would never lie. The Greek explanation for perfect is that we act or do as we should be or act – the way it ought to be.

God told us to be good but never told us to not be perfect so we must strive to be perfect. Perfect our prayer life. Perfect our walk with Christ. Perfect our ability to parent our children. Perfect our compassion for others. But above all, perfect our responsibility to ourselves to be and do what we can for one another.

We have to be accountable for what we do. Don't just pray over things that need to be done or changed and then do nothing. We will spend our entire lifetime praying for the same thing as if God can't hear or understand our need. God can hear and He understands our prayers but we must trust that He will answer in His time. When you signed your name at the foot of the cross to follow and trust in God then that is just what you have to do; trust Him.

Do what you can do, but do it today. Don't sit and wait hoping for an answer from God. Some things you already know to do and if God is leading you, then you will be on His timeframe and pace. It is God's wisdom and not yours is which we prosper and have our being. It is God's love and it is God's Spirit which leads, comforts and guides. Our human spirit is contaminated and corrupted with evil and sin. Let us be like Christ. He followed His Father and He did His Father's will.

I believe God completely and I am not going to stop this outreach ministry because it may fail. I will continue to follow God's will and leave the results to God. I truly believe that when you accept Christ then everything that God says will be. God's word is true and His will, will be done. When Jesus was on the cross He asked not for His will but for His Father's will to be done and that is how I see Christ and God in my life; to do their will for when I follow Him who leads me then nothing is impossible.

With Christ, I believe that I can change this world. With Christ, I believe I can change the hearts of people with God's leadership. Many of us sit back and procrastinate about doing things and equate procrastinating with failing, but there is not failure in God. We as Christians don't get things done because we stop and think about it first or scrutinize it and then set it aside waiting for God to do it all. We must learn to go and God will act for us; open our mouths and He will speak through us.

I believe that before we can reach our children or other people we must be able to relate to ourselves. Before we can expect respect, we have to respect ourselves. We cannot live in our past but we need to go back and look over our mistakes. We need to look at how we took care of the things that God entrusted to us; whether it was our children, our mates, or our finances. Look at how we carry ourselves before Him.

I believe that there is no reason that we have to compromise our beliefs, our respect or responsibilities. There is never a need to do anything illegal before man or God or stooping to lower levels in order to achieve our idea of greatness or prosperity.

I believe there are many questions that you must ask yourselves.

WHO CONTRIBUTED TO ME?

This is about people that I met in my travels. It's about the experience I had in life. It's about my observation of people, about people. It's about things I have seen and places that I've been. Really, I'm doing this book because of an ad that I saw on TV that I thought degraded me. That ad said that if you couldn't read or write, you were nothing. I'm sure it didn't mean it like that, but I heard the "nothing" part of it. That was the only thing that got my attention, that if you couldn't read and write you weren't nothing. Now I thought of it and I realize what the art of it was saying. It was saying that if you didn't know how to read or write, that you would probably not accomplish or achieve very much on this earth, and it looked like to me that she was saying, "If you can't read and write, you're ignorant, a fool or a nobody." But I've met people all over this nation that could not read and write. Back when I was a boy people would be a little shy, but most of them would tell you, "Would you write this? I don't write or I don't read." But this day and time since so much emphasis has been put on that, most people that can't read and write you'll never know because they feel defeated before they even get started. They don't recognize the wisdom that they've gathered up over the years. I knew and believed that I had something in me that was worth while telling or speaking about. I felt that I had some experience that I'd come in contact with people all over this earth and that I did have something. You know when you're ignorant, you ask an awful lot of questions because there are a lot of things you don't know, especially when you can't read and write.

I never learned to read and write, but I learned to survive. I learned early on about God and didn't accept Him as my personal Savior, but I knew that there was a God because someone was always talking about God wherever I was and how important He was. And some of the experiences that I have had in life as a young child, a young boy growing up in the south, only God could've gotten me out of them. I got to thinking about me as a farmer, being a farm boy early on in my life, and I got to realizing how important food was, how important the farmer's role was in life. And I knew when I was a boy that I played a great part in that, and my grandfather, and my great grandfather. People in our lives, most of them couldn't read and write but yet they contributed to the most important thing on this earth. Outside of God, they contributed actually the life substance. No one could live on this earth without eating, without food. God made it that way. You can't survive if you don't eat. I felt like that I was very important in this society.

I played a great part as a boy. As a matter of fact I have never felt so useful since then. I felt that I had something to do with the development and the survival of the people in my community. I felt like I was contributing something to it. When I was on the farm, I felt that I was doing something important. Not only that, it didn't take a whole lifetime to learn how to do what I was doing. When I was cutting wood or plowing - what I was doing was important. My grandfather and my parents were there. I knew something about their lives. I saw what they were doing. They didn't tell me to go do something, they said, "Let's go do something." They showed me and they were my leaders and my teachers. I didn't think that I was anything. I thought I was important. When I reflect back on that TV ad, I felt like they were attacking me personally.

I took it the same way that I accept Christ in my life now. I feel as if Christ died for me personally. I'm His intimate and personal servant. When I go in the room, I'm in there alone with Him. God and I have a personal and intimate relationship since I accepted Him in my life. I felt that way about me and my grandfather when we were out in the field plowing while we talked and he told jokes and told tales and we were plowing side by side. And before then I walked behind the plow and held onto the plow when he was teaching me to do those things. We had a relationship. We had something that was important. We cared about each other. I saw it and knew it. We didn't allow our friendship and love to drift apart, we kept it intact. We had a relationship that was most important.

WHAT BENEFITS US?

When we talk about God and man's relationship to humanity, we're not just talking about our individuality. We're not just talking about what benefits us as an individual; what benefits me - not just alone what is good for me. You may have a particular situation today that affects you and you may have to address that as an individual and it is personal. It might even be intimate. That's different than making decisions that affect those of us as a people, especially in the environment in which I live in.

I've got to be concerned about more than just myself. I have to be concerned about those around me because everything around me should, and will, most likely affect me in some way; the environment in which I live in - the physical, the mental, the spiritual. They are going to come together at one time or another in my personal life. So if you happen to be making a decision even though it is in your personal life, if you don't consider how that might affect those that are around you then maybe you ought to rethink it because we don't live in this world by ourselves. If you are making a decision about what your child needs to do today and how he should go about a given project, that's an individual decision in your individual family. You have a right to make that decision as long as that decision that you make is in the best interests of the child and his surroundings.

When we think about any given thing (I've learned this and I have learned this in the hardest possible way, by trial and error), you have to be concerned about everything in that cycle. In training your children, you have to get them trained not just to get along in your family but most likely they're not just going to be isolated in your given environment in the homey resources in your family house or on your plantation, wherever it may be. If you are in charge of that or that is your personal land or personal estate, that place of business, place of recreation, even the home that you live in, is an image of who you are and what you are. It can affect more than just your life. But the things that I call more personal to use as a people are men and women who – I use one particular thing – that are in the market; manufacturers that make worldly goods, things that we sell. We don't have much of a consumer protection anymore. We used to have it pretty snug. But the politics in the business world have lobbied so hard until they are practically free to put whatever they want on the market without the consumers having much to say about it. But, if you are putting something out there on the market you're not just putting it on the market that you're going to use yourself, but you're putting it out there for all of us. And you don't have the right, because that's your merchandise, to just throw it out there without being concerned how it's going to affect my life because we all use the things in this world that are made by our manufacturers and the individual things that we put out. The services that we perform are not just for ourselves. We must be concerned about how it's going to help us as a people, how it's going to help our community.

I don't just live in this community by myself. It doesn't make any difference whether I'm a sinner or whether I don't believe in God or I believe in one religion and you believe in another. We're not separated where I have my tomb that I live in and I don't go outside of that. Whatever you do and whatever you put in this society, whatever you put out in the environment, it doesn't make any difference whether it's an automobile, or a plant, or a bar of candy or suit of clothes. It may be your lifestyle that you put out here that may contaminate us in some way. We're subject to life contamination that changes our lifestyle for the good or for the better.

The market value – whatever we have – either lifts us up or pulls us down. You're not making progress when you're just sitting there and you're not making progress when everybody is not accomplishing something as we travel along the road of life. Progress carries us all along - some at a little faster pace. But those of us who have the energy and foresight and vigor to fight for what we believe in also have a right to say something about what we put out there in the world or the language that we put out there. We just can't pass laws in this nation to fit a certain portion of the society and to exclude other areas of the society. What I am talking about is being concerned about everything around you; taking other peoples concern under consideration. Feelings are something that you have to examine. Feelings can lift you up, they can put you down, they can lead you in the wrong direction, or they can lead you in the right direction. You have to have counseling. Sometimes you need the inspiration of God's spirit moving in you. You reach that from being concerned about yourself. Examine yourself and see if you feel that you made the right decision and get the right teaching and right training.

All of these things are more than just an idea. It is more than just wanting to make money. Everything I hear people talking about is money. I asked a young man the other day, and not just that young man, I asked the question in a group of young men and women, I asked them, "Why are you going to college?" What is the purpose?" And they replied it was to "make money." I said, "Is that the only reason"? "Well, yes", they responded. If that is the only reason and the only way you think you are going to be successful, is to make money, you may not be as successful as you thought you might be. Because it's a foundation that needs to be built long before you get to college. Somebody has to be concerned about the individual regardless if whether he's a Christian, whether he's been saved, where he goes to church, or whatever. We've got to try to reach our people in the best possible way we can. Television is not doing the job that it needs to do. The media that's open and has the most strength is doing the most harm now. Flashing lights and pretty things and ornaments and all the glitter and things and the funny mess on TV, that's good for five or six seconds to look at. But you can go from channel to channel, ten, fifteen, twenty stations, and you may not find anything that is positive and that has some value to you? But images are a powerful thing. What the eye sees can destroy an individual, a community, even a nation. Why on Earth do you think the Chinese government has their leaders' pictures that stand out before the people every day? Stalin had his picture stand out before the people. Sadam's picture standing out before the people and Mussolini's pictures standing out before the people. I notice lately our President's picture flashed during the war on the screen many times. I don't know how many times, but a lot.

Image is a powerful thing. The eye takes a picture and holds it in the mind. The brain captures it. Images are much stronger than words. All of these flashing images on the TV. They have nothing but money in mind. You can't finish one commercial, then before you get that, there is another commercial and another commercial - just money, money, money, and money for what? What are you going to do with the money? Why is so much money so important and we don't have any of it? If money is that important it looks like we ought to be saving some, instead of having all these *things* around our walls. If I would have learned that when I was much younger in my life, if my parents would have taught me the value of a dollar; not just for my pledges, not just for me, not just for my excitement. You can do a lot of things for people that may be not as conservative as you are, maybe not as economical as you are. If you have money you can teach people how to be economical. We would be a wealthy nation today. A lot of us, like me, could be doing well, really well, if I hadn't thought so much about buying clothes of all kinds, kind of flashy man in the city partying all the time. I was doing that; doing that for me. If I wanted to go to this place, I'd go. If I wanted to do this, I did it. I never did very much for anybody else. Now that I am where I can see that I need to do something for somebody, to assist somebody in some way and I look for people to assist now. I see them and I am always wondering about I don't have the means to do anything for them. I do whatever I can. Now that I want to help I have nothing other than the little wisdom that I am trying to share.

Don't just do it for yourself; be able to fix yourself, to repair the broken pieces that we have in our lives, that we can pull ourselves together where we can not have that individual private thing. We've destroyed our families by it. We don't want our families with us? People live alone. If we could come together as a family and be a unit, it tells me that the Godly thing that a lot of us claim hasn't taken root in our lives.

I just don't believe that we're everything that we say we are in this nation. This is about us as individuals, as Christians, as people who make the laws and rules and regulations in this country, and who are in places of education. When we say we believe in God and He's the most important thing in our lives, and on our money we say "In God We Trust", I believe that word is a fraud. I don't think it needs to be spoken of in that term. I think we need to say, "In God I Trust", because I can't speak about "We" as a people. Because when you tell my child that he cannot read his Bible in school and he cannot say prayers because you're afraid he will insult some other person that believes in something else, I don't care what anybody believes in. If they don't believe in God that's their problem and their business. But if I believe it, he doesn't have to pray if he doesn't want to. You're not making anyone pray, you're not making a law that people pray, but the school should have the right to pray and a child on his recess or any teacher; she should have a right to pray or read and she certainly should have that right. If Jesus Christ is important to us as a people and as a race and as a nation and as a world, we certainly ought to be able to quote the scripture in the schools. If they can openly pray out loud and openly in the Senate and in the

Congress with a priest, minister or clergy - however you want to put it, I don't see why they ought to have it in the government offices in Washington, D.C. In the federal buildings they can do that but we can't do it in our local schools. Is it something we're afraid of? Is there something our officials and our lawmakers are afraid of? How can any constitution tell you that we believe in God and this country was built on Godly principals and refuse to allow our educators to be able to quote the Bible? Do you think that God is a phony? Do you think He's a fraud, that He's not real? Are we sure we believe in God? Why would we swear on the Bible in the courthouse and you can't use that same Bible in the schoolhouse? It seems to me that you don't believe what you say you believe. And if you do, you don't want to be reminded of what you said you believed.

Do we believe that prayer is more important in the Congress and the Senate if the United States that having prayer in our local schools? Do we feel that we can explain to our children that God is the most important being in the world and yet the children are not allowed to pray openly?

Remember these men and women in Congress and Senate are suppose to be fully developed and brilliant people and a child is one is just being developed on a scale of one to ten, who do you think needs the most prayer?

Ladies and gentlemen, I have asked these questions not because I have the answer to them but because I have asked myself the same questions. By doing so I was forced to have self-examination and I was very unhappy with the answers that I gave to myself. I found myself troubled. I hope you won't have the same feeling but I put these questions out for your personal examinations.

GROWING UP

When you are grown and especially when you're a Senior Citizen and look back over your life and you haven't accomplished the things that you needed to achieve. You know, perhaps, that you should have achieved those things. If you're not careful, you'll find out that you'll use every excuse that you possibly can to give yourself a reason why you didn't excel. If you're not careful, none of those reasons may be the right reasons.

As I go back over my life and truly think of my beginning it's not nearly as complicated and as tough as I first thought. I think if we try hard enough we all can find a reason to blame our problems on somebody else. But when I look back over my life and examine it with integrity and honesty, I didn't have as bad of a start as I first thought I had. I was born in Virginia in Isle of Wight County. My parents were born in the country on the farm. I was born in a time when it was said the economy was in pretty bad shape. The thing about it is that my grandfather and my grandmother had lots of children. A lot of those children were at home at the same time. Remember, my mother was the baby of all of the children. You find a span of many years from the first children down to the last one; because no child could be born much closer than a year apart. Of course, in those times many children were an asset because you used all of them on the farm and you didn't have to pay for your labor.

When I was a young man living in the city of Newport News, Virginia, there was an area called Harbor Homes where most of the high class working blacks lived. The end of the street was Jefferson Avenue. Black businesses covered downtown. We had nice nightclubs and, of course, some dives but not as bad as today. There were Jewish businesses too. We couldn't go to the white hotels and establishments. We had to deal with our own people. We had our own theaters. If you went to a white theater, you sat upstairs. Movies weren't but a quarter then. When we integrated, so to speak, we got a label of "integration" and we left our black businesses alone. We didn't try to keep up with the competition. We let the white and integrated businesses take ours. We do not give our business customers the quality they need. We have been freed from segregation. But we separate ourselves today by allowing fear to drive us away from our neighborhoods. We threw our young people in a pit. We show them nothing but the glitter. We haven't shown them through the trials and tribulations to avoid drugs. We're afraid to speak up when somebody disrespects our families, cursing and swearing in every direction.

My sister's son-in-law spoke up the other night because some guy was cursing and swearing in front of his family. The kid wouldn't stop so he called the detective on him. Some members of the family thought my nephew-in-law was wrong, that he was putting gas on the fire. But I believe if nothing's worth dying for, nothing's worth living for. He stood alone with nobody to help him. We've been driven out of our communities. We are pushed by the drug culture, gangs, and hip-hop clothes. Instead of fixing the problem, we are allowing these to take over the community.

This courageous young man who spoke up happens to be the husband of one of my nieces—and guess what?--he's not even black. His skin may be white but I'll always remember what my dear sister told me happened that night. I'm glad I wasn't there because if I'd been there, I'd have to do a lot of praying because nobody, nobody disrespects my sister and her family in front of me. Nobody! And I've been that way all my life. And to see our communities and to see our streets that I used to walk on and feel safe covered in bars--I can no longer stick my head in the sand. I don't care how much you say I'm illiterate. I love God and I love my country and I love my community and I'm tired of seeing them torn down! I'm tired of seeing people attack their own people. Every time a black man murders, steals, robs, and goes to jail--you cannot build up. You can't just up and move because you're making a few thousand dollars more than you did last year, you can't move away to your tomb and lock yourself away from that chaos that's following you because it's going to follow you everywhere. I have so much more to say. But I am limited. God bless you.

If my mother had been married when I was born and had had a child, she had been through some rough times. I don't know how my mother met my father. I don't know what the situation was. I had never been told. But I knew he never spent any time with my mother. I have a feeling that they was kind of passing in the night, so to speak. I don't know if he saw my mother any more until I was 12 years old. What kind of rearing did my mom have? What kind of supervision did she have? I don't know. I do know this; that she had to be a child raising a child because she wasn't even grown when my brother was born.

Back then it wasn't a big problem for someone to marry a youngster; especially black people. You could get married as young as 12 years old. It didn't matter. If someone felt that this child that was 9 or 10 years old and some elderly fellow saw her and they wanted her, they went to the father, especially a girl and asked the privilege of marrying that child. It was 'Yes, we know it's a child but I'll take care of her. I needed to look out for my children. I need a girl.' It wasn't unusual back then for a parent to give a girl to an elderly gentleman or someone that was in their 30's or 40's. He would be a family man with lots of kids and if his wife died or was killed he would find a young girl to "marry" and she would help him raise the children. He would treat his wife like she was his child; raise her up. It was not an unusual thing back then. If we look forward to today and look at our children the way they are coming up. We see the trials and tribulations that they are going through. Back at that time, a girl child didn't have very much to say about how her life started out.

We need to examine our foundation some time. Sometimes we have reason why we do certain things. We need to feel ourselves out; what is our temperament? What kind of experience did we have when we first start out? Who prepared us? What kind of foundation did they have? In other words, what kind of training did my mother have? It doesn't seem like she had very much. It seems like her life was built on a shaky foundation. I don't even know what type of lifestyle that my grandfather Lewis had. I don't know what kind of foundation that my grandmother had. I know that if you allow a child to get married when they're nothing but a baby, you're not starting them out in life with the preparations that they need.

When you get to be grown you can't look back on that lifestyle and allow yourself to stumble over that. I don't think I did that bad when I realize what grandpa showed me in life. I think as a child I did rather well. I think I was responsible. My parents did not have a rough time with me. I was not rebellious. My rebellion started well after I left home and didn't see the necessary responsibilities that I needed to guide my life in the right direction. Now I realize some of those things are due to trying to get out from under some of the pressures that were caused by my parents. Once I learned about how to survive and what to do and learn about integrity, which my grandpa George taught me. I can't put those stumbling blocks on my parents. I was quite an important citizen and I was doing things that made me feel proud of myself and made other people feel proud of me. I had a place of business. I was doing fine. I had that self-pride that overcrowded my mind and took preference over almost everything. Now don't get me wrong, pride is a wonderful thing to have. It's great. But nothing is much worse than false pride. False pride can get you in trouble.

You put pride over justice, kindness, love, and humility. You've pushed it ahead as a stumbling block for you. I put pride over my education. I put pride over a lot of things in life but when I look back and take the total inventory of my life, I'm one of the most blessed people on earth. I'm just realizing. Sometimes you can make a lifetime journey and never understand the maneuvers that you're going through. That's what I think it is. I think its lack of maneuvers for a battle that you're training for; the battle of life. You're going to have trials and tribulations as long as you live. Trials and tribulations give you muscle like an athlete in training. I think if you don't have those trials and tribulations in your young life then all of the sudden you're 40 or 50 years old, well you've been on a bed of roses all your life. You haven't had any trials or tribulations that you've considered were problems except for the few things that you couldn't get when you wanted them. All you have to do is go to somebody else and ask them for it and they give it to you on a silver platter. If you've been through life that way you're going to have a rough journey when you get to be a Senior Citizen like myself.

I am so thankful and so grateful now that I had that rough road. I don't know whether it was put in the front of my life intentionally but I do know I made the decisions. God may put you in training but He's not going to make up your mind for you in which way you go. He'll give you wisdom and intelligence to be able to make decisions and the right and wrong ones. You'll be able to do that. You're going to have to see the vision but if you see the vision through God's regulations, through His supervision, it will be a much brighter light shining in your path. Your hopes and dreams will be put on a foundation that doesn't float all over the place. You see, it's different to have a dream that you're longing for than to have a fantasy. Fantasies can take you to unlimited distance, floating all over the place as I have most of my life.

But a dream that you examine and look at it and find out the meaning of it; look at it and try to find your motive for having these dreams. It gives you hope and a reason to examine life. It regenerates you. Sometimes it gives you an understanding of yourself. It lets you know sometimes that you can have unlimited thoughts and ideas. Dreams will give you a lifeline. It gives you a signal about hope. It allows you to examine the word *hope*. Just to sit down and say 'I hope I can do this', 'I hope I can do that', 'I can hope and hope and hope.' That's not what hope is about, I don't believe.

I believe hope is something like this: If I'm successful in being what I think I need to be, then I'm going to try to make things better on this earth. I hope I can make a difference on this earth. I hope I can make a difference in my life. I hope that my dream can show somebody how to be proud of themselves. I hope God will take my path and straighten it out a little bit. I hope somebody can teach me how to read God's word. I hope somebody can teach me how to understand the things in life that seem to be a mystery to me now. I don't want to live in a fantasy world. That's what I've done most of my life. I build opportunities and realize that God is in charge of my life; that I don't have a whole lot to say about it. If I go His way, that my vision should not just be for me and me alone, but love should shine in my life in a way that I want to amplify it in the families of this nation. Not only that, I should look at my life as a foundation for somebody; a foundation for my family. I should be the roots and the person to build hopes and dreams, not just for myself, but I should show God's hope in the hearts of my children that this world is not just made for an individual but it is made for people. It is made for humanity to see each other's problems and try to share them with them and get the muscle and the love of God and let it be in the front of them as they walk forward through this world.

Yes, there's an opportunity for people. But it is more than an opportunity; it's a realization of putting your shoulder to the grindstone and pushing forward with the hopes and the dreams of God's passion and God's love.

You see, this thing that you call the gospel represents everything that is pure to mankind. Salvation is not just something that's got a name to it but salvation is a way of life and I don't have to go through the Bible and name chapter after chapter. I can think about and talk about Jesus Christ's lifestyle by the way that I live my life on this earth. You set a standard by the way you walk through this world not the way you read through this world, not the way you write through this world but the example that you set - the holiness that demonstrates God's love. You've got to ask yourself hard questions on this earth. And then when you ask the questions if you can't answer them, then you have to go to God to get the answer. The first place to go is on your knees and hold your heart before God and let him anoint it with his son, Jesus Christ. That kind of preservation will make a way for anybody on this earth. It doesn't make any difference whether you can read or write, whether you're crippled or blind, or whether you don't have any hands or any arms. God does not go by the condition of your body; He goes by the condition of your heart.

You're not just born on this earth to set your standards. But you are born on this earth to set God's standards. I don't care who you are. I don't care if you're an atheist. I don't care if you don't even know who God is. You have an obligation to yourself, to your family, and to whatever nation that you live in. You have an obligation to your community. You do not live on this earth alone. You do not have a right to do just anything you want because it pleases you. You have more on this earth than just you. You walk with a nation of people. You walk with a generation of children on this earth. Everyday that you move you're setting some type of standard for somebody. It doesn't matter whether you're Christian or the biggest sinner in the world.

Ladies and gentlemen, I want you to be open to this. God does not love Christians more than sinners. He loves us all. We belong to Him. We don't all receive the same reward and we all don't receive the same blessings. If God did love sinners, I wouldn't be where I am today.

I may be using the wrong word when I say 'set a standard'; maybe you set an example. If people like the way you look and the way that you're acting they may just want to conform to the way you live your life, if it looks good to them but it doesn't mean it is good.

Each of us has a certain amount of time allotted to us, for a certain period of time. It is not ours to use and do with it what we want to do with it. We're supposed to use it for what we need to use it for; for God's purpose, for humanity's purpose. When we help other people we help ourselves if we help them in a positive manner. You don't just go around and throwing away bread to the dogs just because you have it and just because they ask for it. You need to know something about their needs. You need to know something about their lives. You need to know something about your purpose. You need to know who is leading you and who is teaching you. You need to know a little about self-motivation. I believe self-motivation comes in when you allow yourself to accept Godly principles in your life. I believe that will motivate and activate the love in your heart. I believe that develops strength, encouragement, and energy. I believe that you will have all the vigor that you need to push on forward. I believe the purposes that God laid out in that Holy Bible will give you the connection to humanity that you need.

You see, if you search for the lifeline, God will throw it to you. You won't have to ramble around in the dark like I've done most of my life. You'll have something that you can hold on to that will give you that survival aid that all of us need at one time or another.

INCREASING OUR CAPACITY FOR GENUINE COMMUNITY

When we think of the word "community", images of the areas in which we live and make our homes comes to mind. But there is much more to community than meets the eye. Webster defines community as a unified body of individuals. Community is not a new idea or concept; it has been around since the beginning of time. In the first book of the bible (Genesis 1:26), we find the Creator of the universe in conversation; "Then God said.'Let Us make man in Our image." On the surface it appears that God is having a conversation with himself and in essence that is true because He is the "One true God". But a deeper examination exposes the fact that there is a plurality involved.

Notice the words "Us" and "Our", from which the doctrine of the Trinity is derived. This clues us in to the fact that God is singular and yet at the same time plural. This provides an amazing insight to the fact that God, in whose image we were created is not just concerned about community, but also rightly defined, God is community. Since God himself lives and operates in a communal state, it should not surprise us that human beings, created in the image of God have an internal wiring that makes us gravitate toward each other.

People need each other. That is a fact of life. We are different in design but we share the need to interrelate. We define our lives by the relationships we have. Women tend to draw definition from the relationships they share intimately. While men tend to define themselves by the relationships they share corporately. It is certain that there are exceptions to the rule but overall we can identify that the need to relate is the core of our being.

How we relate is an entirely different science and mechanism. Because somewhere along the line, no doubt due to the entrance of sin into the world: we have lost something that was originally intended. Again Webster's definition of community begins with unity. So in order to be a genuine community in a unified sense, I must care about you and you must care about me. We see evidence of this in scripture as Jesus endeavors to lead us back to our original state. After salvation's cleansing work, Christians are urged in John 13:34 to "...love one another as I have loved you." The apostles taught throughout the New Testament that we are all members of one body. The supremacy of this concept is that in order for us to ascend to the level of genuine community (plural) we have to condition ourselves to remember that we are all a part of one mechanism called humanity (singular).

This concept is not only true for Christians, while its pinnacle is manifested in Christianity; this is also a timeless truth for all units of humanity. It is just as true for the smaller family unit as it is for the larger elements of communal society. And so in order for us to increase our capacity for genuine community we must educate ourselves and others in reference to the definition and origin of community, understand that we have been created with an insatiable desire to connect with one another, and from there we must move towards understanding that the cement which holds us together and serves to make us productive in whatever we do is the infusion of "love" in our thoughts, words, and deeds.

When we can grasp these concepts individually and collectively and seek to write them on our hearts and in our souls, then we will see levels of genuine community expand within our society and we will ultimately reap the benefits of such.

By-Rev. K. L. Long

I find Pastor Long to be an upstanding young man. I use the word "man" for "minister." I have heard him teach. He is an excellent teacher and preacher, a magnificent minister. He is an outstanding gentleman. He truly loves God's Word and he knows its meaning. I had the opportunity to talk to him and he loves the Lord. He opens up the hearts and minds of people. I think Pastor Long's wonderful literature has expressed what most of us believe.

By Guy P. Darden, Sr.

INSIGNIFICANT

How insignificant are the things that people think are insignificant. The things that people walk by each day of their lives and they are so small until people find them unimportant. The reason is because they're not shiny; they are dull and flat. They don't stick out above the greatness in America. The people on this earth that we assume are unimportant; we feel that that they are none of our business, that they don't concern us. Those of us who think we know what is truly significant chose to treat others as if they were insignificant. To the individual that overlooked the finer points of life, I believe personally they've lost some of the essence of life and some of the facts. They have lost some of the muscle that might even make them a stronger individual.

Things that are not important to me do not mean that they are not important to someone. People don't always shine. We have people on this earth that carry a glitter about them. Some of them even wear window dressing, so to speak. They look good on the outside. They have oratory and they make a lot of noise, but are that significant? Is that important? Yes. I believe to be able to make yourself known, and the ability to represent yourself well and be able to look good and put on a good show, at times. Sometimes we need to show ourselves and present ourselves in a glamour-like way, in an exciting way if we are working towards a positive effort. But is that all that's important?

Sometimes that same thing can cover up the real essence of what something might be, or might not be. We need to exam all of our thoughts and ideas. Sometimes people fool themselves. They mislead themselves and they follow people who are misleading them. They pick up habits and ideas from other people that are not real.

What I'm leading up to is, I think we all need to find out about ourselves, examine ourselves. I think a Christian man or a Godly man that believes in God and believes in those things that are visible; that they have a visibility about themselves where you can touch it and examine it. I don't always mean the physical touch. Sometimes the mental and insight on the vision of life can lead you to the insides of a situation and allow you to examine it from the core. I believe when you have a Godly respect and Godly love that you can see and understand that type of essence. When I use the word essence, I mean the core of something, the inside, the heartbeat of it, the motor, the thing that makes it move, and the action of it; the things that are real in life and sometimes, as Christ used the word – I remember once that some things you have to fast and pray to make yourself have the type of faith that you need. You need to know that you have a God that operates on faith. And for you to get the things out of life that you need, as a God-fearing person, you have to have faith in God because He's not going to come down here, in most cases, and stand in the front of you and just physically take you and carry you here and carry you there. He'll give you a spiritual ride through life. But I'm not just talking about Christians. God believes in people. I'm talking about people who have a responsibility on this earth. I'm talking about people that believe in integrity and decency and honor, and fair play. He has the same responsibility as anybody else on this earth. If you're talking about someone that might be counted a fool by the Almighty God, or even maybe by you, by the way he lives his life, and stupidity has taken advantage of him; you're not going to be able to reach him anyway. You're going to have to live your life in the front of him so that he examines your standard in life and sees that you really do have something that makes sense. You might influence him in a way that he may come over and start asking you questions. You may have an open door to his heart. You may be able to reach something in him that he hasn't been able to touch; by your Godly love and Godly principles, or just manly principles. And what I call a man is one who respects integrity and honesty to the gills. You believe that right is right and wrong is wrong, and he made his mind up that he is going to do the best he can as long as he can.

I'm going to use some things that I call *toppings* and then I'm going to use some things that I call the *dressing*. You know when you make a layer cake, you take those layers and put them in a plain old pie plate and put them in the oven and bake them and they come out nice and brown. You may make a 3- or 4-layer cake; maybe 4 or 5. They don't look all that appetizing at first. But, you usually put coconut or whatever you decide to put on there; it might be chocolate. I remember my mother making applesauce cake. She would put all that stuff on it and it didn't look all that appetizing until she would take it and put all of the beautiful whip cream and stuff on it. It might be chocolate or whatever she would put on it, but it would be so beautiful when she finished it. But down in the center of it was where the real nitty-gritty tasty flavor was. That was when you went through that topping and got down to that, that was truly a tasty and very, very important cake, but all of the beauty was on the top - all of the lovely things. Some of those toppings were delicious and wonderful but if you just had the toppings and didn't get what was under the topping, it might not be so good.

I think there are things in life like that, such as titles. We love titles, the American people. But titles do not necessarily show the essence of who you are; they are more than just titles. I'm talking about things and examining insignificance - significance and insignificance. Ph.D.s -that is a topping. Doctors – topping. Lawyers, school teachers, ministers; you could take that line, presidents, vice-president, senators, congressmen, mayors, governors and you could take a long line all the way back to kings and queens. Gods, and I means gods with an 's' on it, gods; there is only one God, really and we're not talking about that type of god, that type of title. You could have the first layer, such as our blue collar workers, steal mill workers, engineers, porters, maids, nurses, until you came down to the chamber maid. We don't hear that word much any more. Most people don't even know what it means. (In case you don't know what it means, that was the lady who emptied the urine and the stools.) Then there is your kitchen worker who cooked, washed the dishes, cleaned the toilets, scrubbed the floors, and did the gardening. Some of those people are considered unimportant in certain times and places.

Now let me tell you how I mean that. Guy Darden, you promised the president that you were going to call him Tuesday. You called him. There is no way that you would neglect to call him. If you couldn't you would have your secretary call or in some way let him know you could not make it. Would you put the same emphasis on the importance of integrity to your gardener, maid or a child as you would to someone of a higher level.

The little boy that you promised to give a nickel to or bring back some candy, you overlooked it. It wasn't important. You didn't put priorities on it. The people that you see every day that you tell little stories to, you don't call them lies, you say - I told you a story yesterday son. I promised you I was going to bring you some candy. I promised you I was going to take you for a walk. I promised you I was going to take you to the movies. I promised Sally I was going to call her – I told a story, I didn't call her. Those are not stories.

Those are just a big lie as if you would have told it to the president. Your word is your word, no matter who it is.

Your priorities are to your God. Your obligation is to your God. Your obligation is also to the people that you make commitments to. Your loyalty is to yourself because when you abuse your word, you're abusing your integrity, and everything that you are, has been put on trial. When you accept the responsibility of being a Godly person, living for Christ, living His lifestyle, that's not a job. Being a minister is not a job. That's not a job. You have signed up for service. When you accept Christ in your life it's not a job. That is a lifestyle. You are in service. When somebody asks you to do something for them and you decide you want to pray about it, you pray about everything. You pray about everything on earth that you do; you pray. But this is a corporation prayer. It is a prayer that you made at the foot of the cross. Now you are asking God to give you the guidance to have priorities in your life and make decisions. But as far as doing what you need to do, you are automatically under orders to do that. You are under orders by God Almighty. When these times and things come up, you know what you're supposed to do and what you're not supposed to do. Your leadership is Christ and you prayed this morning and you pray that God will give you the guidance to do the things that you ought to do. You don't stop in the middle of doing something and say, "well, I can't do this because I haven't prayed." You are in service.

What I'm really trying to say is that these people, the way we have treated the certain classes of people sometimes gives them, not just you – I think this is more important than any other thing that I have to say – regardless of what anybody thinks I am in the cycle of life, I need to know personally where I am because I am dealing with my life. I'm the one that's going to control my life other than God. If I'm going to control it, I need to have some order to it. I need to have some priorities to it. I need to know a little something about myself; not just a little something, I need to know a lot about me. I need to know what my capabilities are; what I am capable of doing and what I am not capable of doing. I need to know when I get to be a Senior Citizen I should have some ideas of what I am qualified to do. I should know something about my life according to my past. I should set my footstep according to my path, to the way I am, and who I am. I should know enough about the stand that I have with God because He's already given me an opportunity to believe in His faith.

As a Senior Citizen and as a Godly person, I don't need to just sit around and have pity parties about what I didn't do. I need to do, now, what I need to do; not just what I want to do but what I need to do. If I have some wisdom and some experience and some accountability, I need to express it openly and boldly. Because I've been in my prayer closet and I've been asking God to give me the information that I need to do what I need to do, if I'm influenced in the way I should be by God Almighty, I may have a great feeling for the desire of the want to be what I need to be.

I believe that the world today is suffering a lot because, we as Senior Citizens, have not spoken up. We've decided that we need to keep our mouths shut, if it's good for us. Because if we keep running our mouths, people may get upset with us, and if they get upset with us they won't give us any handouts. They'll stop our Social Security. Our children won't come to see us. They'll get upset with us. We need to let the people know that we're not just a tomb; some old man, some old woman, withering away, having a pity party. I don't care if you don't believe what I say I'm going to tell you anyway. And you may stumble over something that might help you in life. I'm going to say what I need to say no matter how people feel, because I didn't say it when I needed to.

People talk about not paying us any attention, people won't listen to us and young people won't listen to us. We separate our classes and our Sunday school classes. We segregate the men and women, the children by ages. We don't have any relationship. We don't have anything to talk about that we understand about each other. We need to come together as a people and talk with each other. Young people and old people talking and gathering and understanding each other, not putting each other down, but listen to each others conversation and trying to understand what each other means. We don't know anything about each other. We are strangers. We are strangers in our own houses with our own children and with our own husbands and wives. We are strangers.

This is a unity time. That is the reason today that the Indians of this land don't own their own country. They separated themselves. You cannot and will not be successful when you do that; not in a productive way. I'm talking about black people and white people getting together. I'm talking about people getting together. I'm talking about people. I don't care who they are. Let them be of Mexican races or Black races or Negro or whatever you want to call it; I don't have any problem with "Negro". I don't have any problem with "African". I don't have any problem with "Black". I don't have any problem with anything that has to do with togetherness and working together as a team; honesty, decency and integrity. I have no problem with that. I don't care what race you are or where you come from. But I think we need to have a common goal of how we live on this earth and what we do on this earth and what we do in front of our children and with our children and with our families and in front of our families; that's important to me.

SEEDS

I've heard people talk about the seeds that we plant. I've heard my son say his son is his seed. Actually, you're the product of my seed. This is very controversial. You are not the seeds but the product. Parents are to teach you how to plants seeds. Seeds planted in good soil flourish and those that are planted in poor soil will not flourish. A product of the bad seed will have a lot of work to be done on it. This does not take away the importance of it. The seed does not produce a seed, it produces a product. If the product is not developed properly it will not have good seeds that will be productive. The seeds that develop from the product are not going to be productive because the product is what plants the seeds. In order for a product to find the proper seeds to plant it has to come from the parents who are the product of a seed.

We have to do an analysis of separation here. A seed is planted and it then becomes a product, such as a stalk of corn. Remember there are many, many fields where seeds have been planted. A fire may come along and burn it up and that stalk will not produce anything. There are other stalks of corn in the field that we may not have put enough fertilizer on or did not properly nourish it. That stalk stills develops seeds but they are not good. We still have more stalks in the field that have been fertilized, nourished, and cared for properly and they will produce good seeds.

In saying this, the same can be said for man. I am planting seeds. I am the product. Hopefully, my seeds will grow into other products that will produce more seeds and continue the cycle of life. If you plant seeds that are good, good products will flourish. If you plants bad seeds, bad products will grow.

A CORRECTIONS STORY

Growing up in the Deep South, I lived in a small community where racism and segregation are still a part of life. Being a black male, even in a small town, has its drawbacks. I remember going to school defending myself against whites. You were always wrong no matter what it was about. Luckily I had parents, grandparents, and great-grandparents motivating me to be a law-abiding citizen, telling me right from wrong.

Once I finished high school, I started working in a factory making minimum wage and working overtime. The money wasn't worth the work but at the age of eighteen years old, it was all you could do besides selling drugs and stealing. I worked in that place for sixteen years before it packed up and went to Mexico. In an instant, my life was turned upside-down trying to find a new job to support my life and pay my bills.

One day a friend came up to me and asked me to ride with him to put in an application at a prison facility. I really didn't give it much thought at first, but once I got in the place and all the checkpoints that we had to go through just to sign up to be seen, I was thinking at one time, was it worth it? After a couple of days of interviews, we were accepted.

With the state that I work in, you have to go to school for four weeks. It's called Basic Correctional Officer Training. The classes that I took teach you that the criminal justice system in America is built upon the philosophical foundation that a person may be punished by the government only if it has been proven by deliberate process that the person has violated the law.

The criminal justice system has been divided into three components: the police, the courts, and the corrections which each have a distinct task. What each subsystem does and how it conducts its business directly affects the work of the others. The courts can only deal with those whom the police arrest. Corrections deals with the ones that are delivered to it by the courts and how successfully corrections reforms the offender will determine whether or not the police must deal with them again after they are released.

Perhaps the most striking fact about corrections is that it serves as varying degrees of punishment for the convicted offender while the services or programs that accompany the dispositions work toward reintegrating the offender as a law-abiding citizen into the community. If the offender prefers to go back into society, there are courses and classes that they can take to help them with their problems that got them there. Being punished for the crime that they have committed has helped some. I have seen offenders get certificates for computer classes, anger management courses, self-development skills, plumbing, electrical, carpentry, even a GED.

At the facility where I work, we house fifteen hundred offenders on a daily basis. Eighty percent are black males, eighteen percent are whites and two percent are other races. The ages range from eighteen years old to into the seventies. The *average age group is 20 to 35. Most of the young offenders that are housed in our facility have disciplinary problems. They have little or no respect for staff.*

We have weekly disputes between staff and offenders and daily disputes with offender-on-offender conflicts. But this is normal for two men living in the same cell coming from different backgrounds and forced to live with each other. I know the living conditions they were used to have changed, but they have committed a crime and it is my job to control their environment and make them behave in a manly state. Blacks and whites are housed together in the same cells and the same dorms. No one housing unit or dorm has the same race to itself. We have gang members housed among the rest of the prison population to keep the violence down. It is working so far.

The biggest concern we have is homosexual activities. I have to ask some of the offenders, "Does being locked up mean that you have to have sex with another man?" I think some of them think its okay to do if they don't get caught. But when they have a conflict with the lover, it comes out in the open. We have staff that come around and talk to the prisoners about HIV, AIDS, and having sexual partners in the system, but it doesn't keep them from doing it. I have seen inmates that have been caught in the act of having sex with another man and went on visitation to see his wife and kids. It is a sick feeling to know when and if he gets out, he will go back to his wife and be around his kids, possibly with some kind of virus. And it's mostly young black males that we see being brought into the system who then start having relationships with other men. How can we stop it? Can it be prevented? The more you try to talk to them about it, the more they deny that it is going on.

It takes between $25 to $50 a day to house an offender, but what other choices does society have when a crime is committed? Some offenders start off at an early age and never grow out of a life of crime. Some learn that it was wrong and never go back to their old ways, but what about the ones that don't care? They don't mind stealing, selling drugs, killing, raping, and taking advantage of someone. I have seen at last ten offenders return to serve more time in our system since I've started my career in corrections. We say it is wrong to have so many in prison, but what should we do when they break the law? Some think its okay to commit a crime. "I'll do a little time and I'll be back on the streets in about two to five years." It's like people have their values crossed up. Blacks don't seem to care about the outcome of their race. I have learned to respect a person for the respect that he gives me. No matter what he or she has done in life, it's not my job to judge a man or woman. Just get along with them in a neighborly way.

By A Georgia Corrections Officer
Guy Darden's Grandson

People like prisoners need to know that their actions contaminate the family as well as their communities. People who commit crimes, especially those that have a family, need to realize that with all of the protection that we have given in the prison system, there's a lot going on in the underground world known as the prison house. There may be homosexual activity. When you are forced to meet certain segments of society, it's like a university of crimes to be committed from A to Z. Believe it or not, when you put yourself in that position, you don't care about yourself, let alone our family. Many are teachers of crime, intentional or not, by sharing their lifestyle. But that can be turned around if they decide to choose a positive path.

By Guy P. Darden, Sr.

GOING BACK TO THAT OLD HOUSE

Be a part of our environment to allow Him to teach us and let us be influenced by God other than just being influenced by the things and the people of this earth. I think we need to know before we know anything else what part that we are supposed to play on this earth. I think that we need think about what condition we are in. How well have we been trained? How well have we been taught about Jesus Christ? How well have we been taught about serving mankind? Have we been taught about serving mankind? What is our primary duty on this earth? How much can we give that is not ours to give? How much do we receive that's not ours to receive? Whom do we feel is motivating us each day and each night? Who has the most influence on our lives? If we were in trouble today what human being would we most likely to talk to? Who has influenced our lives the most? What preservation have we made for tomorrow other than things? What priorities do we put on our spiritual life? Is it the first thing we think of when we wake up in the morning and the last thing we think of when we lay down at night? Or is it something that just comes into play when we are in need of something that is special to us?

Once we examine those aspects of our lives, I think at that point, we have something that we can discuss openly; not only about others, but about ourselves. I don't think you can learn a lot about other people until you know something about who you are and what you are. This thing – life – is more than just a dream. It is a place that we fix things. We fix the broken pieces in our lives. We look out to those people that we feel that are wiser and have more wisdom and have more knowledge than we do to give us some teaching so that we know for sure that we are heading in the right direction.

We make sure that we can identify Jesus Christ's inspiration; God Almighty, that we know when He is talking to us. He made the statement that my sheep know My voice and they follow Me. The reason they know His voice and the reason they follow Him is because He feeds them. That is more than idle chatter. It is a commitment. It's more than just talking and being impressive in a conversation. It's having that reason that makes people want to listen to you. You've got to have something coming out of you that touches people's lives and changes their lives. You can do that when you are involved in God Almighty's lifestyle. When you deal yourself a hand from the world, you don't have so much. Things and things are not going to give you the strength and the will that you need to serve God.

We need to realize and understand the commitment that we make. That when we make a commitment, it's not just to a church building, there should be more going on in your life than going to church and to Sunday school. That should be the place where you find out how you are supposed to act and how you're supposed to live after you get out of that building. That building is the mechanical factory that makes you and prepares you to do the things that you need to do in the world.

We need to have a reality check. There is a judge that I listen to sometimes when she's on TV and she tells them that she's going to give them a realty check. You see God gave us that when He sent His son down here to die for us in order to save us from a dying world of sin.

Last summer I went back to Virginia where I was born. I went to the home place where I grew up. I wanted to see that place. I had some problems that kept haunting me. I don't like going back to my childhood. I just don't like it. Some of the things that went on back there make me think so negative until it handicaps me from doing some of the things that I need to do. When I think too much about it I feel it takes something away from me. Anyway, I needed to see that old house once more. I went back there and when I did, that old house that I used to live in as a child, I walked around it. The house had fallen down and caved in but the chimney still stood there. If the rest of the house had a good foundation it would still be standing there too.

I had some memories there that had destroyed my confidence in humanity somewhat. You know when you start judging you don't really know what you're judging because the funny thing about it, you're not a judge. Most of us are not even human judges, let alone talking about judging mankind for God. But I was trying to judge my parents from some things that happened when I was a child that I wasn't that proud of. I needed to recapture, I thought, some of me that was still in that old house. That old house still seemed to trouble me. I couldn't understand what was going on in my life.

I remembered back when I had a nervous breakdown and tried to take my life; and some things that my niece had said to me. She came to the hospital to see me and she brought her two little girls. I think they were five and seven years old. Those two little girls prayed for me. Then after they finished praying, the mother prayed; my niece prayed. She said, "Uncle Guy, what on earth is wrong? Don't you know we love you?" She said, "Uncle Guy, we love you. We love you without any reservation; unconditionally. We love you just the way you are." I looked up at her and she had a tear in her eye and that tear dropped. It was as though I felt like I had committed a sin against her. She seemed to love me so much and I had attempted to take my life as though that was going to solve the problems that I had. Then I began to think and see that I wasn't just making trouble for myself but I was making trouble for those people that loved me and cared for me.

They took me to the hospital and later that night they moved me to another hospital where I could get better care. At about 3:00 in the morning I began to yell out, "I killed him. I killed him. I finally killed him!" The nurse came running back there and she said, "Mr. Darden, who did you kill?" I said, "I killed Guy Darden; I killed him. I actually killed him." They were upset and called the doctor. The doctor came and asked if I was alright now. I said "Yes! My suicide was successful." I was now born again!!!

I remembered what my niece said. She said, "Uncle Guy, I love you unconditionally. We love you just the way you are. You don't have to do nothin' like this." And as she told me that and I saw that tear, it came to me then as I was lying in bed there that night. It was about 3:00. I said, "That's the way Jesus Christ felt when He gave His life for us." That's the way He feels now. He loves us unconditionally. He loves us and He doesn't care what we do, He still loves us. He's willing to forgive us for our sins. It's not because we've been so good but because God is so good and He's willing to give us a second chance.

I remembered that as I stood there looking at that old house that had decayed and looking at the bad things that I remembered in my life. Immediately my mind left that house and began to think about the things that I did in the fields and the community that I enjoyed and loved doing. I began to think about my grandfather and how much he loved everybody and how much love he gave us as a family. My mother wasn't his daughter. My mother – God bless her.

Love and sadness; all the tragedies that deal with life has a price. Even the good times that we have, have a price. Good or bad has a price. When we know God as He is and when we know Him with the strength and when we know that this world is a training place. We know that when we accept Christ in our lives as our personal and intimate Savior, that He will guide us and lead us. If we submit to Him, He will make great things come onto our path. He'll open up our mind. He will not only allow grace to be in our lives but great strength and great inspiration. He'll allow us to have great admiration for mankind. As well as God's love, we have to let people see God in us in the way we live our lives on this earth.

Just being alive on this earth gives us a great responsibility especially when God has allowed us to stay here so long. Those of us who think that retirement is a pleasant and exciting time in our lives; it is. But it's not a time to go back, lie back, and take ourselves out of action. It is a time to look for the world's excitement. It is a time that we take a survey of our lives and look at the world's people that haven't been as fortunate as you have been. Look at the blessings that God has bestowed upon us over these years. Look forward to having the time now to serve God in the service of God. It's time to make your life shine. Not only in your path but let God shine through you into somebody else's path. They may be going along the road that you went over a few years ago and you have some experience and knowledge. You've been blessed to gain some wisdom. Let that be the things that you might be able to do. Let your life reflect back over the things that you can do for somebody, not necessarily about the things that you can't do. You have to recognize the things that you can't do and understand what God will allow you to do. That's my opinion.

You know, I still have to go back to that house and remember the good and the bad so that I can have a better reference about what happened to me in my life. What motivated me all through my life up until this point? I need to find something back there and up here that works together for the benefit of me and you. Hopefully we can do something to help each other.

Yes, I'm going back. I've got to go back to that old house where so much went on in my life. I grew up there on the riverbank of a farm with one of the most wonderful grandfather I've ever known or any kid could have. He was the godliest human being that I've ever known. I don't remember going to church with him. I know we went because I remember us being in church. I'm pretty sure he went with us. But he certainly read the Bible to us every night. He talked about how God was in his life.

As I think about my life, maybe the reason that Christ has allowed me to live to an age of 78 years old now...I thought of this book over 20 some years ago. I just kept trying to put something together. I thought I needed to say something about the way we were living our lives as a people. I ask the question I think will mostly give you an idea to go back over your life and take a survey. I don't answer very many questions. Most of the questions I ask are something that most of us already know. But I think we need to re-evaluate them and find out how well we have been blessed. How much we knew about life that we didn't take care of when we got there? We thought the pleasure and excitement of lust meant more to us than the things that we needed to do right.

I believe it's a little different with the youngsters and youth of today. I believe it's a little different because I don't believe they've been taught like we were taught. I don't believe they have been taught about integrity and morale values the way we were taught. I don't think they see the interaction with me and you that we saw back there. When I go back to this old house that is sitting here with the chimney and only a foundation now; when I come back here and look at the land structure and the road and highway, I can see the people coming down it.

I can hear the old carts clicking and clacking and the chains jingling. Sometimes it would be carrying a drunk. Nobody was in the wagon and horse knew the way back home and was going home. We would say, "Better go out there and see if that's Mr. Dick Fowler and see if he's okay because that sure is him." He would go out there and walk up to the mule saying, "Whoa, Pete, whoa." He'd say, "How are you doing Dick?" He said, "Uncle George, I'm drunk as hell, but I'm okay." Grandpa cared about all people. It didn't matter who they were and he was frightened of no man. He had no fear in his life. I don't think fear existed in his life. When he got angry, people feared him. He would say, "Dog. Bite it." I never hear him say, "Doggone it". If he would have said "Doggone it", we would have probably run away from home. He had a glorifying speech that made people have reverence for him; white and black. Even the Ku Klux Klan had reverence for my grandfather. He wasn't really my grandfather, he was my step-father but he treated me like a son.

I find my roots more on that place than I do anywhere in life. I find more things that he said that kept me alive on this earth, kept me from being a real bad stinker. It kept me from stealing and robbing and it kept me from a lot of things. I believe it kept me out of jail. It kept me out of prison. It's not that I didn't go to jail a couple of times. I was in prison a couple of times, but the total time in my life being in jail was about 90 days. I got put in jail one time for stealing my uncle's pistol. I told the boys I had a gun; they didn't believe it. I had to prove it to them and I took it to them. He found out after I took it there that I stole it; at least he thought I had. I was the only one in the house. He called to police. I threw it away and my dad came and asked me, "Boy, did you take that gun? I don't want no lyin'." I said, "Yes, sir." He asked what I did with it and I told him I had thrown it in the ditch and I told him where and he went and found it. He carried it back with him. The judge gave me one year of probation. At that time, it just killed me to think I had done something to the kindest man I had known; my uncle was very, very kind. I didn't hang around him anymore but he never did hate me for that.

 I go back to that house, I see people coming down the road that are drifting from one place to another. Perhaps they got in trouble way down in Georgia someplace. They were running from the white people many times; trying to escape. Sometimes they would get in trouble with the Ku Klux Klan or something. My grandfather took them in. Sometimes they just stayed there. Sometimes they died there. They just lived there. Nobody ever told them to leave. That's the way he was. Young men would come along and want to spend the night and they never left. They would just stay there and work on the farm and be part of the family.

 That's what I think about when I try to make money and save it and put it away. Every time I would start doing that somebody would come up and ask me for something and I'd let them have it. Every time I thought I needed to do something for myself or save something up in a big bank account, somebody would be in trouble, they would ask me for something, and I would give it to them. It didn't bother me. I didn't feel bad about sharing what I had with somebody. I made good money for that time. I worked hard. I got paid a top salary for the farm. When I went away I got paid pretty well too.

 I've been a tailor now for 59 years; almost 60. I've always been able to eat and make a living for myself. Not a lot, but I've been able to survive. I've been able to be around good and nice people. The times I got in trouble, for some reason some things back then were kept secret. I never heard anybody talk it except for now in my family because they said I went away. Nobody ever knew that I spent any time in jail. I was a polite, nice, quiet, church-going kid, when we went to church. When I grew up I went to church quite often for a while.

Then I decided the church people were doing things that I wouldn't dare do. I would see them with people's wives and getting drunk and staggering, cursing, and swearing. I never did that kind of stuff. So I thought, 'what the heck.' I know God and I know what He wanted and what He did. I knew I was doing something wrong. I knew I'd change it whenever I got ready. I did not see what I did as being so bad because everybody I knew was doing stuff much worse than me, other than my grandfather.

My grandfather on my mother's side didn't seem to have such a good record except that he was a nice, respectable person and everybody loved him for being like that and he was always looked up to. But I saw the things that nobody else saw happening around there. I saw things that they didn't think kids knew about. That's something I want to tell you and something I need your advice on. Try to live you life the way you want your children to live theirs. Be careful what you do in front of your children. Be careful what you do when you think your children don't see because they see a lot more than you think. They are a lot more intelligent than you think. They know a lot more about things than you think they do.

In all the churches that I've been to, I began to realize that people trusted me. They saw something in me. I thought that what they kept telling me only a good person could have. I know differently. I knew that I wasn't near what they thought I was. I had become an actor. By that time I had become a performer. I kind of resented, especially the intelligent people, because I was doing the things that they were doing and getting a lot of praise. I didn't even know how to read and write. I heard them putting down people and talking about how stupid they were. I saw young people making fun of people who couldn't read and write. There was no way I was going to let them know that I couldn't read or write. I began to get talking books so I could listen to them. Besides that, I had a photographic memory. I could remember anything anyone would tell me or that I heard; I memorized it.

I saw all those church people doing all those things at those speak-easy's and I saw my mother at the speak-easy and I saw her doing things that even the regular men she was dating didn't know she was doing. I thought that they were doing things in order to impress people. So for me to be a good person then all I had to do was do good things. So whatever I saw good people do, I did it. But behind the closed doors and where I didn't see them, I did whatever I felt like I needed to do if it was socially acceptable by the individuals that I was doing it with. I never drank very much at that time, and as a matter of fact, if I took 4 or 5 drinks a year that would be probably the most. I had never been around children to play with them and socialize with them very much; only my brother and I was quite a bit older than he was.

I learned to be a good communicator with people. I could interact with anybody. I just followed my lines and whatever good people did, and I saw them do it; those were my lines. You can become addicted to that. But the one thing that it doesn't produce is pure, unadulterated love. You can't act up enough to get that. You can get an appreciative shake. You can get a pat on the shoulder but true, Godly love, is based on Godly principles. I didn't know that at the time. I knew enough about God that I joined a church when I was 12 years old. I didn't go back many times afterwards except when I met someone that had something that I needed. I felt like going to church would impress them. If I knew they went to that church, I'd go to that church.

I tried to change from that and turn my life around. I began to like people and to love them for what they were. But the Godly things, I never got the picture. I didn't know that much about Jesus Christ. I didn't know that much about the inward part of God. I only knew the surface of God, the one I hear the preachers talk about all the time. The things that they talked about and the things they did were different. They talked about discipleship. They talked about helping your brother and loving your brother as you loved yourself. I'd never seen anybody do that other than my grandfather.

I began to become disenchanted. I became radical and proud and excited about some of the things that I was getting; cars and jewelry that I never cared much for. I found that I had the same thing and got the same respect that the people that had money did and as long as they didn't know that I couldn't read or write. As long as I could keep a conversation with them and discuss something with them and talking about a given situation, then I was way beyond the average person who went to school. I could talk politics. I could talk about God because I had a lot of talking Bibles. I had begun to really be respected very highly.

I began to learn how to connive and scheme with the money thing. I didn't believe in being dishonest very much. I learned early in life with the stealing of the gun and I took a suit of clothes from somebody. One time I was hungry and I stole some food out of a lady's refrigerator and the police came along and took fingerprints and everything. They did this because someone had come along before me and stole some money out of the house and when I got back there the place was covered with police and I knew I was going to go to jail. Somebody stole a half a gallon of dimes. I was frightened to death but the Lord blessed me and got me through it. I really thought the reason He did it was because I had been doing so many nice things for people.

I was never one that was thievish and cheap. I was always a giving person to my friends and neighbors. Whatever I had that they wanted, they could get it because I could get anything I wanted. People trusted me with their cars, their daughters, and wives. I was very trustworthy.

Then I got religion again. That time I accepted Christ in my life. There are times when everything was fine and beautiful.

TECHNOLOGY

I want tell you what I mean by technology having us instead of us having technology. I want to explain some little things that I know you already know. There are just questions that I'm putting out there to let you examine. They are just thoughts that are being put out there that I've seen happen all over this nation. These are the things that I've seen go on. These are about people that I've talked to. These are about things that I see happening every day. It's not something minor. It's not something that you can just overlook.

Technology is good when it's being used properly. Technology is excellent when it's used for the good of all. But when a few take technology and use it to their advantage and to your disadvantage, then I think that technology has us at that time. I'm going to give you an example. You've kept your house too long. You took care of it too well. You've taken care of your property too well. You have your house remodeled and you put a new roof on it. You've been doing it for several years. As a matter of fact, you've been living at that place for over 40 years now. You had the electric wires redone, kept the lawn up, kept the trash picked up and you kept the place neat. It's a beautiful home. It's a beautiful place. It's not modern. It doesn't have all the technology in it.

You even have televisions in that home that you've had for 10 or 15 years. You took care of your television and you didn't have people throw it around and you kept it clean. You haven't bought a television in 10 to 15 years. You've had it too long. You need to replace your television because of the technology.

That phone that you have that you bought last year, it's obsolete now. You need another phone because of the modern technology in order to serve you better. In the last 5 to 10 years, you might have had 5 or 6 phones because of the technology. But prior to that time, "Ma Bell" or whoever had the telephone company; you could keep a telephone for 30 years – the same telephone – and you wouldn't have any problem.

That house you live in, you're only paying so much tax for it because you only paid so much for it. But since you own that house, the tax rate has gone up. Really, I don't want that house sitting there that you paid $10,000, $14,000 or $25,000 for 40 years ago. I want to put a $200,000 home on that spot.

That's change in technology to make money, not to make things better for us. When we change technology in manufacturing that replace 25, 30, 40 or 50 people – sometimes one piece of equipment can do the work of 20 or 25 people that had to do it manually. That technology has nothing to do with trying to make things better for the country or for the people. It has to do with money, money, money, money, money! That's what I'm talking about.

I'm talking about those areas where you bought property 30, 40 or 50 years ago, that land didn't have the value it has now. I'm saying that those houses now; we can't collect enough taxes to pay for you owning that house or staying in that community. Furthermore, you've got more land than you need there. They don't want you building a $25,000, $30,000, $40,000, or $50,000 house on that lot that you have there for your son or your daughter. They don't want you to be economical by letting you and your son go out there and build a house by buying your own lumber and assemble it yourself. They have to have all these inspection laws, licenses, and sorts of other stuff. That's why I loved the farm so much when I was there because the farmer was the most independent individual on the earth.

The farmer was an individual person. He was someone that you couldn't buy out. He saw the land as being a part of God's creation for man to till and sow the land as being something that needed to be respected. It was more than just a piece of ground. It was more than just a place that you made money off of. It was a place that you could feel proud of. You could plant a seed and see the result of it. Hard work and tilling the ground as it should be was a recycling process. I guess the farmer did the first recycling on earth because you planted the seed, the seed came up and it produced thousands and millions of seeds. You fed it to the horse. The horse ate it. It came out as manure. You put it back on the soil. It reproduced. It fertilized the soil. You could recycle it. Next year you had a crop in another space. You rotated your crops. You knew when you picked up an ear of corn and you took it to the market that that ear of corn was going to keep somebody from going hungry. It was going to feed somebody. Some of the oil that came from the corn was going to cook some food some place. You knew that people all over this world, you were helping them to live. There was no one that was going to come to you and buy your land for no money when you had everything on that land that you needed. There was nothing that money could buy that you didn't already have.

So, technology took over your farm and stripped it out of your hand and gave it to the money grabbing people of this nation. The farmers are not out of business because he had a rough time or because of the famine. No. His honesty did some of it. Trusting people did some of it. Technology did most of it. I know no farmer in my community when I grew up could afford the tractors and farm equipment that they were buying. Most all the farmers that I knew went into debt to buy the equipment that they bought to replace the mule, horse and wagon. He was the most independent individual and nobody could buy his land. He wasn't going to sell it. Since he wasn't going to sell it, then we have to work out a way to steal it or to take it. That was done by getting him in debt knowing that there was no way possible that he was ever going to be able to pay for it. The interest would always be there. He would always be paying interest. Most of the farmers paid interest and interest and interest.

They said the reason the farmers went out of business was because they over produced. The farmers never over produced. Those small farmers that had farms all around did not over produce. The people that over produced were the people that were trying to keep the farmer from planting too much and they were planting millions and millions of acres of land, and they were exporting their products all over the world. Then after they sold it out of the country, a lot of the stuff they sold out of the country, the country they sold it to sent it back as an import to us. We did that with our goods. We did that with our wools. We did that with our textiles. We would have a textile mill over here making fabric and we would ship it overseas and allow them to put their stamp on that fabric and ship it back here and we sell it as imported fabric. You know the word imported rips off people. That fabric may be made right up the street from where you live and you send it overseas and it's called imported. Well they use, I suppose, the same word over there; imported from the United States or England or Germany. It doesn't really mean anything.

There used to be a time when we sold our merchandise, in this nation, especially the farming community, sold their merchandise as cheap as they possibly could in order to make a small profit, to make a living. We had manufacturer's that did that. Sears and Roebuck was one that did that. Walgreen's was one that did that. J.C. Penney's was one that did that. We had great companies all over this nation that tried to be fair and honest until technology came along. Now technology has us. We do not have technology.

HOW DO WE GET THE JOB DONE?

The solutions to the issues that face all of us whether they are personal, community or global in nature will rely on working collaboratively and cooperatively. It is the nature of the society that we live in that the solutions or results require that persons, agencies, political subdivisions and even countries search for the common goals that bind us together and act to strengthen those goals not destroy them. Too much in our society and culture pits person against person or entity against entity for limited resources, recognition or opportunities. Breaking the cycle of competition is the first step toward developing a healthy and vibrant individual, a growing and exciting community and a caring and positive global environment.

What is collaboration? What does it really mean? These are two questions that often never are answered and therefore never permit true collaborative efforts to occur. Collaboration as defined by Webster Dictionary is united labor. Therefore it is the joint efforts of many or more than one to produce something. It is results oriented. It is not just discussion or talking but creating an outcome that is tangible and quantifiable.

If the definition is so simple why does it rarely happen and why is it such an accomplishment when it actually happens? The answer I believe lies in the reason or purpose for which someone enters into the collaborative effort. Is it really an opportunity to produce a result? Have each of the participants come to the table and identified their needs and desires, or are there, as a mentor of mine always asked, "hidden agendas". All participants must be upfront about what they wish to gain from the collaborative effort. That does not mean that if someone gains someone must lose. It means that each party whether they are an individual, agency, community or country must accept that others will gain something from the collaboration and that the gain may be unequal. Each party must also see that there is something in it for them or there is no reason to make the investment. That is why it is important that each entity understand what is important to them from the collaborative effort and be willing to invest to achieve their goal. One must trust that the results of a collaborative effort are bigger and more successful than any individual could create on their own. It is the acceptance of a loss of some power in an effort to develop a better solution. Collaboration is not the loss of individual identity but the success that comes from the process.

Collaboration is about communication; it is about sharing and opening up to other possibilities and understanding of the situation. So we return to the question of why is collaboration important? It is what affects all aspects of our lives. What is a marriage but a collaborative relationship between two people to achieve a common goal? What is a community but a collaborative arrangement of persons working together to create a common vision for the future. When there are issues of conflict or dissention that arise within those arrangements the solutions must be achieved through open communication, a sharing of each one's needs and desires, the willingness to give up something in order to achieve a larger goal. In a marriage both partners must want to work together to find a solution. Both must see that there is something in it for them to keep the marriage together or it will not work.

Similarly the members of a community must understand there is something of value in the community itself. That may be safety and security, companionship, comfort of other resources that can not provide individually, the support of other institutions to provide service larger than one could provide on your own, such as water and sewer system, electricity and similar items. By living in cooperation with each other we have more than we would have living individually. But this also comes with a price. We must be willing to accept the differences between people; that we have different likes and dislikes, that there are different traditions and cultures, that we each value our individualism yet support a collective society.

The need to collaborate in all aspects of our lives continues to grow as our society and the issues we face become more complex. No one person, agency or organization can solve many of the problems or issues that face us today. As detailed by Russell M. Linden Working Across Boundaries, we must be open to hearing from all persons that come to the table regardless of their opinion. The process must be open and credible, based on a conclusion that the stakes are high and that people are interested in working to find the solution. For example, we can not stop the crime in our cities simply by putting more police on the street. We must work with families, neighborhood, social agencies, police and other enforcement entities to address the issues that created the crime and that continue to support it. This means commitment from the individuals that crime is not acceptable. It must be a goal that many want to achieve; a commitment that addressing the crime in the community comes from various levels on the community and in an open and accepting manner. Lastly, people need to accept that the solutions may not come from traditional locations or organizations.

As a government official it is important that these concepts be considered in all the aspects of what we do. It is in this type of an open and communicative organization and community that issues can be resolved and solutions identified. It is not possible for every situation to be collaborative but it is possible for every situation to be thought about in a collaborative manner. Always keeping in mind the other persons or entities interests, goals and desires. It is the old adage of "putting yourself in the other person's shoes". There are times when the "line gets drawn in the sand" that people will not move from their position. When analyzing those situations they are ones when open communication does not exist; when one or more entities will not share *information, where trust has not been built or where the concern for the loss of power is great. These are the situations that divide and can destroy the entities involved. These are the situations that destroy communities.*

Collaboration can be the solution to many problems but it is a journey that will shift and change with time. It is not in itself the end but a means to achieve a stated goal. In government we must be careful that the means does become the end in additional senseless bureaucracy that simply exists to serve itself. For each of us to continue to evolve and for communities to continue to grow collaboration must be a tool that is used to break the cycle of competition and to create the future we each envision.

By Rita C. McMahon
City Manager, Painesville, Ohio

Ms. McMahon is a government official that I have high regard and respect for. I agree with her in most of the things she stated. The only place that I might disagree with is in regard to the many of our officials, locally and nationally – if in order to agree with someone means to waiver in your integrity or principles that you truly believe in order to cooperate with an individual or group then personally I think maybe you ought to re-think it. I have not found that to be true of this lady's administration. I find her to be a decent and upstanding individual.

By Guy P. Darden, Sr.

GOOD AND BAD

I make so many controversial statements. I want you to know that I am trying to talk about the things that I know about personally. I'm speaking on my level. I'm not trying to reach out above myself and talk. Now, some of the things I say may be rather contrary or you may think they are old time or out dated. You make think that I'm not with the times. But there is one thing I want you to know, that I am with God and God is with me.

I don't want to hurt anybody or cripple them in life when they have to struggle to go on. If I say something that might hurt your feelings, I'm not going to feel like I've committed a crime by doing that because everything I say to those of you that are listening to me or are reading this book; I want you to know that I love you and that you are special. If it wasn't for the people on this earth, I don't know what I would do. I love people. I am a people person. They are the ones who have kept me alive. You've been my family. You've been my mothers and fathers. You've been my uncles and cousins. I have so many people that love me on this earth.

You know, I'm one of those guys that can't go around feeling sorry for myself now. A lot of things happened to me in my young life and caused me to get bitter. I never got so bitter that I didn't like people. I think I got angry with myself. I didn't trust myself. For a while, I didn't trust people. That's no blame of yours, it's mine. That experience taught me something that I ought to share with you. I don't want to do anything but make you think. Sometime I would like you to recycle yourself. Sometime I would like you to retrace your steps and get some of that experience back there and bring it up and give it to somebody else.

When I am talking to you like this, I'm talking to you seniors. I'm talking to the people who have had a tough life behind them. Some way or another God brought them out of that hazard that they were in. Now they have some wisdom that they can share with somebody. They have some experience that they can go on. They have a history and sometimes they need to share it with somebody. If they made it out of a deep swamp some place, then they need to let somebody know how they came from back there to up here. That's all I'm doing.

God and Man's Relationship to Humanity

I'm talking to everybody on this earth that I can reach. I don't believe there is anybody on this earth that doesn't have something good they could share with somebody or that they don't have something bad that they can tell somebody that happened to them that might turn that person's life around. What I want you to do is not just look at what you passed up on the road but I want you to tell people about some of the things that happened to you that caused you to struggle and stumble and fall. I want you to let them know how you got up. If it was easy or bad, be brave enough to share some of your life with somebody. If you feel like you have something that was negative at the time but the way you put it out now can be positive, I think you ought to share it. That's what I'm doing here.

I'm not a learned person. I don't have any degrees and I can barely write my name. But I do have some experiences that I want to share with you. I want to prove to you some way or another that God has a living purpose for you. He has something bigger than failure, bigger than defeat, and that He wants to lead you someplace that is better than where you are. That's what I am trying to say.

When we get so that we are intelligent enough or that we have enough wisdom, especially we Senior Citizens, we're going along through life and we pick up nuggets along with way; something that may help us. There is someone that can use the same information that we use for ourselves. We need to share the things that we know about in life to others. Some of us can't process everything the same way. We learn ways how to process the information we get. We're able to use our senses in a better and more constructive manner.

The things that we sometimes think we need, it's not what we need at all. It's what we want. If we're just getting what we want all the time and neglecting the things that we need, then we need to re-examine our status of information that we have. We need to examine our surroundings, our motives, and find out what those motives are to do whatever we do. We want to be sure that we don't have a stranglehold on our progress; that we're not strangling ourselves when we're trying to progress. When we're going somewhere, we don't need to be just going without some destination. We don't want to allow false pride to take over our lives, as I have allowed. We're so afraid about what people are going to find out about us that is wrong that instead of trying to emphasize and show those things about ourselves that are right. Instead of hiding so much of the things that carried us in the wrong direction – I'll tell you something else that gets in our way sometimes. We meet strangers or you could say we go into a new environment, like moving into a new city, or like coming into a new neighborhood, or meeting new friends. They look at us as someone extremely fine.

Our lifestyle has changed from the way they were back there. We really are doing the things that we need to do today. We're doing the things that we should have done years ago. But now we've changed our lives and people are patting us on the back and they are very proud of us. They can see something in our lives that inspires them. Now we want to keep the image. We don't want to lose that image. We don't want to reach back there, in our wisdom, and pull up some experiences that we had because we are above that; we are beyond that.

Just for a moment, I want to jump to something else. You know, I hear ministers and psychologists and psychiatrists talking about forgetting about the past, and don't dare go back there and get anything, and be happy; just find happiness. Christ wants us to be happy. Yes, He wants us to be happy but He wants us to be workers in our vineyards. He wants us to share our experiences and sometimes it doesn't make us shine. It doesn't make us feel so good. It doesn't make us look good. But it isn't what you used to be, it's who you are today. If you can relate to some of the things that are happening out here, that means that you can do more about fixing it. You may be able to repair something in my life. When I understand that you've been where I am, and you came out, maybe you need to tell me and explain to me what happened.

Do you understand where I'm coming from? I don't want you back there wallowing in your pity. I don't want you back there strangling yourself with yesterday. I want yesterday to be an experience; a learning process that you can pass on to somebody.

THE POWER OF SIN

I deem it impossible, or nearly impossible to have a discussion about God and man's relationship to humanity without looking primarily at God's Son, Jesus. It is of paramount importance that we accept the trichotomy in salvation that Jesus provides. Salvation is a simple "act" of faith, but very vast in applying this simple "act" to every area of our lives. Many Christians get saved and start the Christian experience with enthusiasm, energy, and effectiveness, and often find themselves uninspired in a short period of time. You may ask the question, "what is the disconnect?" It is understanding the totality of salvation. When we get saved, we are totally saved from the Penalty of sin, the Power of sin, and ultimately, the Presence of sin.

First, the penalty of sin: Someone who lives in our affluent society may ask the question, "why does man need salvation". The answer can be given in a short three letter word, "sin". The Bible reveals several basic truth's about this. First, sin is universal. **Romans 3:23** *says, "all have sinned and come short of His glory!" This allows us to not judge other humans, because we all are in the same dilemma; from the individual who lives by the highest code of ethics, to the one who derives his livelihood from crime.* **Romans 6:23** *states, "the wages (payment) for sin is death"; so the acceptance of Christ as Savior brings a pardon from the "Great Warden" of the universe, God.* **Romans 5:1** *states,*
"We have peace with God". This "peace" <u>**with**</u> *God is twofold. First, it is forgiveness, or "Peace with God". The senior saint in the African American culture would ask the powerful and penetrating question, "have you made 'Peace' with God?", which really meant if you die, will you go to heaven? Do you know Jesus?*

The second peace is somewhat controversial, because it's relational and simply put, states after accepting His finished work on the cross, we are "friends" with Jesus, and when we sin, we break fellowship, or the peace <u>**of**</u> *God (relationship), and it can't be restored until we repent, or change our direction and apologize. Now, the controversy comes because many believe you get put out of the family of God, or lose your salvation when you sin, when in reality you lose fellowship with the Son of the living God!! This is powerful because knowing you won't get dismissed from the family will help you recover and reestablish your faith walk, because of a love relationship, rather than a "law" obligation. He loves us no matter what we do (and yes, He will chasten us when we are wrong), but He also longs to reestablish relationship with us.*

Now, this brings us to the second point, which is the "power of sin". I am of the persuasion that this is an area of struggle for most believers. "Let not sin reign" **(Romans 6:12)**, *control, dominate. The Message Bible says, "don't give sin a vote. The power of sin leaves a devastating destructive wake in its aftermath, and it has been evidenced by a society which is out of control. How can one man, (Hitler), destroy* *so many Jews (six million by some counts), and control so many? The "power of sin". How could America and Americans allow the tragedy of slavery to devastate a nation? According to an 1860 census, the lower Southern states had 2,312,352 slaves, or 47% of the total population. The upper south had 1,208,758 slaves, or 29% of the total population, and the border states had 432,586, or 13% of total population. "How?", you may ask. It's simple. The power of sin. Finally, 21st Century America is being destroyed because of the absence of absolute truth. We now have an America which will spend more to incarcerate than to educate; an America which has more African American males in prison then in college... why? The power of sin. Needless to say, this power has now taken us to a new realm of debate as we see those practicing gay and lesbian lifestyles becoming more demanding, television supporting them wholeheartedly, and our legal system locked in battle as gay and lesbian same sex partners are licensed and married. How could this happen? The power of sin. It is evidenced that unchecked sin in the life of an individual, family, church and society will destroy character and numb the senses of absolute truth.* **James 1:5** *states, "sin when it is finished bringeth forth death". We as a society are paying for the "power of sin", but, we don't have to be controlled by it. The Message Bible says in* **Romans 6:13,** *"don't even run little errands that are connected with that way of life", and* **verse 14** *says, "sin can't tell you how to live." The application is simple, yet so profound. The evidence of God in our lives is revealed by how we live our lives in relationship to humanity. It can only be done consistently by breaking the shackles of sin -past, present, and future, and move into the love of our new landlord, which promotes harmonious living.*

Finally, the "presence of sin". There is a struggle with allowing God to forgive us (penalty of sin"), and there may be a struggle with allowing God to change us ("power of sin"), but we must live as citizens of another world, and be active change agents in this world. As we see life mutating toward its ultimate end, as we see the devaluation of humans, and disregard for God, let us be mindful that god and man's relationship to humanity is a team effort. The all-powerful God has partnered with His Son and us to empower us to allow heaven to live in us. We must demonstrate love where there seems to be none, where self doubt is prevalent, we must replace it with the confidence of God. **I John 5:14** *states, "and this is the confidence we have in Him, that, if we ask anything according to his will, he heareth us".*

Whatever humanity's struggle, it has already been remedied by Christ, with the promise in **John 14.** *"I go to prepare a place for you." Ultimately, we will be in a place where there is no sin, sorrow, pain, and disappointment. We will be removed from the very presence of sin and live in community with God the*

Father, God the Son and God the Holy Spirit. This is the zenith of God and man's relationship to humanity.

By Rev. Roderick A. Coffee, I
Union Community Church

I search all through the United States of American and I found few people of God that work to assist humanity other than Sunday morning and Wednesday evening. Most churches only open their doors on those days. Reverend Coffee does not operate that way – the doors are always open. People need help on the other days of the week too. I thought that the church was a place that you went to in order to learn how to work for humanity outside of the church. I have found that to be true with Reverend Coffee.

To say "all" really means most. "All" covers too much.

By Guy P. Darden, Sr.

Union Community Church
10959 Johnnycake Ridge Rd., Concord Twp. OH 44077

Mission Statement
To bring people to Jesus and **membership** in His family, develop them to Christ-like **maturity**, and equip them for their **ministry** in the church and life **mission** in the world, in order to **magnify** God's name.

Vision Statement
Our ministry will be characterized by a willingness to love God as creator, and His Son, Jesus Christ as King and Lord of every individual who has a desire to be part of this ministry. We will teach God's word, read God's word, and model God's word in every aspect of our lives. We will give extra attention to our senior saints and our youth! We will be intentional in our efforts to Evangelize, Disciple, and Exhort those in our fellowship and community. We will use the gifts of our people, as well as financial gifts, to enhance the kingdom of God. We will constantly practice using discretion with those we place in leadership. We will constantly assure that the entire church strives to be mature and full of God's spirit.

SAW SOMETHING I DIDN'T LIKE

I wanted to write a book many years ago. I saw something happening in this nation that I knew was wrong but I was doing so much wrong myself and the things I wanted to talk about was so far from what I was doing, but I could see it. I could see my mistakes and I could see that the value that I had put on myself wasn't there. I could see that trouble was on the horizon, that something was going wrong with me, and not only me, this nation was losing its foothold on life. I could see something going so far wrong that I begin to wonder why the people weren't in the church talking about it. I began to mumble and grumble and talk to friends and when you start talking about values and problems you can find almost anybody will hold your conversation, especially on the criticize side. There's always somebody that can tell you what's wrong with that person, what's going on in somebody else's life. I wonder why somebody doesn't do something about it. Especially they start pointing at the church, they start pointing at people they feel are religious. We don't want the blame, so we find somebody else that ought to do something about it. If we don't put it on our churches and our ministers, we put it on the government or we put it on the city official. We put it on the police and we certainly put it on our young people. We can always point the fingers and talk about how bad the people are. But as I look back on my life I didn't find anything that I had done to help the situation either. So I began to think about what I could do about it. How could I talk about it? How could I bring it up to disturb somebody's conscience, to make people look up? Well I got to thinking, and after awhile, I found that I had convicted myself.

I understood one thing; the reason I wasn't doing anything was because I didn't think I was worthy. I didn't think that anybody would listen to anything I had to say, because I had been living the type of life in the world that I just didn't think anybody would pay me any attention. But as I went on through life, throwing my dream behind me, what I'd like to do in this Earth; you know sometimes sinners can think up some of the greatest ideas and sinners are not lost for ideas and thoughts. Those of us who have accepted Christ in our lives need to realize that most people know when you're doing wrong and they know when they see us doing wrong. Those of us who are criticizing the part of the world that we don't feel that has accepted God in, in their lives, the way we have, they know and they understand. Just because you accepted Christ in your life doesn't mean that you're not acting stupid. It doesn't mean that you're not acting ignorant. It doesn't mean that you don't do things that are not pleasing to yourself and others that are around you. It doesn't mean that we do everything we need to do because we accept Christ in our lives.

I believe that we are very lazy, some of us, as Christian men and women. I think we have more lazy Christians than we do diligence; you know people who are full of energy and fight for what the really believe in. I think we believe a lot of things but for some reason we don't want to do what they know is right to do. And we look for somebody that got a lot of letters behind their name to bring because we feel that they are to be the ones that are leading us. But you know what? God can take a donkey and teach a man a lesson, I'm sure He can take somebody like me and you, if we know about Christ. If you know about Christ and you know about Christ's lifestyle. Whether you believe that He was God's son or not, you know that He was a fantastic leader and he was a great teacher; if you know anything about the Bible. Now all I'm saying, if you know about the Bible then you then you know about what God wants us to do on this Earth. You know something about your responsibility. You know it does not end by going to church on Sunday. I started asking myself a few questions and one of those questions was, "When I pray, do I know what I'm praying for? And do I know the essence of my prayer? Are my prayers blind?" And what I mean by that is am I asking for the things that I'm supposed to be asking for? Am I asking for the things that a man who loves God needs to have in his life? Am I asking for strength to help all of us or am I praying for my personal and intimate friends and my family alone? Am I praying for just the things that I want or am I praying for the things that we need for the world? Do I get up in the morning and get down on my knees by my bedside and ask God to bless my family, or do I get up in the morning and call my family together with me and pray about the things that I need for them and the things that I need for myself? Am I praying about our government? Am I praying about the things that I complain about all the time? Am I praying about the people that I think don't know what they're doing? Am I praying about the people that know what they're doing? Am I praying about the people that just won't change? Am I talking to God about the things that I need for my children? Am I praying in a way that is not selfish? Am I praying for my nation? Am I praying for my police departments? Am I praying that when the policeman goes out in the morning on his job that he'll have a safe day and am I praying that the policemen that serve us in our city will reach up and ask God for strength and wisdom to do what they need to do?

Do I look at my minister and instead of criticizing him, am I asking God for wisdom so I can come before him and be a testimony by the way I live my life in the front of him? Am I someone that lives the kind of life in my community that would make the people in my community take up and look at me and feel that I am somebody that they can set their lives in a way that they could influence me someway? Am I praying that the person next door to me would see something in my life that might inspire them? Am I talking to people during the day when I have an opportunity that I could have some kind of influence in their lives? Am I living my life in a way that I would want my child to live? Am I an example for the people that know me? Can I live my life in a way that if I decide to talk to a neighbor about something that I might think that he has been mislead in that I set him on the right track and he would feel within himself that I have enough foresight and enough care and enough love that I care enough about him that I would want to assist him in some way? Or am I being a busy body, just being nosy and interfering in his life? Can I live a life with enough integrity that people would believe what I have to say? Have I talked to my minister about the things that I believe in? Have I tried to influence anybody about the lifestyle that I want for everybody? Have I been down on my knees long enough that God has convicted me that, sort of, I can seek for wisdom and knowledge to be able to touch somebody's life? Is this day that I live in now important enough to me to realize what God has given me this day that I can not only pray for what I want, but I can thank God for what He's already given me? Are my hopes and dreams out of line with God's values? Have I mislead myself to the point that I've been doing something a certain way so long I've got in the habit of doing it until I believe it is right? Or do I go to the source of all things and pray to God to let me know for sure that whatever I teach or whoever I talk to, that I know what I'm talking about?"

I want to ask you, how often do you pray with your children? How many times have you prayed for the school teacher? How many times have you prayed for the President? How many times do you pray for the Senate? How many times do you pray for the school official? How many times do you pray for the child that's walking down that street going the wrong way as far as life is concerned? Are you doing more than just discussing with your friends about how bad the neighborhood is? Are you looking at the people in the neighborhood? Are you searching for hope? Are you looking for something that can lift you up on to this mountain, other than man? Has your life been imbedded into Christ's life? Have you accepted God so far in your life until you know where you're going because He guided your footsteps? Where are we in life now? Where are you in life? How far can we go until we don't know where we're going? Have we got onboard of the hopes train, this train that is a dream train, and that we're just going where somebody told us to go and that there might be a pot of gold at the end of the rainbow? Have we forgotten our roots that were embedded in so many years ago? Don't we know where we're going? Are we just feeling in the dark? Do we know that there's a foundation that we can put under our life?

We can put our life on a ton of foundation that's embedded in God's spirit that will keep us afloat and show us where we are going. Sometimes I believe that money has taken over our lives. I believe that things, and things, and things are guiding us wherever we go. I don't believe that these school officials are doing what they need to do to make this nation a better place. Do you know that the professors, the school teachers, and the ministers, and the government; do you know those three or four organizations can be the downfall of this nation or the up-building of it? How can a person tell you that they want to put education ahead of everything? They feel that education is the most important thing in this nation today. They believe in good education, a solid foundation as far as education is concerned, and yet they take our surpluses and give people a tax break when they should be building new schools or better security systems. It doesn't take an educated person to know that our teachers are not being paid enough. We pay our ballplayers in this nation millions and millions of dollars; ten times much more than they are worth. And yet the school grounds that these people, that some of these ball players play on, and in the cities that they play in, in the colleges that they go to, the teachers are not being paid well. The kids are not being protected. Don't you know that the schools that are in this city and the teachers that are teaching don't have the materials and the things that they need to do the jobs that they need to do? They are the foundation of this nation; the school system. This is where they learn to be men and women. But yet you take the power out of these places and leave the kids that feel there is no God. If you can't talk about God in the school, He must not be important. If you can't play in the school, it says to the kids that this is the least thing that we are in this nation. We take power out of the most important place in the world. It's where we teach our kids. We have taken away the foundation of the greatest thing on Earth, and that's God Almighty. We have taken Him out of the place where our children first begin to learn how to process themselves through life and we say, "You can't have God in here. You can't discuss God openly. You can't preach about God. You can't pray about God; not on government property anywhere." But yet they do it in Washington, D.C., which is phony and irresponsible. They must think it's terribly important otherwise they wouldn't do it everyday before they open up. It tells me it's something about God that you don't want them to know about. It tells me that it's not the most important thing in this nation.

You can't tell me that a nation is built on the principle God Almighty, and then take the God out of the schools where the kids start their first foundation outside of their parents; and some children don't get it any place else but in school. It's the only place they get attention and the only place they get a sense of closeness is in the school from the teacher. What happens to a child that the family never talks about God? Maybe they drink booze all the time or they are on drugs all the time and they go to school and the kids don't get it there. He hasn't got any place to go but to prison when he leaves that school. It's not being taught; the principle that you say this nation was built on, is dying. You can't say you believe in God and don't fight for the right for Him to be in every segment of life. I don't understand how we as church people, as people who claim to have accepted Christ and claim to have Christ guiding us through this nation can stand up in our churches and be independent of all the things that are going on around them. They don't go to their council meetings and they don't know what's going on in city hall. They don't go down there. They separate themselves from that segment of society. You don't participate in your city government; you don't know what's going on in the government, and then you tell me I'm the ignorant one because I haven't ever learned how to read and write.   I believe there's something wrong going on here. You ask me, what are your credentials that give you the right to talk about God? What do you know about the bible? I know what you've been teaching me all my life. I know what the churches and synagogues have bean teaching me all my life. I think by now I ought to know something. I'm in my seventies and I've been hearing about these things that you're supposed to do to make man develop into something that can produce and have moral standards and have integrity; you've been teaching me that all my life. I think I ought to know something unless I'm a total fool. I got to be a nincompoop not to know something about God. And if I know something about God and I keep my mouth shut as most of us have been doing, then I don't think we really believe in what we're teaching.

LEADERSHIP THROUGH FOLLOWING WELL

To be a good leader in God's mission in the world, we must first know how to follow. This essay is on the art of "followership".

Leadership is a popular subject. Entire courses and schools are devoted to it. Business and military training includes leadership theory and methods. But no one ever talks much about how to be a good follower. That's a shame, because good followers are vital to the success of our churches and faith here on earth regarding our relationship with God. We certainly know there are many more followers than leaders, but—are we following well?

As I investigated the art of being a good follower, I couldn't find much written on the topic, so I went to the experts—followers. Based on conversations with people of faith and love for God and my own personal philosophy, I've come up with a "guide" for successful followership.

First of all, we must truly understand God's word and His values and those of His chosen leaders within our faith. Through this process we must look at our own values and how they coincide with our God. The leaders of our churches teach us His values through the written words of the Bible. They are the guiding light that shines the way in which we must journey through our lives.... if we truly understand and follow well.

We must be flexible. Change occurs so rapidly today that followers must be willing to take on a variety of missions within the church and must keep an open mind. We must learn to anticipate problems in our church and in our faith and be able to move through them with courage. We must learn to stay the course while adapting to unfavorable conditions.

We must learn to be patient...with our neighbors, our church leaders, and ourselves. We must wait for the right moment to shine and to blossom into one of God's leaders.

Loyalty is another true mark of a good follower. This entails supporting our leader's decisions whether we agree or not. We can disagree with a leader—we're free to have opinions—but in the end we must act according to our leader's decisions.

Wise followers do not criticize their leaders. Criticism is a negative act; it solves no problems and can be destructive to the church.

Successful followers are positive thinkers. They don't gripe about problems they solve them. If they aren't in a position to make decisions, they go to their leaders with suggestions for resolving the problem. Get along with your fellow Christians. Internal strife means less productivity.

Challenge yourself and keep learning and studying about God's teachings. Know more than others expect you to. Stay tuned in to important and changing situations in your church. Get to know your fellow members of your church and learn what they and other churches are doing.

Be active in your local community as well as your church. Get connected. The contacts you make can help you in a number of ways and you will grow personally by sharing your knowledge and ideas.

Carry more than your share. Don't be satisfied with just being "one of the masses." Ask for difficult assignments in order to show your skills and your understanding of the workings of the church. Strive for excellence in all you do.

Above all, learn to communicate well. Listening often takes a back seat to talking. Good listening skills are vital to the successful follower. Listen for content and watch body language to get the full, correct meaning. Learn not to be confused by conflicting signals. Misinterpretation of a message can seriously damage the communication.

By now, you may have concluded that the theories for being a good follower parallel those for being a good leader. Should that really be a surprise? Those who truly become great leaders must first learn to follow. Learning to follow sets the foundation upon which we must build our leadership role.

By Christopher J. Collins
Chief of Police, State of Ohio

Chief Collins contributed this poem – author unknown:

GOD IS NEAR!
I will not fear though all my dreams come shattering
Down around my feet for God is near.

I will hold onto Him who helps me rise
Above life's stormy sea

A wondrous and shining light that lights my way
To see the path ahead; this light of love and good
That seems to cover me

I know no fear for God is near.

Chris is one of the godliest gentlemen I've met in a long time. Some cops or officials think godliness is a sign of weakness. Chris is not afraid to show his beliefs. Not only is he a community leader but he is also a scholar. Boy is he a scholar! I've been told in my church and others that we all have to be of one accord even if you don't believe in what they are saying. Christ is not one to go along with that. Chris is not a go-along person. Chris is one that is grounded in the gospel of Almighty God.

By Guy P. Darden, Sr.

IF CHRIST WERE ON EARTH TODAY

Now listen, I'm going to tell you some things that I believe are happening and you can tell me whether I'm right or not or whether you feel the same way. You see this is my opinion, and everybody has plenty of opinions, but I want to find out from you, do you believe if Christ was on Earth today, would He agree with what I have to say? Would He answer yes to some of these questions? I believe the reason that some of us are so quiet is because we're afraid. We are frightened to extend our opinions. Because if we extend our opinions we're going to step on somebody's toes and we're not going to be so popular. And I believe the reason that some of us that are leaders in the church, and some of us are ministers in the church, and some of us are teachers, and the reason we are so quiet is because we don't want the government bothering with us. I don't think we complain enough about prayer not being in the school. Because I believe if we taught prayer everywhere we go and that we believe that prayer should be in our schools, then we'd be fighting towards that. I believe we feel that if we interfere with the government officials too much and we try to push our ideas of religious backgrounds, and if we try to teach about God and Christ that the city officials, the federal government would take away some of our tax exemption, that our churches may be attacked for tax exemption. We wouldn't get our tax exemption. We would not be free to do what we want to do inside of our church building. Some of the things that we do would be restricted. If we're not talking about the way we serve Christ, but the way we run our business and some of our organizations would be threatened. I feel that the city officials and our government don't want men and women; they don't want us too much grounded in to God's belief to the point that it would influence those of us who work in a city government office. That if we had the Ten Commandments in the hallways of our city halls or if we had some scripture on the wall in our courthouses and on our government official's grounds, that it might influence somebody; it might work on some body's conscience. Some of the things that are allowed to go on in our government officials lives, it may have a lasting effect on them. It may mess with their conscience.

How can we say that God insults some religions? If God is the most important thing on Earth, it looks like to me He ought to have a place in our government. If God is the most important thing in our nation, and if we believe that and if we believe that God is in charge of everything and that He has an influence on everything, don't you think that we ought to speak up for the things we claim we believe? At least you ought to know enough about our government to become involved in our government action. If we believe all the things that we claim we believe on Sunday morning in our churches and yet go on so silently about our activities, why are our church buildings so empty during the week? Why is it that most of the churches in this city don't have any activities going on during the day, except a nursery or something that is going on that will generate profit for our churches? Why not have every type of actions going on in that building during the day? Why aren't economics being taught in our churches to some of our people that hardly even know what the word means? Where are we teaching somebody like me that doesn't know how to read? Why aren't we trying to push an educational program for adults? Why aren't we trying to teach Head Start in every church in our community? Why not every chance we get, we don't have something going on for the homeless people? Why aren't we looking for people to help instead of waiting for them to fall dead on our doorstep? Why aren't we looking for young people and inviting them into our churches? Why don't we have leaflets going on all over this city from our churches asking people to come to gather as a people regardless to their race, or creed, or color? Why aren't the churches of this city asking all the churches to throw in the pot, something that we can bring people together; children of all races and all kinds. Why aren't we trying to do something other than just generating funds? Why aren't human resources being volunteered? Why is that we are not becoming involved in our communities as a church people, as a Godly race of people, as a Godly nation of people? These are powerful questions about human well-being.

Those of us who claim to be Christian – I can understand why those that don't know about love and about the kind of love that God taught on this Earth – I could understand them not leading or spearheading it. But I can't understand how the churches of this city and how the Christian men and women can lock themselves up in the church on Sunday mornings, or on Wednesday or Thursday night; just a few nights, and then let the world just forget about them during the week. We don't want to know about the problems that are going on, no more than talking about between each other. How can you keep talking about how bad these children are when you're not trying to help them or meet them in a mass group of people trying to influence this society? Why aren't we trying to bring them together in some form? How can we call ourselves Christians and put ourselves ahead of everything? We are first in everything. The preachers are first. The deacons are first. We, as Christian men and women, are first, and we put the sinners that we call sinners, last in our lives; last on our agenda.

The Bible tells us that we ought to treat our neighbors as ourselves. Do you only call your Christian friends neighbors? Are they the only neighbors you have? Are they the only people you care about are the ones that you know personally? As a nation of Christian men and women, are we just thinking of ourselves when we take up money on Sunday mornings in our collections? Is that money just for foreign missions so we can get a tax credit? Or do we have a mission right here in this city, in our community that we need to be helping? Why isn't a homeless shelter here where I live? Why isn't a soup kitchen going on every day? Why are we looking for somebody else to do what we need to do? Maybe, if we would start a program ourselves, it would put so much pressure on the city officials that they would try to start something. Maybe we could influence somebody. But all we are is just like I am doing right now, just talking.

I know that what I am saying isn't in the beautiful English that you like to read. I know that some of the words that I say are mispronounced. *[Remember, this book was dictated and transcribed into print.]* But, if you are as intelligent as you claim you are, I think you understand what I am trying to say. I think that you know that I'm trying to give all of us a guilt trip. I'm trying to make myself feel guilty for what I am not doing and what I haven't done. Don't you know I can't mention these things that I mention without messing with my own mind? I just want somebody to say things that need to be said. I'm getting tired of seeing the preacher riding around and just talking to us on Sunday mornings. I want to see somebody talking to me during the week. I want to see somebody that's bugging me so much until I have to do something about what they are talking about. I'm tired of seeing senior citizens, like myself, sitting on the porch in their rocking chair, minding their own business, getting so stiff that their arthritis controls their lives. I want to see us all trying to do something; coming together. We claim we have so much wisdom and we're so holy and we're so sanctified, but we're not doing anything with it. Those of us who claim to have the

Holy Spirit, we can dance all over the world and scream and holler, but if we're not doing anything for the people of God, we're not doing what God told us to do.

You know what? I sometimes think we're a bunch of phonies. We think we can fool the world by pulling the holy quilt over our head. I don't think we really mean what we claim we mean. I don't think we are really what we need to be. I know I've been phony all my life because I haven't done anything. And you can't live on this Earth for a whole lifetime, especially as long as I've lived, and not do anything for the world and say you couldn't do it. We just keep passing the buck. Those children that we talk about a lot out there, they were babies at one time. They were in our homes at one time and most of them are still in our homes. But we've got a lot of them in prison, and we've got to take some responsibility for that. When we allow these things to happen all over our nation – those neighborhoods that we call bad neighborhoods, they were once decent neighborhoods. This country was once a place that you felt fairly decent in. You felt fairly safe. There isn't anybody that can tell me that they are Christian and they love God and can walk around feeling that they've done everything they're supposed to do, or that they are doing things that they need to do, or they are doing things that they could do and just won't do it. Not because they're sick, not because they don't know what to do, it's because we're not talking about these things enough to bug us, annoy us, so we can't sleep at night; loving somebody that's suffering and dying and being murdered and being raped. How can we sleep as Christian men and women and feel so comfortable and let this world go to Hell right at our back door? We just keep talking and pointing our fingers.

I don't think most of us deal with our families. I think when we come home from work, we're so tired and so busy looking at television and all the other things that entertain us that we forget about the cycle of love and kindness and talking personal with our family. I don't think we believe we need to cut the television off and not allow it to come on for so many hours in the evening when we are home. I think the television should be a luxury hour. It shouldn't be a necessity. I think it catches us, and grabs us, and leads us. The television ministry today is just taking over the world because it's good entertainment. We look at the dancing and the shouting and the singing and all of that, and we get caught up in it. I'm not so sure we're getting what we need to get out of it. We're getting a good feeling out of it. I think those men and women that scream and holler all over the nation in these churches are real wonderful men and women, but that doesn't tell me what they are doing in the communities that they need to do.

When we're taking up money, are we taking it up for the right purpose? Shouldn't we take care of our own first? Doesn't the Bible say something about get the plank out of your own eye before you get the speck out of the other person's eye? We did that thing about politics; everybody's government was wrong but ours. And then we have all this mess going on in Florida and we have all the scandals going on in Washington. We have our government officials just looking out for themselves. This is supposed to be a democratic government. It's not a democratic government anyways, it's a republic, and that's even questionable. It is supposed to be built on Godly principles. It looks like we traded places with the communists? And the next thing about it is that they are all trying to look out for themselves. All our government officials are fighting against each other. They are not fighting for the good of all. Our nation has walked away from our obligation to our nation and to our people and to ourselves. We haven't prepared ourselves. We haven't armed ourselves with the things we need to work with. We don't have enough God controlling our lives to make us want to do the things that we know we need to do, and we can fix this nation.

We can fix our community. We live in this city. We should make things right here the best we can. When we say we can't do anything for someone, we ought to know we have done everything we could have to do something and now we leave it up to God. But we take God with us when we go to deal with the problem in our community or a problem in our family. I have many problems in my family that are going on and we need to pray about it in times we can't do anything, especially when we try to do it alone. But if we come together as a church people instead of trying to build up this church and make it look pretty, and this guy, and this organization and that organization; we don't need all these organizations. What we need is a group of Godly people trying to serve mankind as God wanted us to serve each other. I'm not who I need to be. I'm not who I want to be. But, I've got to try to be the best I can in the way I know how.

You see, God teaches us some things, if we listen to him. It doesn't matter how much education that you don't have. Don't think about the education that you don't have. Think about the education that you do have. Think about the knowledge that you do have. Think about the wisdom that you do have. Recognize the things that you don't have, but don't trouble yourself; anything that you need, if you serve God, He'll give it to you. He'll prepare you. He'll help you to have the nerve. He'll help you to have the faith. He'll help you to kindness. He'll help you to have the finances that you need to do what you need to do. He'll help you to have the patience that you need. He'll help you take away the selfishness. He'll help you take away the jealousy. He'll help you take away the greed. He'll help us realize that in our weakest point; sometimes it is our strongest point. You know, I'm going to keep making noise until somebody gets so angry with me that they start cursing me out or telling me that I'm wrong and I don't know what I'm talking about, or to either tell me that I got something that makes sense. And if I have something that makes sense, why on Earth won't you listen to me? Let me talk to somebody, somehow.

I believe the relationship to God and Man is the only hope we have. I believe God and Man's Relationship to Humanity is the only means that man has for survival. I don't believe you can survive on this Earth without having God leading you and teaching you. **I believe your survival for justice and hope and freedom for all men means that we have to fight for all men**. We are all men and women on this earth and our allegiance – especially when we are in God's army - we are in the service. What about me? What about myself? When you work towards the victory of your brother, you automatically have hope yourself and you'll have a victory. Somewhere when God sees you doing what you need to be doing, not what you want to do, but what you need to do, and what He is telling you to do – we're under Commandments to do these things, to talk about what we're not doing, not always talk about what you're doing. What you're doing will stand for itself, whether it is right or wrong. Just look for guidance. I'm sorry, in a way, if you don't know what I'm trying to say. You have more intelligence than I'll ever have; most of you, especially our religious leaders. I want you to help me where I need help. Guide me where I need guiding. Pray for me that I may say the right thing at the right time.

I was trying to find out what people thought about humanity and about what people's opinions were about what was going on in this nation and why were we having such a vast problem with men and women being locked up and put in prison. I talked to Police Chief Wilson in Suffolk, Virginia. I got to know him quite well and I asked him what he thought was motivating people to walk away from their responsibility as far as the city government and a system of police that would be there for them and what he thought was wrong with the lack of support for the police departments throughout this nation. He told me that he thought part of it was the police themselves; that they didn't have the type of relationship with the public that they needed. They didn't have a connection with the people, and he told me that is was what he had been working for. He said his goal was not have crime happen and then stop it, but he believed in crime prevention. He believed in relationships with the citizens of his city and the surrounding communities. He tried to talk to his officers and revealed to them the idea of a good wholesome relationship with the community and if they had that, that they would have a better police department. He talked about policemen hiding behind bushes and building up, more or less, a traffic trap.

I talked to him for quite a while. He had Godly and Christian principles that he thought worked in every form of society, and if you took away the moral and integrity from the police department, you were disarming them. He wanted to have a task force that could communicate back and forth with the people in the community. He wanted to have a good relationship with the police that did the patrolling of the city and the county. The people that worked with him, he wanted to have a good relationship with them. Most of the police that came in that had been trained in public relations and knew a little bit about psychology, he said he could talk to the young police officers but he had police that had been on the job so long and they couldn't walk away from their tough, strong manhandling situations. They wanted to be in control of people – it was kind of like a bully pulpit type of thing and that you weren't a good policeman unless you kind of manhandled people a little bit. You didn't need that social service type of time to compromise and bring the community together as team. He said, he thought that when the community worked with the police department and city officials, and they knew what you were trying to do, that they would be more likely to cooperate and become a part of serving the community as well as the police. They would be more likely try to help and assist and that it would work in crime prevention rather than waiting until the crime happened and then going out and manhandling people, but showing people that they are human as we are, he said. He also said that he wants to feel that he's part of the community. "I'm a citizen of this community as well as a policeman in it, and I have to have all of the citizens' freedom and justice comes before anything else. I must allow myself to be a citizen first and be human and feel and see people as a part of me."

When the time comes to place someone under arrest, he wanted that person to be treated humanely. He wanted that person to be treated with respect. The officers were only to use force when it was necessary. He believed in the rights of the criminal as well as the rights of the law abiding citizens. The officers were to keep the peace in every sense of the word. He wanted his officers to be gentlemen and to treat all people with respect. He wanted his officers to be treated with respect and he felt like if they treated the public, in general, with respect and then it would be more likely that the public would respect them in return. He didn't believe in the good old boy and this buddy-buddy thing. He believed in being fair to all people. He said he was fighting for that right. He spoke with Christian principles and he wanted his police department to be outstanding in integrity and to have the public interests foremost in the forefront. He seemed to me to be gentleman. If I had to talk about officials, I would speak about the chief of Suffolk, Virginia, and his men that I met. I met several of his men who seemed to be trying to do their job in the best way they knew how. The Chief is a man of deep, strong conviction. He believes in being the right kind of policeman, protecting the citizens from the criminals and the people who would come down on them.

This nation is threatened by the criminal element. A lot of our policemen have allowed the criminal's to influence their lives. You can't judge everybody on the same ground. You have to judge each individual for who he is and what he represents. I find there are police departments all over this nation that are doing a good job, and there is some doing a bad job. There will come a time that the ones doing a bad job will be thrashed out and put out of business. I certainly hope so. We as citizens have walked away from our policemen. They feel alone. The criminals corrupt them. We see somebody's home being broken into and say, "It's none of my business." I don't believe our nation is hopeless. But

I feel that our police department and our city officials need support. They need to give us support too. Before they will give us support, we've got to act like they work for us instead of us working for them. We need to work with them, but we pay their salary; and actually we are their bosses. We're the people who are supposed to be there for them when they need us. We should care as much about the policemen's family as we do our own families. They have got to survive and they need our strong support. But they've got to know that we hold them accountable for their actions because they are there for us; they're supposed to be there for us. But we have to let them know that we are watching, we're looking, and we hold them accountable for their deeds. We are responsible citizens and that we know something about what's going on in their lives. If we are blind to what is going on and we close our eyes to the way they are suffering with the chaos that they deal with every day of their lives, the problems that our police departments have to deal with each day of their lives, the city officials need to know that we care about them. But in return, we want them to care about us. We want them to see more than just what they see at city hall. We want them to go over these streets, not just in the daytime. Our city officials don't just need to know what their police officers report to them; they need drive these streets in the middle of the night and find out what's going on in the community. We need them to know firsthand what's happening.

We know the drug lords and the gangsters and the people of this nation that are violating the law are doing it with some of our official's consent. Not necessarily consent by mouth but there is so much going on and we care so little about it until it gets in our community until it makes them become desensitized a lot of times. They feel like we don't care what happens, as long as it's not happening to "me". What goes on in your community, if we keep letting it happen, it's going to be going on in my community. We've got to have enough relationship with our city officials and our police department and our organizations that govern our state. We have to know enough about it to have some kind of participation in it. We've got to ask our officials to let us know what's going on in their lives as far as the city government is concerned, and as far as the state government is concerned.

We've got to wake up and care about what happens in this nation. We've got to notice that whites and blacks are going to prison because we haven't given them the protection down here that they need. Sometimes we need protection from ourselves. Sometimes our children need protection from themselves. They're put out on the street to walk alone sometimes because we don't know what's going on out on the streets. We go by what we hear. We are so frightened to death because we think we have to walk alone out there. We don't have to walk alone. We can come together as a people and have some consensus that pulls us together and have a Godly principle that means something to somebody outside of ourselves. We need to try to protect somebody's home outside of protecting our own homes. We need to protect somebody's community outside of just our community. We need to be concerned of every form of life in our cities, and in our states, and in our country, and in this world. But we need to be concerned about our nation and the development of our young people in this nation, because today's youth is tomorrow's future. Our hopes and our dreams are no good unless we have some kind of regulations set up in our lives to make them come true.

I don't want people to make the mistake I made. I spent most of my life trying to struggle for myself and for my personal family because I didn't prepare myself when I was young and I had the opportunity to learn about what was going on other than just my selfish self. I needed to know what was going on that I could have prepared myself for the job that is ahead for all of us. We are instruments on this Earth, and instruments have to be in a condition so that we are able to use them, and use them affectively for whatever job that they are made for. Each one of us is made to do something. Each one of us can do something rather well, but when God needs to use us, we need to be prepared for that. We need to ask God to prepare our families because the youth of this nation; our children, our babies, don't know what to do on this Earth to get them started out in the right direction. So that means the preparation has to be started some time before the child is on this Earth, we have to be preparing ourselves so we are equipped when the child gets here and to be able to raise him in a proper manner.

You see, some of us as parents are not prepared to take on the obligation and the responsibility of a family. We haven't had the Christian background. We haven't had the teaching that we need to make us what we need to be. I sometimes shed tears; I cry because I can't do what I want to do, but I have to do what I know to do. I didn't have the opportunity to go to school when I was young and when I was at home as a child. But after I grew up into a man I ought to have learned from the problems that I was having, that I needed more than what I had, that I could teach myself and let myself grow into manhood knowing something about life. I should have gone to some school and let them teach me so I was able to do something so when I had something to say, at least somebody would listen to me because I had some kind of credentials that would make them recognize me. The only credentials that I have are God's wisdom and God's knowledge and God's strength, because mine has now faded. My old age has taken over my physical being and all I have is a little mental capacity to fight for the things that I believe in, and the things that I believe God has taught me to believe in, in the later years of my life.

I don't intend to die on this Earth and go to Hell. I don't intend to go to Hell for anybody and I don't intend to be on the Earth and continue to do nothing for humanity. I intend to do something, somehow, somewhere on this Earth that will help somebody on this Earth. I hope my life will be an example in the late years that I spend here on this Earth. I hope somebody can see that I made a big mistake by not protecting myself and for preparing myself so I could do something on this Earth; where people would listen to me because I had moral background, that I had the integrity and that I had the spiritual life that I had lived that would make me be what I needed to be. But now, since I didn't get the education and the schooling back then that I needed, now I must let my Godly life shine enough so somebody can see something in me that they would want to have. I should be worth something on this Earth to somebody. We are an instrument and you can't use an instrument if it's broken. You can't use an instrument if it hasn't been well kept. There are different types of instruments for different types of jobs. I'm planning to give a statement in the rest of my life what a man should be. I hope God will give me the strength in the time to do something on this Earth that is worth something. I hope my light will shine somewhere on this Earth that would be valuable to somebody. I hope that I've learned something from the wrong things that I've done on this Earth that will help somebody. I hope I've learned something from some of the right things I've done on this Earth to help somebody. I hope somebody will believe in what I'm doing by the examples that I set in my life.

As I talked to that police chief and I saw tears in his eyes being concerned about the people. I saw him talking about the people that had condemned him for trying to bring peace in the community and trying to have his police officers treat people like they were human beings. I saw him get a vote of no confidence because he was trying to do what he thought was right, and treat people in a nice way and a respectable way; give people dignity instead of making them feel like they were no good or worth nothing. He wanted his peace officers, regardless of who were, to treat them with respect and treat them with dignity. Let the law stand for something. I believe that God meant for all men to be respected and that all men were innocent, in this country, until they were proven guilty.

Ladies and gentlemen, I love you. I hope my love shows. I hope my anger shows in places. And if I'm angry, it's because I haven't done what I needed to do and I'm angry with myself. But I'm not angry in an ugly and nasty and threatening way. I want you to know that there is something on this Earth worth saving. Our youth is worth saving. Our humanity must stretch out farther than just the Christian world. Our churches have to reach out to men and women in every segment of life. I'll talk with you again in a little while. God bless you.

FOUNDATION

I'm going to talk about some things now from a segment of my life that I don't like to go back to and I don't know why. It's strange how our lives change a lot of times by the negative side of our lives more so than they are by the positive side. I think it's because sometimes we like to dwell on the negative side rather than the positive side. Sometimes I think it's because we want sympathy; we're looking for sympathy. We look for the things that we get the most attention from, I think. It means I believe that's what has happened in some of the things that bother me in my life. I remember part of my childhood, but for some reason it annoys me and it makes me sad. I very seldom talk about it. I wanted to know what set my life into motion. I wanted to know what makes great men, great men. Why did life deal some people such a magnificent and exciting hand and look like others went through the torture of hell in order to develop into manhood? What creates the opportunity for someone to be a valuable instrument to society? What helps create men and women to be what they are? What does your childhood have to do with your development? I wanted to go back and find out what made me the way I was. Why didn't I get an education and try to work on myself to be a cultured and an intellectual individual that I thought I ought to be? What kept my life from blooming into the enterprising young man that I could have been? What makes young men what they need to be? And what is the one strike against a person from being the best they can be? What made me what I am? Why wasn't I what I thought I needed to be early on in my life? What made me not develop into a prosperous, wealthy, young man? It seems that I was intelligent enough. I don't think I was a stupid kid. Maybe not that smart, but not that stupid either. I think I wanted to be something. What happened that caused me to come up and not be the great man that I think I should have been that I believe I should have been? Was it something back there that was different that kept me from thinking positive? I think I always wanted something.

Now I remember. I remember that my mother was sad all the time. She was sad until a man came along in her life called Presley Darden. I remember him taking her a lot of places. I also remember her leaving me a lot and going with him. She used to leave me at a lot of different people's homes when she went away with… and then he was her boyfriend. I don't remember her playing with me. I don't ever remember my mother playing with me. I don't know why I get so sad and I don't want to remember things about my childhood. I wonder what it would have been like that I could remember my mother spending time playing and having fun with me. I wonder what it would have been like to have a father take me out some place and spending some time with me. I wonder if that would that have changed my life and made it different? I'm sorry if I seem emotional. I wouldn't talk about my childhood for a long time because I didn't want my emotions to be on tape, but somebody told me to tell it how it felt. When I think about my childhood, I get angry, and I feel cheated, and I feel like I've been robbed of something. I remember my mother taking me to many a place and I remember how people used to call me by different names. One time they called me, "Guy Stags," I go some place else and they call me, "Guy Holland." I had so many names I didn't know what they were. I didn't know what to go by. I remember them calling me, "Guy Ricks", "Guy Scott"; I never knew what all those names were about. These were the men that my mother had been involved with. I don't remember any of them. I remember one time, I think, seeing a man called Butler Scott. I think that's why they call me Scott. Whoever the last name was of the person that my mother was going with, that was the name I got, I learned later. I remember mama having a lot of friends and them saying that how much they liked her and how good a friend she was to them and they would always invite me to stay. I was a little curly haired kid; they said that I was cute.

    You know if the only foundation you got is how cute you are and how curly your hair is, or what color your skin is, I'm not so sure that you have the foundation that you can build on. Foundation should be built on moral principles and deep integrity, and character that are built on God's liberation and foundation. You'd have to be understanding of what God means to you. You need your child to know something about the Almighty God. His look should not have anything to do with his character. I was challenged by that and I was always shocked by how nice people said I looked. But I don't believe it had anything to do with who I was and what I was. And that was a strangle hold on me, most of my life, how well people thought I looked. I think I needed to know who I was. I'm not sure I ever found out. Maybe now I am just beginning to understand.

    I didn't get to talk to any man as a father till I was about seven or eight years old and then he used to talk to me a lot about the Bible and he would read the Bible to me. Grandpa

George would read the Bible every evening. And I remembered everything he read to me. They said that I had a mind that didn't forget anything. They said, "Be careful what you say in front of that kid cause he don't forget anything." I remember everything that someone said to me when I was young. He used to read a lot of things to me and he used to teach me about honesty, integrity, being fair, and always being honest. I remember him telling me that he'd be there for me for anything, if I was honest about it. But he would say if I ever stole anything, don't even talk to him about it, don't even come to him. He hated a thief worse than anything on Earth. I remember him talking to a man one time and borrowing a quarter from him and told him he'd pay him that Saturday. Saturday would come, for some reason he didn't have it, but he got in his horse and wagon and drove about five or six miles to tell the man he didn't have the quarter, but he would bring it to him just as soon as he'd gotten it. I remember him telling me, "Always give a man a good day's work." And after I had given him a good days work, then work some more. "Always measure out a good measure of corn to someone." Then after I had measured out a full measure, then give them some more. "Always be sure that I paid my debt." I followed that pretty close for a long time. He was the basis I suppose for the morals. But as he would read the Bible and talk about the way he came up, talk about how his grandfather used to talk about slavery and talk about how they would hang people for just talking to a white lady. They would hang a black man for just talking; holding a conversation with a white lady, sometimes a man could get hung for that. And at that time I saw white people being very cruel and mean people. I saw them as being unfair and dishonest people. But one thing he taught me, he said, "Everything you do on this Earth, if it has to do with a black man, you got to do it twice as good as the white man, to get half as far". You've got to always be honest and respectable for your race. You can never do anything that would be disgraceful to your race. Anything you do, your brothers and sisters and mothers and fathers, are going to be held responsible for it too. That I was not only responsible for my actions, but I was responsible for other peoples' actions too. What I do could affect somebody else's life and that I wasn't just only responsible for myself, but I was responsible for my race as a whole. What ever I did for myself, it was also for my neighbor. What I ever I did that was dishonest and disrespectful to me, the reflection of it could bear on my neighbor or my friends that were black. We didn't know much about and we weren't taught too much about togetherness with white people. But we were taught to respect all people regardless to their race or creed or whoever they were, that loving God and doing what God demanded in the Bible would set the standard for your life, all through your life. And what you were to yourself, you were to your neighbor, whether you knew it or not. I really believe he lived that way.

    But in between my development as a teenager; I think maybe about six or seven years, I'm thinking that's how old I was, that my mother, Grandpa George got worse, and my mother had to go back to where he was living. We moved in there because my Grandfather got so he just couldn't help himself at all. So we had moved into the house with the man who turned out to be my stepfather; we had moved into his house with him and his family at that time. So now we have to move from there back to my mother's father's house and live there. My stepfather-to-be, he couldn't stay there. My grandfather, you know, was quite strict in that way. But I remember my grandfather was so sick and so bad a shape that he was dying. I don't remember much about how but that one time that my grandfather called me into the room, and he was dying; they thought. He hadn't spoken in two or three days. He was supposed to be in a semi-coma. They said he had a death rattle. I went in the room where he was and I looked at him, and he looked so bad, and I started to back out of the room and for some reason he must have recognized me. He called me. He said, "Guy?" I said, "Yes, Grandpa?" He said, "Come here." And I went by the bedside and he moved his fingers and I caught onto his hand and he said, "Son, would you do me a favor?" And I said, "Yes, sir?" He said, "Will you take care of your mother for me? I want you to take care of your mother for me. Will you promise me that?" I said, "Yes, Grandpa. I'll take care of mama." He says, "Okay. Now you be a good boy." And I left the room and I don't remember grandpa no more. You know, it's a strange thing when people die, for some reason my mind shuts off and I don't remember the funeral. I don't remember anything after that about my grandfather.

But you know when I was trying to put this book together and think about my childhood, after so many struggles, I remembered something. I kept feeling the title that I was trying to come up with. It stayed with me so strong until it was like torture: *God and Man's Relationship to Humanity*. I would go to sleep at night and see that in my dreams. It appeared to me for days and months, everything I thought was about God and Man's Relationship to Humanity. It dawned on me one day, I want to write a book and I don't know how to read and I don't know how to write. How on earth would that phrase mean so much to me? It seems to me that we're talking about the world. We're talking about all mankind regardless of race or creed or color. We're talking about a world of people and things that revolve around them. What on Earth would I be doing concerned about it and why is this torturing me so? And I remember what I promised my grandfather. I promised grandfather that I would take care of my mother and I didn't take care of my mother. When I reached eighteen years old, I left home and traveled abroad and sometimes I wouldn't come home for seven, eight years at a time. But when I came home I always paid their bills and brought some money. But then I was on my way somewhere, drifting and floating all over this nation. Could this phrase be attacking me about a promise I made my grandfather when I was five or six years old? If God wanted me to do something like that and be the man I should be He had the power to make me do what I need to do for my mother. He had all the power. What excuse does he have for torturing me all these years when I didn't have a father and sometimes I didn't have a mother? How could he hold me responsible for something I said when I was five or six years old? That bothers me. It's put a stranglehold on me. I began to think, and bounce in and out of my childhood back to adulthood, again and again, and as I remember over the years of accepting Christ in my life and if I had really accepted Him from what all I had...all the talking books and talking Bibles and I had heard over the years. Then the memories come back into my mind what my grandfather used to read to me. I had a photographic mind and I remember everything I saw and heard, but yet, I couldn't help remembering my mother promising me that I was going to go to school next year. Things bouncing in and out of my mind about the reason I couldn't go to school, because I didn't have clothes. But they found time to do the things that they needed to do, but I couldn't go to school. I couldn't get on with my life thinking about the things that they allowed to happen to me when I was a child. Every time I would go back to that time it looked like I had an excuse to not go to school as an adult. I was finding bits and pieces of my life that didn't add up. They said I was a good kid, an obedient kid. They said I was a smart kid, I wasn't lazy. I worked all the time. I kept myself busy. What happened that once I became a man and got away form home I would work on a job for six months and go to another one and drift and float and drift and float all over this nation? I guess I need to quiet down and think some more about this. This is troubling. I knew I didn't want to think about my life as a child. I have to go out of here. I need some rest. I can't think about this any more. I've got to think about the things that I need to do.

WHY WE ARE WEAK?

The United States of America is now well over two hundred years old and at the dawn of the twenty-first century. The past few decades have seen incredible advances in technology and medicine. We are living in a world of wonders and possibilities our forefathers could not have imagined even a half century ago. Why then have we stagnated politically, scientifically, and culturally? Forty years ago we put men on the moon and haven't been back since. There was an oil crisis thirty five years ago and we are even more dependent on the substance than we were then. Crime is rampant in the country despite the fact more and more people are being put in prison than ever before. The USA is no longer the unquestioned world leader and we seem to be losing ground every year. Our federal deficit is rapidly nearing an almost inconceivable ten trillion dollars and our government may be bankrupt within our lifetime. Culturally there exists little respect for our elderly, our traditions, our institutions, our country, and most of all for each other. We are a nation of self centered, apathetic, entertainment saturated individuals who's first and only question when presented with a new idea or problem is "What's in it for me?" How did this country, which was founded on a combination of high ideals and hard work, arrive at such a state? Part of the problem lies with our own success. Each generation wants its children to have an easier life than the one they experienced. It is only natural for a parent to wish to protect and indulge their child whenever possible. Because of the advances in technology and wealth over the past decades these children have become more and more spoiled, coddled, and dependent with each passing generation. During the Great Depression in the nineteen thirties many people refused to take handouts and insisted on working for their food. Nowadays government aid is a common thing. We are one of the few countries with fat poor people. Everyone has television, a car, a roof over their heads, more toys than they know what to do with, and many other things that were considered luxuries just a few decades ago. Want something as a child? Throw a temper tantrum and mommy or daddy will get it for you. Want something as an adult? Put it on a credit card and declare bankruptcy if you cannot afford to pay. There are no longer the hardships that faced many Americans in the past just to get the basic necessities of life. Without adversity there is no strength. Everyone looks to someone else to solve their problems and someone else to blame for their failings. Parents expect the schools to teach and raise their children and yet will call out the lawyers if that child is disciplined. Our congress is comprised primarily of wealthy, self-serving, well connected aristocrats that can get plenty of pork legislation passed for their districts but cannot balance the budget. They are away from Washington for months during the year, have a golden retirement plan for themselves, and are regularly bought off by special interest groups in exchange for campaign contributions. We have only ourselves to blame for this situation. We choose who is to lead us by our votes and yet many of us do not vote. Worse yet, the votes that are cast are for the same corrupt, incompetent individuals that have failed us in the past. People have lost their sense of civic responsibility and no longer take an active interest in the affairs of their own government. Everyone is absorbed pursuing goals for their own self-gratification and personal success and yet no one seems to have the time for others. We are a country full of whiners and excuse makers. Where else could you sue McDonalds for making you fat? You made you fat, no one else. People hide behind their race, their gender, their religion as excuses for why their lives aren't perfect. Take a look in the mirror, there is where your problems lie: with yourself. Each of us has the ability to change ourselves and make the world a more pleasant place to live. This starts with thinking beyond your personal wants and desires to the needs of the community in which you live and the other people in that community. Turn off the television and volunteer your time to a person or group that can use it. Discuss and learn about political issues and then go vote intelligently, the government is only as bad as we choose it to be. Most of all, take some time out of the day to help others and you may discover the pride, strength, and satisfaction that this country has sorely missed.

By W. Bill Peden

Ladies and Gentlemen, Wow! If we had men and women that could think like this gentleman, we could change this nation overnight. If we would put these words into action we could change the world overnight. I hope it motivates us and give us a vision that we can fulfill our thoughts and ideas like this. I don't feel I have much more to add to this brilliant and intelligent man's writing. God bless you.

By Guy P. Darden, Sr.

FOUNDATION FOR LIFE'S JOURNEY

When you go back in your life you don't go to find out about trash or to judge people. You go back in your life to find out what kind of soil that you built your foundation on. Was your foundation built on solid ground? Was it built on a rock? What kind of essence was put in your beginning? Sometimes the way people are brought up they miss their foundation, structure. They miss the essence of who they are. They miss the human part of the structure of their lives. Some people have bounced over whole generations of people. Maybe back there somewhere you had a great-grandmother and father that had everything that you needed for you to draw on and make you what you needed to be. But then, somewhere along the line, you lost the material that it takes to build a foundation. Maybe it was not passed on from generation to generation and we lose a lot of muscle if it does not get passed on.

We need to know how to build a foundation now. It's been so long since we've had a foundation that was grounded in God's spirit and had that stone and rock that it takes to build; the stone of honesty, integrity, and the adhesive that seals you together as a family. Sometimes we bounce over that. We lose a lot of traction because now we are wondering and pointing our fingers at this person and that person and blaming this person and blaming that person. The reason for that is because we haven't' researched life and found those tools and that material that it takes to make a life. Before you can build a house, especially the foundation, you've got to have the material to build it. You've got to know where to look. You've got to search for the right material it takes to build a life. That is your mother and father. It could have been a grandmother or a grandfather that didn't have the teaching or the structure in life. They staggered through life and they drifted and floated. They may not have had the stuff it takes to make a life. If they didn't have it, you are going to have to be extremely blessed. Your blessing is going to have to come from someplace else. It's not wasteful to go back and check and try to understand what happened. All you're doing is trying to find pieces of your life and find out why they are strewn all over the place. If you haven't been taught about discipline and what discipline is and the meaning of it and what you use discipline for – discipline is one of the tools that you need to put your life in order. Priorities are one of the tools it takes to become unified; to get something in some kind of order. You have to learn the meaning of the word. What is it? Is it something that separates you or is it something that gives you some kind of order in life? Priorities just laying out there somewhere – no, you need to examine it and find out what part of it is a in your life or if it is at all. Are you just grabbing things randomly? Whatever comes, you grab it and accept it? Whatever looks shiny or whatever feels good to you; that's what you accept first?

Find out what kind of tools you have to work with. Do you have any tools at all? Are you trying to build a foundation with bare hands and no tools? Are you just finding a place to build a foundation just anywhere? You haven't examined it? You haven't researched that piece of ground that you're going to build your life on? You haven't looked out there in the world and decided because you didn't get it back there. There is no reason that you should go through life completely without it. Should you be seeking out someone that can give you some knowledge?

Of course knowledge is not enough to take you where you need to go. You need to have enough knowledge that is refined enough to allow you to know that you need wisdom. Usually wisdom is gathered up by your years and if you're very, very young you're not going to have a lot of experience. You need to search out people that have experience. That's where your minister comes in. The word minister, well I suppose it means that you've got somebody that will minister to you. I believe that the word pastor has a little more value than the word preacher has. I believe a preacher has to be turned into a pastor and be taught how to be a pastor. I believe a pastor is one who looks over his flock, the people that he has to work with, and adopts them in his life as his family. It's a part of the unity. It's a part of his extension. I feel that a pastor is appointed by God not by some group of people in some conference. I believe a pastor has to have more than some schooling some place. He has to have drawn power from God Almighty, where he's able to look in the hearts of men and women and not just on the surface or by just being impressed with their personality or by their glitter, but their soft and quiet and searching for the essence of communication with their congregations. They empower the congregation. They don't take away from the strength, the wisdom, or the knowledge of the congregation.

A pastor feeds off his congregation. He has a relationship with them where they draw from each other. A pastor will look over his congregation and start a research campaign. He'll start to research the heart and then he starts to research the character of that individual. He looks to see how much integrity is involved in that person. He looks at the physical individual. He checks out their physical ability. In his quiet, searching and Godly way he searches out their mental capacity. He examines the man from inside out. He has a feeling for that person. He regenerates himself and looks into their heart, through God's vision, not man's vision. When he looks out at the congregation and when he looks at people, he sees souls. He sees suffering people. He sees people in need. He learns their body language. He learns how they function with each other and how they get along with each other. He becomes concerned about their family's orientation, how they feed their family, and he starts to see that person through their own eyes. He starts to see the person in the way the person sees himself.

God will blend and amalgamate their minds and hearts. He's not just dealing with a man; he's dealing with the spirit of God in the man. He deals with the church in the man; not the church building. The minister that is searching for a person's character, personality and foundation will undoubtedly receive from as well as give to those he speaks with; an exchange of humanity. Now we are not just getting a foundation built by me that's suffering and struggling. I see some hope. I see a shadow of hope. I see the teaching in my pastor. I see the love in my pastor. I see his concern for me as a whole person, not just someone that's given him money.

We've put money at the forefront. We keep telling people how they're robbing us and how they're robbing God. But I want to see men and women. We are human resources. I want to see them doing physical things for each other. I want to see them searching their hearts, not just 10%, but 100% of themselves to God and God's work. When you give yourself to God and God's work you give yourself to your family. You give yourself to your community. You give yourself to your nation. When you give to others you are also ministering to yourself. You learn that God will teach you and show you how to work with your family, your community, and your church. I like to use that word: church-people.

I think people are getting hung up on the building. That's the place that you congregate. That's the place that you meet. That's the place that you do your research work in. That's a research building. That's a repair shop. That's where you go to get the broken pieces put back together. That's where I go to find something that I can't find anyplace else because I have people that care about me, not just themselves. They want to know how I feed my family. They want to know how best I can function in my community. What am I doing in my community? What is my qualification? Am I capable of doing anything there? My pastor and those of us that are Godly people, we need to know what our economical ability is. How am I capable of working out a budget so I can see that my family gets the resources that they need to function off of? What am I doing about the world around me, the drugs in my community or the officials in my community? Is my community suffering? Am I suffering because of my community? Do my officials that run and operate my local government, city and county, are they getting the things they need to function? Are we cooperating with them? Do we know anything about what is going on there? Do we know anything about their character or are we just going by hearsay about how wonderful and good this person is? Have we examined them ourselves? Have we checked out ourselves and found out how much we know about politics? How much do we know about governmental functions?

We're talking about being a total person. We're talking about being an organism in our family. We're talking about being an organism in the church. We're talking about the church being an organism in our community. We're talking about the church doing more than just asking for something. When they ask for something that people believe in and that they're honest and trustworthy and that they just don't receive but they also give. The reason we know they give is because we see the results of it. We don't just see all these churches; one here, one there, 20 or 30 different churches in one little community and each one is begging. None of them have come together perhaps, and joined hands and said 'what can we do as a Godly people, as a church-going group of people', 'how can we come together and have some kind of consensus?' Why do we have all these leaders here and there and everywhere? I call it tribal-orientation. If I can't get anything out of it, I don't want to do it.

If I can't get the credit for it, I don't want to do it. I don't want to cooperate if my church name isn't represented; if it hadn't been represented.

Ladies and gentlemen, we're talking about re-evaluating a nation of people. We claim, those of us that are in the church, those of us who have accepted God in our lives, have accepted Him as our Savior and our leader, are we trying to lead God or are we asking God to lead us? Are we willing to submit to God? Does our willpower; is it so strong that we are not willing to give our will over to God? Are we scared that He won't do by us for what we need to be done for us? I know why we don't submit our will to God because He gives us what we need rather than what we want. A lot of times God doesn't give us what we want. He'll give us what we need. Then a lot of times we have to earn it, and not by God paying us, but we show the people around us that we are real and that we have actions in us that we are willing to share. We have knowledge that we are willing to share and that we have wisdom that we want to give, and that we want to give and give and give until it hurts. People should be judged as individuals not just one group of people so they can minister it out there but where we want to give individually to individual people, to individual organizations.

We want to come together, that's it. If you are being led by God, you cannot and you will not treat me the way that a lot of us treat other people. You will not tell me that you are a Godly person and I don't see anything that you are doing for God. I don't see you doing anything for Godly people. I see your tribal system; you over here and you over there. I'm over there. I can't live by your rules and you've got to live by mine so I'll get my own group and this is the way we are going to do things; the way I want to do it because I have a group of people over here that will listen to me. They believe in me. They trust me and I can do with that group of people what I want to do, not what God wants to do, what I want to do, or what I say God wants. In other words, I make up God's mind and decide what He wants me to do. Well, you can't do that you know. But we act like we think we can.

I'm talking about a power structure here. I'm talking about foundations. Foundations have to be in a family. Foundations have to be in a people. Foundations have to be in a nation of people. Foundations have to be in individuals. Foundations have to be in individual city officials. You've got to be willing to sacrifice something. Sometimes you've got to be willing to cut down on your salary. You need to check out some time and talk to people and ask them if it's possible if we can do with a little less in this city, and get some priorities. Is it possible that we can bring people together and have some community meetings where we can talk about giving people jobs? Some of the people volunteer for the city, doing some of this work for the city and not charging them anything. Maybe there are certain types of businesses here that are not big business, that we could bring back some small businesses in this community and that community, wherever it may be.

Wal-Mart, Kmart, and the rest of these stores that have ten stores in one, has put the small businessman out of business. They're not helping the community anyway. They are cycling up the wealth. Have we decided that we rather have handouts than to work for a little less money an hour? Have we decided that we would rather steal and rob rather than to work for $4, $5, or $6 an hour? Have we made that decision? Can't we decide and come together and tell these grocery stores and some of the other places, 'Look, we'll work for less if you'll charge less for your things that you have here.' Let's form some kind of consensus in this community and see if it catches on. If you'll charge me less for my rent, I can work less for my boss. If you charge me less for my gas, I can work less for my boss. If you'll charge me less for my phone, I can work for less for my boss. If you charge me less for my car, I can charge less for my work. If you charge me less for gas and let's help us all.

We, after all, we are the workers of this nation and we did have the willpower of when Martin Luther King, Jr. was around, God bless his soul. He at least talked to people about coming together. Sometimes it caused conflict but they got people's attention, and in a positive way. What I am saying is that we've got to stop being *I, I, me, me, myself, me my family, me, me,* and even *me my city, me my county.* There might have been a time when we said *me my country.* That's what President Bush did; *me, myself. I'll* make the decision to do what *I* want to do. God bless his heart. I'm not so sure that he should have done that. I'm not so sure that did the right thing. I'm not so sure that he's convinced he did the right thing. I'm not so sure. But if he did, it's going on awfully strange to me. But since I'm "400" years old and I'm not supposed to have the intelligence that these technicians have, I'll just keep looking and seeing and learning. I hope you'll do the same.

Search your heart, pastors, members of the clergy, the church, members of people who go to their prayer house and their church, let's just think about what we are put on this earth to do. Let's see if we can still survive and strive for success if we keep on letting babies have babies, letting children have children without any instruction; just throwing them out in the world without knowing how to build a foundation under our children.

How on earth can that young lady that are 15, 14, and some as young as even 12, having children and they don't even know how to take care of themselves? God bless their hearts. You cannot blame a child for that. Do you really get the essence of what I am saying here? I am putting a note in here because these children are having children. They're going to be leaders someday. Is that what you want for their foundation? I believe that when a child is that young and has a baby that that should be some kind of control on the parents. I think there should be some kind of discipline on the parents. If the parent hasn't disciplined the child, I think the parent need to be disciplined. I don't think you can just back off say nothing. I don't think we can allow the cities and the police departments to tell us how to discipline our children and at what age. As long as we're doing it in a decent and orderly fashion and we're not persecuting them. Sometimes our children need to be punished and they don't need to be beaten to death but there is nothing wrong with spanking a child. There is nothing wrong with using a little switch on a child. I have never known in my life a switch; not spanking them but a switch, in the history of the world have I ever heard tell of a switch causing a problem for a child. It may happen somewhere where a child was allergic to something or they had certain infection from a little cut from a switch. But a switch will hurt a grown mule; but I've never seen it harm anybody. It's just a sting; no more than putting a needle in your arm. We need to bring our children under submission without giving them things and things and things in order to do that. The bribery needs to stop. Supplement the material things with love; God's love.

This is where I'm heading. This is the direction I am going. This is what I'm talking about. I'm going to talk about it until death do us part; not just that subject but I'm going to follow it wherever it leads. You hear the people say when they are looking for a criminal or somebody that has committed a crime and they don't know where it started at but they are going to follow it wherever it leads them. That's what this book is doing. It doesn't flow. It may stop talking about this now and start talking about it somewhere else.

We don't have to make our children think that they have to be angels or that they are angels. What we want our children to know is that they are extremely valuable, and that they have something that is important in them. We want them to know that they are unique and each one is made special and has unique qualities. They have special values. Each one of us is set aside to do something special on this earth. We have an obligation to that. God will give us that opportunity and He'll put someone in front of us that will lay out the standards that we are supposed to go by. If we search in ourselves, God will reveal who we are. The spirit of God will allow us to know what our mission is on this earth. He doesn't just discriminate and throw you in the world and say go for if yourself. He gives you a value system and a way to survive in an orderly and productive way.

Our family is the seed of the beginning of all of us. Ever since that day that man was driven out of the Garden of Eden, ever since God gave man the responsibility on this earth, ever since God gave man a mission, he has not been alone. God will send His angels to help you. Even if a family lets you down, you still have some hope when you have the knowledge of God Almighty. I realize that some young people on this earth are the only people that they're going to get to know perhaps or get any script from. Maybe the only people that they will get the wisdom and the knowledge that they need to survive on will be from the church family. That's the reason that when a pastor comes into a congregation - I believe that one of his jobs is to teach them that they have an extended family and that is the church family. I believe that he is supposed to teach each member about that so when that member leaves that church he can't just assume his responsibilities are for his family and his family alone.

We have to be concerned about the families of this nation, especially those that we have our hands on. If you were in our church, that we need to exercise our feelings towards each other and that we have a special commitment. We have a special mission. Even if you never heard the word of God and regardless of where you would be, you still have an obligation to work towards the effort of being successful in your nation. If we are not successful as individuals we cannot be successful as nation builders. We can't be productive in our families. We can't be productive in our nation. We can't be productive in our cities.

We can't be productive in the county of which we live in. Everything we do has to have some integrity in it. It has to have some essence that means something more than just to us alone. The way we survive as an organized people; they call this nation a "United" nation, well maybe we ought to see if it's united. What is it united with? What is it united to? What is the meaning of this country?

Our country will depend on our youth of tomorrow. It doesn't matter how young you are now, how much youth you have now, how much authority you have now over our governments and city officials and our states in this nation. Some day you're not going to be in control. The youth of today will be in control and the foundation that we give them; the raising, the training, the love, and the hope are what they will have to depend on. The way we live our lives today should be a good impression. It should make a good impression on our youth. It should identify and allow them to understand the meaning of what love is. Is it just another word we throw around when we are affectionate towards someone, or when we say we love, we meant it. We say we love this nation enough to fight for it and die for it. We need to love our family at least that much; at least that much. This is our own blood. We'd die for our own nation. We ought to have at least that same dedication to our families and our children.

We should have learned from the tribal orientation that we have experienced from the American Indians. We should have learned something from the nations of Africa that tribal mentality has destroyed people all over this world. We know when a nation is disorganized and does not unite with its people that you are going to see the strong ruling over the weak. That has been maintained since the beginning of time when we see our churches that are developing that same attitude. They don't come out and say it, but you find people all over this nation creating that type of atmosphere. When you do that nobody is going to win until we organize our hearts and minds with the inspiration of God and not just talk about it, and not just use the words, and not allow ourselves to be influenced by that type of atmosphere, we are going to continue to be uprooted. We're going to be roaming all over the place. We're never going to find a home that has a solid foundation.

We think that what we do in our personal lives is just personal to us, period. That's not totally true. I found out those things in a hard way. We have an obligation to each other as a people because that the one thing that we have in common is that we live on this earth together. We are all here at the same time. We have to find a way to tolerate each other. We need to find a way to love and care for each other. I personally; I speak for myself on this, I do not believe that you can truly love your fellow man fully, absolutely and completely, until you have loved God. Not until you have accepted God in your life as your guiding force and that you allow Him to lead you. It took me many, many years to learn that. I haven't known that a long time. I feel that we have an unknown personal obligation to each other that we haven't fully recognized yet. Going into Godliness and dealing with it as a people, I think survival, getting along; trying to understand each other's needs is going to be extremely hard. Just because you haven't accepted Christ in your life, or that you happen not to be a believer in God Almighty, doesn't mean that you don't owe this society in which we live in, your allegiance.

LOVE ONE ANOTHER AS I HAVE LOVED YOU

As we have been looking at the relationship between mankind and God and how far we have come from our basic foundation, how far we have allowed our intellect and our social status to blind us to what is truly and eternally beneficial for our very existence, I have come to see that one vital component of life has been replaced...love.

God is love, God sent His love and God commands us to love, not only Him but each other. We have become a society that has forgotten how to love. We believe that we understand what love is, but I believe if we took a survey, we would find many definitions and attitudes about what love is or how love should act but the reality is that, God gave us the most profound and greatest examples of love when He sent His Son to redeem man by dying in our place. There should be no confusion as to what love is or how we should love one another. Love is placing someone else's needs before your own and finding that your gratification is seeing them happy.

Love is staying even though it is easier to leave when things get too tough.

Love is unconditional, meaning I will love you with no hidden agenda, no tiny clause that says, "only if you do this".

We have become so out of touch with the real purpose of our being here. God created us to have a relationship with Him. He created us also to love one another. Our problem comes because we no longer have a love for God, for when we love God then we can love His creation. We can look beyond a person's circumstance and still love them. We desperately need to return to our first love, God.

There was a time when we feared God, we were afraid to do or say anything that would bring shame not only to our parents, but to God as well. We have come so far from our basic foundation that we feel that we can't go back, but we can. Everything that has happened to us individually or collectively, has been orchestrated and allowed by God to bring us closer to Him, to strengthen us and to remind us who really is in total control. Why, then has God allowed us to stray so far away? To become only lovers of ourselves? To wreck havoc upon each other and destroy all the resources that He has given to us since the beginning of creation?

God has shown us so much love by not giving to us what we rightly deserve, death. But because of His love for us He still is giving us time and opportunity to return to Him and to have a relationship with Him, God is giving us something we do not deserve, chance after chance to start loving one another, He is giving us new mercies each day, while we sit back and continue to disregard all of His grace.

There will come a time where we will not be able to go back, and God will not hear our cries. There is devastation everywhere around us and the only thing that keeps us together is God and the compassion that many have shown since 9-11. But why should we only care then? I remember a street corner that had a little neighborhood store on it and all the kids would go there after school to get candy and snacks. There was no stop sign at this corner but yet a candy store was there in the midst and no one thought of its potential to be a dangerous intersection until one afternoon a 7 year old girl was crossing this intersection and a car driving a little bit too fast couldn't stop in time to prevent from hitting her. The little girl died from her injuries and before her funeral services were held, a bright red stop sign was installed on each corner, great idea but at the cost of a life. We have to stop waiting to be careful, to make a difference when it is too late for some to benefit from it. Too much too little too late should not be our philosophy. Nor should we wait until someone else thinks of a solution, we are all part of the problem so why don't we be a part of the solution.

Let us start loving our children, our neighbors (that means everyone, not just those who live right next door or across the street), loving ourselves a lot more and above all else love God.

How?

Think of what He has done for you. Think of how much He loves you. You do not wake up on your own on any given morning; God gently wakes you with His finger of love. You cannot move a finger, leg or blink your eye without the brain telling it to do so which is willed by God. That promotion, don't think you accomplished that on your own merit, God gave you the ability to achieve.

Love is powerful all by itself. Love conquers everything and love makes things possible.

Love makes a heart sing, a child laugh, a tear dry up, and it is a gift from God to give to one another.

Like the songwriter penned, "What the world needs now is love sweet love, it's the only thing that there's just too little".

Let us rebuild our foundation with love and it is a guarantee that we can change a heart, a mind and a nation.

By Karen Tyree-Sudberry

Maybe I'm a little biased here. Karen is one of the first people in this part of the country that when I asked, she helped me with this book. She went all out in every way to assist me. If this book is a success, it will be largely due to the help and advice from Karen. She is my cousin but never, ever have I called on her and she was not there to help me. She was always there. When you truly have accepted Christ as your savior and signed your name at the foot of the cross you are on the job 24/7. Karen has seen enough in her life that she dedicated her life to Christ's service for the rest of her life.

God bless you, sweetheart! Thank you so much. You are a gift from God!

By Guy P. Darden, Sr.

MANEUVERS

Some of you that have never been in the army would probably not know what maneuvers are. Maneuvers are something that the army uses for skill. They use it privately. They go to any area that is sealed off. They don't allow the public to come in there. They teach you how to maneuver and learn different skills on how to out maneuver the enemy.

God has a plan for him way beyond his comprehensions especially when he set it up. I believe that sometimes God has a special thing for special people and He has to send them to a training field. The funny thing about it; God has an army that we have to join if want to fight the battles of this world. I believe that this particular person has been on maneuvers in his lifetime. You see, when we think of maneuvers, we think of the physical part. But God has a spiritual, a kind of under-the-camouflage of physical sight. And when God deals with the man and puts him in an army, he deals with the spiritual part of the man. Even though the physical may take over, but God is still dealing with the heart of the individual.

You humble yourself to our Father which is in Heaven and ask Him to deliver you from your past sins and to forgive you for the promises that you've made to Him in the past; or maybe you haven't made any promises to Him. Maybe you have struggled through life trying to make it on your wits. Then again, maybe you were brought up in a home that had all of the decencies, loyal background; standards that men and women should go by. In other words, those that look out and see you would think you had an ideal situation. God had blessed you with a lovely mother and father and they did all they could to build a foundation in their lives and your life in order to bring you up in a world of happiness, peace and harmony. Sometimes when that happens we shield our children from the tough times in life. We want to make things easy for them. We want to give them principles of life and just hand it to them on a silver spoon or we give it to them on platter. When you pass a silver platter to someone you don't pick out what you want them to have. You allow them the opportunity to pick out what they want. Sometimes that platter has things that they just want rather than the things they need. Sometimes when you pass out the platter of hope, it has some things on there that you need and it has some things on there that you want. Sometimes the things that you need don't have the glitter that the things that you have.

You meet a situation like that, opportunities are plentiful. But if certain things in life haven't been pointed out to you, you as a parent or a mother have not been out there in that world going through some of the trials and tribulations that we all go through at one time or another. But sometimes, hard work, hard times, and sacrifice for the things that some people take for granted. Sometimes you have to point out those things in life that can strangle a man if he doesn't go the right way. Not because you don't have wonderful parents and great parents and they want the very best for you and they would never do anything around you that would cause you to be destructive. But sometimes we move our children too fast and too far ahead of the foundation that we have given them from the inside in order for you to see your own foundation. Most likely your parents are going to have to point it out to you.

In other words, before you leave that home and start forth into the world, you need to know something about the hazards of the world. You need to know something about the downfalls; not just what you can accomplish if you do, but what will happen to you if you don't. You need to know that there are drugs, murders and people out there that are envious and jealous. You need to know something about the reasons they are that way. You need to know something about your fellow man before you have to deal with him.

Now you can't teach a person something if you don't know it. I think we as mothers and fathers feel that in order to deal with the general public that you have to have them in your building, in your circle, in your home environment, in your church environment. No! Sometimes you need to do a survey. Sometimes you need to go down in those valleys and look around. Certainly after you know that God has endowed you with His Holy Spirit and He has put His angels around you to protect you, then you need to expose yourself as Jesus Christ exposed Himself to the world and allowed them to see Him and see His lifestyle, and to be able to participate with something other than just the glorified spirit of God.

He walked with sinners and talked with sinners and not just in a building, not just in a church, but He dealt with the world. He dealt with sin; unadulterated sin. Christ had that opportunity because He knew whatever, wherever He went, even if death came, He had a

God that could protect Him. If something happened and if He died He would still have a safe haven. Sometimes I think we get ready for Heaven too soon. We need to deal with something on this earth. We need to know something about what is going on around us. We need to know something about what is going on over on the next block from us. We need to know our neighbors. If we don't have a relationship and a friendship, we won't ever do that.

What I am trying to say – sisters and brothers, I'm trying to say to you that before you can work with a situation, you have to know about what's happening with it. You have to be acquainted with it. You need to know your neighborhood. You need to know your community. You need to know what's going on there. You can't go by hearsay. You can't just point your finger and say, "those people down there" or, "you people". But in this nation and in this world and in this community in which we live in that we can touch, we need to be able to put our hand on our brothers and sisters. And what I mean by that – you need to know what makes them function. You need to know what motivates them. You need to know what motivates them towards sin rather than towards God.

Now you say that, "I don't know what's going on in the guys mind. I can't read his mind. I'm not a mind reader." But you know enough about him to stand back here in the pulpit and in the church or the prayer house and point your fingers and talk about how bad they are. How do you know that they are bad? I think that when a man is bad, he is bad from inside of his heart out; not from the outside in. A bad person has become – his spirituality has left him. It is not the temple of God. It is a playhouse for the devil. It is a refuge for the devil – demonized by the devil. He should be able to say, "I know pretty much what's going on in your life."

Sometimes we have to say, "I have not been on drugs. I have not been a prostitute. I have not been a murderer. I have not stolen or robbed, but I did a host of other things that I shouldn't have done." You get close enough to an individual and he knows for sure that you love humanity, not just him, but you love people like him. You don't love him for what they give you. You love them for what God has given you. You show your humility. You don't go down there trying to show them up or try to put them down but by the way you live your life and the way that you talk to them; the way that you walk with them, they see your lifestyle. They feel you. They feel your insides because they feel you reaching out to them.

You know something, I know ministers throughout this nation that have done exactly what I am telling you now. But guess what? Their own personal and private family was going to destruction right before their eyes and they never saw it. That minister, that doctor, that lawyer, that deacon, that schoolteacher, that professor, that congressman, that president, saw everything out there in the world but he didn't see what was happening in his own family because the glitter and the shine or pats on the shoulder were being put on the stage of life; being put on the physical things in life, that the glitter of the world took control of their lives.

I know many ministers' sons and daughters all over this nation that have been neglected under the name of love. I raised you right. I brought you up in my home. I taught your Sunday school. I saw that you went every day. But they never had the five star training. They never sit. They didn't have the picnic. They didn't have the family gathering. They didn't have the nightly reading. They didn't have the baseball games. They didn't have the tennis games. They didn't go on vacations together. They didn't have the love gathering. They didn't have their mother and father praying with them. I don't care how popular you are. I don't care how much you love God. Your family comes first or at least equal to other people's families.

I believe in everything in my being, after God - after God, the first thing that comes in your life is your wife. After God, your children; you build a foundation in your personal and intimate life to stand the rocky roads of life for your children. I believe that the reason that some of the disciples of God's people way back years ago. Paul mentioned something that I do agree with him on. It is better that some people that are leading God's people should not marry. Sometimes when we are married, we have too much emphasis on their family. But you have to remember that you made a commitment to God and your family when you get the family. You made that commitment, I hope, before you got the family.

Now, you're obligated to God first and family second. When I say you are obligated to God, you're not obligated to put God's people ahead of your people. But, at least you treat your family as well as you treat your neighbor. And you treat your neighbor like you want to be treated. Now, it's tact here, right here. You don't need to tiptoe through these tulips but you need to walk softly in life when you come to this point. It says treat your neighbor as yourself. Or does it say treat your neighbor as you want to be treated? You would not want your neighbor to give up his family and come over to see you rather than his own family. You wouldn't mind if your neighbor came over and he saw that you needed some necessary things, to help you with your survival. You would want your neighbor to assist you and help you to get on your feet so you can help yourself.

Are we getting this straight? Do you understand what I'm saying? Your family is being trained to walk through life gathering up the tools and the instruments to survive in life. Not only just for their survival but your survival, and the survival of humanity. You open up their hearts and minds so they can see through the fog of hate and envy and jealously and selfishness, and those things that push men and women apart.

Just this one essence in your life will shine through all of the pride. We can just look inside of ourselves and visualize God moving into our lives. We see all these physical things out there but when you are in God's army and God decides to put you on maneuvers because you don't have the material to fight the battle. Maneuvers are never held out in the public eye. Maneuvers are moved to a private and personal landscape and it's camouflaged.

When we think about maneuvers with the U.S. government, we see that's a physical thing but when we speak about the maneuvers in God's army, we're not talking about a physical thing. God's army is not physical. It is spiritual and spiritual is not visible to physical eye.

Are you getting this? Are you peeping? Are you peeping at my hold card? Are you seeing under the hate and ugliness or the physical part? Can you pull up the canvas of the camouflage (God's grace) that God has over you that you don't even know about yet? Sometimes your life may be threatened – this is a physical thing but God is dealing with your heart. He knows what he put in you. He knows what is there.

The Holy Spirit is waiting for your surrender on the physical things from the outside in the glitter of the world. But down here, under this camouflage, is God delivering you even though you don't even know it. He's waiting for you to surrender from the devil's army and sign up for His and all of this is spiritual because God is dealing with your heart. He's dealing with your spirit and that spirit is kicking you, it's shoving you, it's pulling on you, it's giving you tears, it's causing you to suffer, and its calling you pray even when you don't want anybody to hear you pray. Its saying, help me. You have all kinds of threats and things happen. But it's spiritual! It is not physical. It is not visible. You wouldn't want anyone to see you begging even though you don't know you're begging. You haven't been captured by God yet.

God doesn't go out and throw a gun to your head but the stuff that is planted into you years ago is boiling in your stomach like a gas. It's like you have indigestion inside of your sole until one day you turn around and you decide that this thing that's boiling inside of me – I can't allow it to happen no longer. Until you come back to Christ and you let Him receive you, and on that day, sign up in God's army to fight the battles that life has for you.

Now, you come in as a private and with your past experience, you get promoted awfully fast sometimes. Step, by step, by step. Yes, my friend, Larry Barclay. I've known him now for about 8 years. He's become my friend and he doesn't know it but he's also become my mentor. I love him as a son and believe he loves me as a friend, as his father in Christ.

Larry is a great man today. He has great things to do. He has great promises he made to God Almighty. I believe that Larry Barclay will fulfill his destiny for Jesus Christ. I believe that he has been on maneuvers and he knows what's going on in men and women's lives that have been in the jungle. Larry's been in the jungle. He's dealt with the jungle. He knows the function of the jungle. But after you have been in the jungle and you know how it functions and you know how to survive, when you come back out into society and then you have to function in a society of different classes and types of people. He knows what a sinner is and he knows what a Godly blessed man is. He knows how to talk to a drug addict. He knows how to talk to a drug lord. He knows what danger is. He's seen it. He's faced it. He's faced guns, knives, the traps of life; physically, spiritually and he's been close to death. He has accepted Christ in his life. Yet God restores him to his best part, the standard of opportunities.

I can't speak for Larry, but there are many Larry's on this earth but very few have accepted Christ. He spent a long time being phony, and went out in this world and stayed 18 years to be in that world of every imaginable thing going on in his life. He was in almost everything. He was a man that was brought up in a home of Godly principles where morals meant more than anything in the world. His pride was hurt. He knew that he was putting his family through disrespect. He knew he was dishonoring his family. He cried and moaned. He was losing his spiritual life and close to a physical one. Yet, he accepted Christ in his life and the Holy Ghost lifted him up after 18 years and put him back on the stage of life and gave him his second chance, I call it. The first was when he accepted Christ in his life the first time. The second is when he accepted Christ again. But I believe once Christ is in you, He never turns you loose.

I'm going to allow Larry to finish this up. He is one of the finest men I've met in a long, long time. May God bless him. Larry, I love you and your family. Your lovely wife is a princess to me. She's a lovely lady. She knows what hardships are. She's seen the devil in action and she's seen God in action. She stuck by you through the thick and the thin. She's been there as a woman of God, a woman of stature. Stature means more than somebody that picks you up and puts you on a stage - a pedestal; a shiny thing doesn't lift you up. The power of God shining through a woman can glorify your spirit. This lady, who is a minister of God, shows her tenderness without always trying to wrap you around her title. She shows down-to-earth, unadulterated love and effort through action and motivation. She has motivated her husband, her family to a higher level of integrity, honor, respect, and love. Nothing could be greater than the love that we show. God Almighty in our spouses and in the families.

Almighty God, I ask you to lift us up to this thing that shines for hope, dreams to be found, and love to embrace. God bless you in every way. Mrs. Barbara Barkley, I have been honored to know you and your family, especially your husband that I know so well and love so much. I hope that you all embrace me in God and hold me close to the stone of God in your prayers. Amen.

OUR MISSION - Pastor, Elder Larry D. Barclay, Sr.

Our Mission is to make the life-changing wisdom of the Bible understandable and accessible to all men, women and children.

Our Vision

Our **Vision** is to see people of all nations experiencing a personal relationship with Christ, growing to be more like Him, serving in this local body and be found doing the kingdom work for all humanity.

Jesus gave us the Great Commission: "Go ye into all the world, and preach the gospel to every creature" (St. Mark 16:15)

As you scan the headlines of you local newspaper and see the television news - with crime rapidly increasing and people dying daily (some without God in their lives), I believe you can agree with me that there is a dire need to reduce crime. Jesus is the solution to the world's problems. Individuals the world over need to be introduced to **the transforming power of God.** There is an urgent need for the furtherance of the gospel both locally and abroad.

The purpose of getting the gospel out is to introduce Christ and present salvation to the lost. The more people we reach with the gospel, the less there are for the enemy to influence with crime. The more people who know Jesus Christ as Savior, the safer your neighborhood will be.

Paul said, "For I am not ashamed of the gospel of Christ: for it is the power of God unto salvation to every one that believeth..." (Romans 1:16)

In The Life of Holiness

My Personal Beliefs:
1. In the verbal inspiration of the Bible.
2. In one God eternally existing in three persons; namely, the Father, Son and Holy Ghost.
3. That Jesus Christ is the only begotten of the Father, conceived of the Holy Ghost, and born of the virgin Mary. That Jesus was crucified, buried, and raised from the dead; that He ascended to heaven and is today at the right hand of the Father as the intercessor.
4. That all have sinned and come short of the glory of God, and that repentance is commanded of God for all and necessary for forgiveness of sins.
5. That justification, regeneration, and the new birth are wrought by faith in the blood of Jesus Christ.
6. In sanctification subsequent to the new birth, through faith in the blood of Christ; through the Word; and by the Holy Ghost.
7. Holiness to be God's standard of living for His people.
8. In the baptism of the Holy Ghost subsequent to a clean heart.
9. In speaking with other tongues as the Spirit gives utterance and that it is the *initial* evidence of the baptism of the Holy Ghost.
10. In water baptism by immersion, and all who repent should be baptized in the name of the Father, and of the Son, and of the Holy Ghost.
11. Divine healing is provided for all in the atonement.
12. In the Lord's Supper and washing of the Saints' feet.

13. In the premillennial second coming of Jesus. First, to resurrect the righteous dead and to catch away the living Saints to Him in the air. Second, to reign on the earth a thousand years.
14. In the bodily resurrection; eternal life for the righteous and eternal punishment for the wicked.
15. In dressing in modest apparel according to 1 Timothy 2:9, 10 and 1 Corinthians 11:14, 15.

"Great is the Lord and greatly to be praised in the city of our God, in the mountain of his holiness. Beautiful for situation, the joy of the whole earth, is mount Zion, on the sides of the north, the city of the great King" (Psalm 48:1, 2)

"I will bless the lord at all times: his praise shall continually be in my mouth" (Psalm 34:1)

"And it came to pass, as we went to prayer, a certain damsel possessed with a spirit of divination met us, which brought her masters much gain by soothsaying." (Acts 16:16)

We are living in a terrible time. Many people are going through great trials. These are the last days. There are wars and rumors of wars as Jesus has said there would be. (St. Matthew 24:6)

People are mourning the death of their sons and daughters on the battlefield. People are slaves to drugs and alcohol, crime and anger. Murdering demons are taking over. People are being murdered on every hand. People have hatred in their heart. Men are murdering their wives. Wives are murdering their husbands. Men and women are murdering their children.

I want you to know that, as a nation, we need God! **HE IS MASTER OF EVERY SITUATION.** People are wondering why there are so many perplexities. They are wondering what is causing people to act the way they do. Well, I can tell you-it's the devil. He means to destroy everyone. You need God in your life. There is hope today in Christ Jesus.

We are serving a Savior who is the Master of all mankind. If you want to be saved, He will save you! If you want to be healed, He will heal you! Whatever you need from Jesus, you can have it!

My prayer is, may God bless and keep you, and richly favor you.

By Pastor, Elder Larry D. Barclay, Sr.
And
First Lady, Evangelist Barbara A. Barclay
Greater Faith Tabernacle Church of God in Christ
596 Homeworth Avenue
Painesville, OH 44077

LIFESTYLE

I hope this day has been an exciting day for you. I hope God has blessed you accordingly to your needs. Hopefully, you have been a blessing to someone else. I want to talk to you about something that is on my heart strongly these days more than ever. Let me give you a scenario of four questions; if you were to call them questions: money, schooling, gang leaders, and lifestyle. I think they have some association. I think they touch each other in some way or they could touch each other. I think they will have some significance to each.

I'm not sure when we send our children to college that we're doing it for the right motive. I wonder what motivates us. They certainly need to go. They certainly need all the schooling they can possibly get but what kind of schooling do they need? What is our motivation for sending them? What do we call a decent and good lifestyle? What are our ideas about preparing our children for the future? Have we thought it out quite well before we make decisions? When do we start making decisions for our families; for our children?

The reason I started with the children is because everybody at one time or another was a child. It doesn't matter what nation that you were born in - you were a child. It doesn't matter what part of the world that you came from - you were a child. Even Jesus Christ was a child. Mary was a child. The only person that I know that we cannot visualize him being a child is God Almighty. Since He wasn't a child, He must be the beginning of everything that makes us human. So, if we need ideas and thoughts and coaching, it looks like He would be the one that we should go to.

The reason I thought about schooling is because that is what we are doing when the child is first born; the first day. Even some of our scientists and counselors say it's a great idea to start talking to your baby before it even gets here. That child is inside of you and you have a relationship to it; you three: mother, father and baby. Perhaps even more that three are united with that child. At least you should be and you certainly are before it gets here. Before the child gets to a woman, it's in the man and before it gets us, it's in the woman. What I'm trying to say is that there is nothing on this earth that should be more close to you and that you should be more united to, than your child. That is the most important thing that you have in your life; God, your wife, and your child. These four things are connected tightly; God, man, woman and your child. I want to know what you think about this idea that I have that maybe, just maybe, that we have leaped too far from the womb. Or that maybe we've gotten a great idea about what we want that child to be before we have shaken it, before we have given it the roots and foundation or the soil that it's supposed to grow up in. If you want a good plant, you'll go somewhere and get good soil or you'll plant it in a piece of ground that you think it will make it grow well. We have to look at ourselves as that soil that the child develops from. You can call it a foundation or you can call it soil or whatever you want to call it.

You certainly wouldn't put a flower pot over a volcano. But it looks like that's what we're doing with our children when we send them out in the world to be educated by someone that doesn't even know them and has to become acquainted with them somewhat, and give them something that they may not be trained to handle. There is no professor or school teacher or doctor or counselor or psychologist or psychiatrist that is going to be able to give your child the love that you can give it. No one is going to know your child's emotions like you know them. No one should know your children as well as you know them. Maybe before we get to where we need to go, we pushed it out of the nest too early. We are so busy making a dollar to send our kids to college and the school we don't give them the foundation that supports them when they get out of the college so they can deal with them. They are not able to analyze it. They're pushed out in the world before they have their grass roots training.

We are so anxious to get to our job in the morning we don't have time to pray with them. They don't see us praying in our homes. Some of the most serious Christians that we know don't pray with their children in the morning. (Now for some sarcasm: Of course, I know there's nobody here that doesn't do and I'm sure that you've done that all your life - prayed with your child before he left in the morning. You prayed with your child before he went to bed last night.) I'm sure you did that. If you didn't do that – if you didn't do that – think about what it would mean to somebody's life if you started to do that now with what you have; even if he's not your own child. Wouldn't it be wonderful if we could put some kind of literature out that would teach people and tell people and mess with people's conscience so badly that they would become interested in more than just themselves and more than just the money?

Good, strong-minded people, people who are grounded in a foundation with morals and prayer in their homes continuously – you know it's not enough for our children to see us living a good, strong life. It's not enough for our community to see us living a good, strong, decent, and intelligent life. They need to see something of our hearts. They need to see the spirit in us moving. They need to see some God in us. They need to see some love in us. They need to see some hope in us. It doesn't matter whether he's a sinner or if he doesn't believe in God or a Satan worshiper. It doesn't matter if he's a Ku Klux Klan. It doesn't matter if he's Hitler's best friend. He needs to see something of value in us that stands out so much until it disturbs that person. Money; if that's all you're sending a child to college for is to make money you might have blown it. You might have missed the whole point. I believe that we are here to build characters not only in ourselves but in other people. I believe we're supposed to see something in this world that needs to be corrected because there is enough stuff out there that needs to be corrected that we have great ideas about changing it. It may be our strengths. It may be a light somewhere. It may be a life somewhere.

Our children don't get the attention, love, kindness, or touching sometimes at home that they get in a gang somewhere. They decide that they want to make money and they see so much mess going out there that we have allowed to be out there, that they get involved in it. It has more influence on them than what we have on them because they have more to do with it. They deal with the intimate and the serious part of that individual. They deal with the emotions of that person. When the person is angry or when he's hungry for money, hungry for dope or whatever, they see their feelings and they see their hurt in each other and they've felt it. It can be negative. It doesn't have to be a good kind of nourishment that they get but it's the attention that they draw from them and the lifestyle that we live will depend on who we are and what we are. I don't know what you get out of that but you need to think about it.

Some of us feel like we have arrived and have achieved so much that we have grown past the man that is out in the street; the people hustling, selling dope, and the women selling their bodies. We feel like we don't want to be bothered with that mess. We want that hidden somewhere. We can't say that we don't see them if we open up our eyes. They are begging and crying for help and for someone to talk to, but they don't dare come to a man of the cross or they won't dare come to someone that claims to be a devout Christian. It is because we seem to be so holy that we're untouchable. No one can put their hands on us. We're so high and mighty. If we bring ourselves down to a level of who we used to be.

What I mean is, look back over your life. Take an evaluation of the way you used to be, the way you used to think and how you hurt. There is nobody that hasn't hurt at one time or hasn't had problems at one time or another. Maybe you didn't have the problem that some of the people out there have, the ones that are on dope or hooked on stealing and robbing and misusing people. Maybe you didn't have that kind, but you've had a kind of a hurt. You wanted to have someone to go to talk to. You see, you can't wait all the time until someone comes to you and almost drops dead on your doorstep. Sometimes you've got to make yourself available to people. Sometimes you've got to approach people when it's not comfortable to approach them. Sometimes you can go and talk to people about things that you believe are right; something that you think that they should be doing and if they would do that it would give them a better lifestyle. Sometimes you just have to approach them and break through the shield that you've got in the front of you. Sometimes you have to let people know you really love them. You can't talk about how much you love people and then stand there and see people dying over the things that you know you could at least tell them about. You could tell them about going in a different direction. It might turn their life completely around, and it may not. But at least you had the opportunity of telling them. You took the opportunity to tell them about a different way.

THE CHRISTIAN HOME

When a structure begins to crumble, we look to its foundations for the source of its weakness. One of the foundations on which our society was built was the sanctity of marriage and the home. Today we witness the erosion of this foundation. The divorce courts are filled. Discipline and authority are almost forgotten words in the homes. There is" little filial [parental] respect and love. This lack of respect carries over into society and manifests basic Christian "morality apart from the foundation of morality, a vital faith.

We desire to expose our children to a variety of philosophies of life and so enthusiastically support "neutral" State education. Yet the very concept of neutrality toward Christianity and God is hostile to the Christian view of God as the Foundation of all life and thought. We have left God out of our thinking and so our homes lack stability and are collapsing.

With alarming rapidity we are becoming a generation of dependents and thus are not rearing children with the moral stamina to meet the demands of this fearful, yet challenging age. This dependent spirit displays itself in our looking increasingly to the State as the provider for our wants and pleasures and the guarantor of our security. Like the Roman citizens in the wake of the fall of that mighty empire, we look to the State for "bread and circuses." But like Rome, we too are threatened by a powerful foe. This one has promised to bury us and boasts that it is already ahead of schedule in effecting the conquest.

The edifice of society is crumbling because the foundations of a virulent Christianity have been seriously eroded. If the building is not to fall upon us, we must hasten to strengthen the foundations in making our homes God-centered. We can know neither ourselves nor the world aright apart from knowing our Creator. God has revealed something of Himself to us in the Scriptures. He has shown us the way to life. He has given us principles to guide our conduct. The true Christian, knowing as Lord the One to Whom he must render an account, seeks in his calling faithfully to serve God. He knows the only gateway to the divine blessing in all his family and social relationships lies along the pathway of love and obedience to God. Nor can he lightly permit the individual whom Christ redeemed to become lost in the mass or a slave to the State. This faith in God he seeks by precept and example to pass down to his children.

God has ordained that in the home there is to be a relationship of authority and submission in love. Thus the home is ideally suited to inculcate the relationship of love and submission that should exist between man and God and submission to all duly constituted authority. He who has learned to honor his parents and to worship God in the home (and families that worship together will stay together.) will not find it hard to submit to the authority which God has given to the State to suppress evil.

The responsibility of parents for the spiritual welfare of their children involves training their minds. True knowledge begins with God and relates the knowledge of the created universe to Him. Hence, the importance of Christian schools, with a consistently Christian education, in strengthening the foundations of society. Morals are an integral part of education. It is the Christian faith nurtured in the Christian home that provides a solid basis for morality, without which the pillars of society cannot stand.

In the intimate relationships of the Christian home, parents and children alike best learn the meaning of love as they work, play, and study together. Here the cooperation and non-coercion so essential to the functioning of society are best taught by precept and example.

The home is one of the foundation stones of our society that has been badly eroded. But it is one of the places where we each of us can effectively have an important part in strengthening the foundation. We can do this by making our homes God-centered, truly Christian homes.

By Dr. Gary T. Johnson

The world is in turmoil. Disaster appears to be showing up everywhere. Our nation is troubled from the government, to the state, to our communities. Some of us think our young people have lost control. I believe the young people of this nation are our greatest resources. I believe that when we re-evaluate ourselves, we have to go all the way back to the cradle. We have to go back to our beginning and understand where we come from. What was our teaching and what resources did we have in order to get where we are today? How much appreciation have we shown our parents? What did they give us of value? How well have we been taught? How much have we given in return to the things on this Earth that we have received? How much emphasis have we put on love? How much have we received from humanity? And what is God and man's relationship to humanity? Oh, my God! That phrase has tortured me and troubled me in my soul.

You know, life is something to be examined. Our children are troubled with this world's problems. And most of the problems that our children have today, we made those problems. You see, we've had this Earth ever since God gave it to us. Ever since He gave us this world, we've been in charge of it. Maybe the phrase "in charge" is questionable. Maybe we've just been in the world, but God gave it to us to manage with His supervision. If we have accepted Christ in our lives and He has been the most important person in our lives, then we should have done rather well. But when I evaluate my part on this Earth, I find that I've done rather poorly and that's why I'm angry. That's why I'm angry with me. And to be attacked by that phrase "God and man's relationship to humanity" I thought that even for me to think about the big awesome task that was involved in that, that it was being unfair to me. Was I looking at it the way God would look at it, the way Christ would see it? Have I been a hypocrite all these years? Why is my soul so troubled?

By Guy P. Darden, Sr.

LIVING AND DYING

Hello. How are you? My name is Guy Darden. I'm trying to get a few things out here to our ladies and men all over this nation; boys and girls. One thing I want you to know, I'm talking to believers, unbelievers, and all of those in between.

All of the people that I've met and known on this earth, we all have some hang-ups. We all have problems that are hard to deal with. Living and dying on this earth is not all we have to do; not just come here and live for our personal and intimate life, and die and go away. You see, whatever we found here when we came here, we are supposed to feel for ourselves and others. We're supposed to do the best we can to maintain it, be good stewards of it.

With what I know now about human beings, if this world was perfect today, we would find it a hard place to live in as it is. You can't live on this earth just looking out for you and your family. We've got to realize that we have other people that live here with us. Whether they have our same belief or not, we've got to impress them well enough so they feel that we are not a threat to them.

When you live in this society and you don't care about anybody but just yourself, you're going to have a struggle on this earth because we can't live by ourselves. I don't care if you're a billionaire, you can't live by yourself. You need somebody to help you on this earth. So that is the reason that I say if you really love somebody then you need to show them what love does, whether it's a fascination or is something that is free and that develops in us through God Almighty.

I love me. I've got to love me and I've got to love you if I love me. Now, I'll tell you something, they tell me I'm supposed to love you as I love myself. I have a hang-up and I'm trying to work with it. I've found it to be one of the hardest things I ever tried to be; is to love my neighbor as I love myself. Now a neighbor doesn't necessarily mean that you have to live next door to me but it means that you're human and you're on this earth and I'm to show you love when you come around me or when you come in my environment. Even if you don't, I'm supposed to love humankind. I'm supposed to want you to have this necessity as I do. You need life and the things that it takes to make you viable. To love your neighbor as yourself doesn't mean that you go over to his house and feed him as you feed yourself. But it means if he needs something and you have the opportunity to give him or assist him in the same needs as you would assist yourself; you respect him as you respect yourself. If you were hungry and didn't have anything to eat and you were a healthy and vibrant person, and the only reason you didn't have anything to eat is because you were too lazy and too trifling to go and get it; to go and get the job that you needed to supply yourself with the necessary things that you need to feed your family or yourself – even if you didn't have to feed anyone but yourself, in that case, it means I would come to you. Talk with you and try to show you, try to inspire you in making a living for yourself. I would insist, if you were supposed to be my friend.

I'm supposed to love you and care for you. I would keep right on coming at you in the best way I knew how. And God Almighty will always give us the wisdom and the knowledge that we need to deal with people. People who are just lazy and uninspired to do anything for themselves; I wouldn't want anybody to do anything for me like that. That type of person is not the type of person that God is talking about. Except that you are to love him and love him enough to go out of your way and take the chance of being insulted; take the chance of insulting him. Don't be so concerned about how much he likes you or be so concerned about him cursing you out, as far as that is concerned, or punching you in the eye. God will give you the diplomatic spirit and the diplomatic feeling. The love that you have for him will allow you to deal with him in God's way, not your way.

You see people in your community where drugs have taken over their lives and they are being defeated, or perhaps already have been defeated. They gave up to drugs and they allowed themselves to go even lower than that. They are not even able to have food to eat and they've gotten so weak that they're not even able to have a place to stay. They don't have the means of cleansing themselves and they are gone all the way out where diseases and sin have taken over their bodies. They've lost their pride and go into public places and beg. That individual is not allowed to do that spiritually, physically, or lawfully. All these things that I mention here violate every one of them. When you don't go to him with love and deep humility and do everything that God has for you to do to assist that person in bringing him back to reality, then you haven't done the things that you're supposed to do. When you allow your community to be eaten up by outlaws and drug lords; to allow you community to become destroyed and contaminated, whatever imaginable type of crime that they can do to keep from going out and getting a decent job, you've violated everything that God stood for.

You can't tell me you love your community and you allow it to be destroyed, or you sit around, or move away, or talk about how bad that "those people" are down there and you're not trying to reclaim them and reclaim your community. When the people in your community become contaminated, your community becomes contaminated. When the community is contaminated, the state becomes contaminated. It's like a cancer. If one segment of your society, racial or however it may be, starts pulling everything down around it, then you've got to get the cancer out. You can't just throw words around about I love you. You've got to have some action in your life that has more than just lip service in it. Those of us that say we love God we have to make it visible. People don't know what's inside of you until you bring it outside.

Your body is the temple of God and your heart is where the Holy Spirit dwells. When you have all of that going on in you and none of it comes out, then I challenge you to tell me what your motive is for holding it inside. If you are a Godly person then you ought to be able to deal with un-Godly people. You should be able to ask God to show you how to deal with this. If you want to help people, you've got to help yourself first. You've got to get yourself prepared to be able to go to battle in a Godly fashion; not a manly fashion, not a, 'I'm going to do this my way or the highway', 'you either do what I tell you to do or you do nothing'. No. You do what God tells you to do. You can't lock up your wisdom and knowledge because you're frightened. You can't do that. You can't tell me don't go out there on those streets because it's dangerous out there. You don't have to tell me there are things out there. I know it. I see it every day. But what good is a god if he can't protect you from another human? These aren't gods out there. God's love in you is stronger than the hate in them. Who is 'them'? They are our children, grandchildren, and friends that have allowed themselves to become involved in the wrong aspects in life.

It's not just only the dope addicts, prostitutes, hoodlums and gangsters that are destroying this nation. It's those who say and go around talking about how much they love God and the people out in the world don't see any Godliness in them. They don't represent

God. They represent themselves. The things that you hang on your walls, or the things that you have in your garage, or the things that you have in your closet does not impress God.

You can tell me about God and how to save myself. But until you have shown me some examples, my wheels are going to spin. I don't have anything to draw from, as you say you have.

You know the reason I think that those of you who haven't decided to accept Christ in your life perhaps it's because all the things that we say that we are and say that you are not. I think the next thing is, because we're just talking important. I believe you, as a layman, and you are like me in that we have sat on the sidelines and talked about what other people should do so long. You haven't been blind and you have been watching us because you have some experience about wrongdoing, just like most of us have. We've been out there in that street messing up most of our lives. But we have been doing it behind closed doors. We did so much of it, and so many of our friends that we were doing it with, know what we were doing until we, as a Christian community, are sometimes a little bit embarrassed. We're embarrassed to tell you what to do because we've done so badly ourselves. I don't mean we went out and murdered anyone. I don't mean we've been robbing and stealing. But we've done an abundance of wrongdoing and we handicapped ourselves a little. You were out there sometimes when we were out there too. You just haven't come in yet. You know a little bit about our lifestyle, especially on the sinner's side. Even after we got saved, or so called saved or church-going people, you still see us blowing it. You're not all that excited about what we say. The only way we can move you is by what we do, and we don't do very much.

I've had a few people in a few places that I've made a few talks; they say I'm attacking the church. I'm attacking the ministers. They said they are under attack. They certainly are. They are under attack by the Devil. He's attacking them. I'm not the Devil, but I've been out there in the world the same as anybody else doing devilish things and then coming back in the church and using the Holy quilt to pull over my head. It doesn't work. It doesn't even work for the people that are in the church let alone the people that are out of the church. It doesn't work for me as a church-going person in my intimate and personal life. You see, you're not hiding from God. You hide from me. You hide from the preacher.

You hide from your neighbors and your friends; and you don't always hide from them because they know the same system that you use.

Do you know that some of the people are going through a living hell out there on the streets? We prefer to go through that rather than what they'll get when they come in the church. They say, "I would go to church but I don't have any money. I would go to church but I don't have anything to wear". The window dressing of this world has caused us more damage than anything else on the face of God's green earth, and not only to the Christian community but our society. Oh, am I guilty of that.

I'm so guilty of covering up things; covering up my personal life. Over 50 years I covered up my inability to read and write. It strangled me to death almost. I died a spiritual life so many times. I had to show off and make people think I was somebody special; most of the time it did work. They thought it for a while. But I'm quite sure some of them saw the things I did and the way I lived my life that I wasn't all that I was acting like I was. I lived through a living hell trying to hide everything that was inside of me. I didn't allow myself to purge myself; to bring out the things that were condemning me from in my spirit. I'm not attacking the church. The church is in your heart. The church should stand for love. If a fellow doesn't have the proper clothes to wear, that shouldn't keep him from coming to church. If he has a little odor on him, that shouldn't keep him from coming to church. If he doesn't have a single dime on this earth, that shouldn't keep him from coming to church. You shouldn't expect him to give you any money. You should look for his presence, striving to receive the Lord in his life.

You speak about tithes and offerings. I let you know where I stand. I believe in tithes and offerings. I believe you should give them abundantly. I believe the church building; the prayer house, the repair shop that place where you go to get your broken pieces put back together and someone there to show you how to repair despair and corruption in your life – these are the things that you need to talk to people long before you consider asking them for money. I don't want you to forget and I want you to put deep, deep essence on this. God said money, the love of money – I repeat that – the love of money is the root of some evil, a little evil, maybe no. The love of money is the root of all evil – all evil. I want you to know, just to give you something to look at here.

They didn't bring slaves over here to this country, imported them all the way from Africa and other countries, because they wanted to make pets out of them. There was no place for them to be at over there. The people who sold them over there to the Americans and the English and other countries I imagine, I don't know that, but I do know that this nation imported us as a commodity to this nation. They didn't bring them over here because they thought they were sub-human or they were going to bring them over here and teach them the American way; no. They brought them over here to work so they wouldn't have to hire anybody and pay them a salary. They brought them over here for the love of money - the love of money. That's why. No other reason.

In the North, free slaves, because they thought they ought to be free, it was an injustice that they thought was an awful thing that they did and it wasn't fair. These people are human like we are and they shouldn't be slaves. That's not right. No, that's not the reason. They did it because the South had a disadvantage over the North. They didn't have to pay their people anything for them to work. They did it to preserve the Union. They did it so they could have an equalized economy. They did it for the love of money. They didn't beat up on the slaves for a reason they thought was something bad. They did it because if a slave knew how to read and write, he would learn something about his history. He would have something to draw from.

They read him that part in the Bible that says, slave obey your master – obey your master. They did that for the love of money. That was something in there that made him think that he was being honorable to God; to present himself as an honorable and obedient slave. You are only supposed to be an honorable and obedient slave for God Almighty and doing the work of God. I want you to understand what kind of love we're talking about is a different type of love that all things that control you and make you a slave are really not your master. It's not your master.

You only have one master, and that's God Almighty. He can control you and do what He wants to do with you any time He wants to. He is truly your Master. You're not in command of your life when you surrender your life to God. He's in charge of you. He's in control of you when you surrender your life to God. He's in control. But until you do that, He just gives you His grace to keep you alive and allow you float; kind of like putting you on a level playing field with the rest of the world that is just going along doing their own thing and leaving God out. Grace keeps you alive and keeps you functioning because He gave that to you. He loves you and you're a part of Him. You have His blessing. If you don't believe it, just stop using it and He'll take it back.

I said all those things to lead you into this extremely controversial thing that I must say. And the word *all* covers too much. You can't use the word *all* when you speak about the thing that I am speaking out now. But I can say this without any apologies because I've gone to church after church over this nation. I've heard good teaching and been accepted. I've had bad teaching and been accepted. I've accepted things all over this earth because I made the choice to do so. I made a decision, most of my life, to do the things that I wanted to do, not the things that I needed to do. It's gotten me in a lot of trouble. Now, I'm doing something that I need to do and want to do, and it's going to get me in a lot of trouble. I know. I'm not guessing. It's not a maybe. God is leading me to do this. And for the first time in my life, I'm being obedient to God's command.

Sometimes I would like to open up my heart, open up my being and ask God to allow you to see my heart. Up to this point in my life I haven't done very much to show people the essence of the love that I have inside of me. Some out of ignorance and some out of just doing what I thought I wanted to do. There are very few things that I needed to do, I did. I would consider myself a failure in many things, succeeding in very few. One thing I did rather well, I learned to be a good tailor. I haven't always done that my very best, but I did the best I knew how in my tailoring. I love it. God has blessed me so many times in that regard.

The Lord has truly blessed me in so many ways. I never got in any trouble with the police; only a couple times when I was a child. It never got me in any real heavy trouble. I tried to be law-abiding. Most of my ugliness was womanizing and drifting and floating all over the world instead of being stable. I was quick-tempered and I would fly off the handle. When you do that too much in life, you can stall your young life.

There is something that we've refused to tell our young people, most of us or least a lot of us, especially black people. We have not told how we got from back there to up here. It was due to our forefathers; our mothers and fathers. Maybe they didn't tell us about our accomplishments and things that we had in us that were stepping stones to success. They didn't teach us about our possibilities. They taught us about hard work. When I was a boy growing up my parents didn't see much future for the black person, so they didn't see the need, a lot of them, for giving us an educational background and tell us about how much we could accomplish out on the road of life. Some of them told us about the tough times. A lot of us told our young people about the struggles and how other people treated us. But we didn't tell them about a lot of our blessings. We were family-orientated in that time. Not only that, people in the workforce learned trades. When you went to find a job, you didn't necessarily have to know a lot about it. An employer would, if you couldn't read something or if you didn't know that job too well or if you'd never done that; if he knew a member of your family or knew a little bit about you, usually they would have you come on in. If something needed to be read, you wouldn't have a problem going over to somebody and they would read the instructions. Eventually they wouldn't have to read it to you, you would know it.

They took great pride in that. One of the reasons that an employer would do that is because he didn't have to pay you as much money as he did somebody that already knew it. It would probably take you a year before you would get a raise and then another year before you get another raise. You worked your way up. Once you learned something from scratch like that, you really got it. Sometimes you would know how to do that just as good as someone that was a professional at it that learned it from school. And sometimes, the people that came from school wouldn't have anything but the theory and you could teach him and show him how to do their job even better.

I've taught trained foremen how to do the physical work. I've trained people who had been to school for tailoring and they would come on the job. They just went to school for it and they hadn't done very much of it. They would come on the job and I would show them and teach them. You appreciate people like that, that have the experience.

Money is valuable for the church to be a distribution center; spiritually, physically, and otherwise. But we look at this hand like we hold our prayer hands and bow to the church as if we worship of the church. You don't worship the church building. You worship God in that building and you bring truth and Godly beliefs in that building and you pass it on to the people. That is a building for teaching. That's a building were you teach people how to be disciples for God; to be missionaries for God. Every single person in that building should be some type of a missionary. I failed that test all my life. All I've ever done was just for a few friends and a few members of my family. I failed that obligation; to my family, to my children, to my wife. I failed it miserably. I failed so many times that I know what a failing grade is. Ladies and gentlemen, the church is a place that you go to get knowledge and wisdom about God, his lifestyle, and how he expects you to live. I believe that the ministers are supposed to teach you how to serve the people. You're not in there to not have an open house for Christians only; that is the place that sinners come to get saved too.

You know how it works and you've got to clean it up where He'll come in. He will not come in a filthy temple. He will not dwell in your home; in your house. Your body is the home for God. It is a temple for Holy Spirit to dwell in. He'll come inside of you and live in you and let you shine light on the world and He has shined light on you. Because you don't have any money or you don't have on a suit of clothes should not keep you from coming in the church. Blue jeans, tennis shoes, or even having no shoes should not keep you from coming in the church. Being a sinner or having no money to give to the church should not keep you from coming in the church.

You shouldn't, I don't believe, put so much emphasis on money in the church. Everybody that's able should give money to the church building. You should give money to the church leaders. The people of God that are serving in that church need money to do the service that they need to do and they need it abundantly. But what I don't understand is if they need money so bad why they aren't giving some to the community that they are in when they do get it. Because there is no way that the leaders of the church can give without receiving – no way. The more you give, the more you receive. In other words, it doubles and triples over what you do. Now, if you know that, for me and you say that to me, why you as officials of the church system don't use that same thing when we're talking about you as leaders of the community.

If your church's Godly people are doing what they need to do for themselves and God, as a leader of God – people, if you are a leader of God's people, then you'll teach them how to be a distribution center. You'll teach the church people how to manage that church and its funds to not just help the people in the building, not just help the pastor, or the leaders, but give them the muscle to go out in the community. Give them the audacity to take surveys of the community. If you are a Godly people, there is nothing wrong with having a business of a kind that makes money and generates funds to turn back into the community. To bring in the funds for you to have some kind of enterprise that generates funds that you can give the profit and assist the people that need it in the community. Pick out people in your congregation that know about finances, know about leadership, and every capacity that is needed. Find those in your church families, if you can. And if you can't, generate enough funds to have people to come in. Volunteers or how ever you can get them that can teach you and show you how to do the things that you need to do in the community. Then you start to move out. You can't just lock up everything we get and hold it in here for a pretty building and the pretty people.

Let's not have any misunderstanding here where I stand on this money situation. I believe if you and I are who we say we are, and we have accepted Christ in our lives, that we won't only just give 10%. We won't only just pay our tithes, but if you are a Godly person and you are being led by God and you are going by God's will and not your will, we will give every single dime that we can possibly give. We will give until it hurts and then we'll give some more. We will do everything in our power to see that God's work is getting done.

On this particular subject I believe that every human being that has money or works or doesn't work or however you get the funds, that you should give to the church as much as you possibly can. I believe the leaders of the church should respect that. But I don't believe if you don't have a dime, you don't need to feel bad because you don't have it to give. Give when you have it. If you don't do that then you're not doing God's will. So let's get that out of the way.

If the church does not have money, the management of that church is not going to be able to do the things that it needs to do. But in return, the church is supposed to give and share in that community to the fullest extent of its possibilities. It should do all it's supposed to do in the community. When you live in a community or have a congregation of people, you should be teaching them how to serve the community. Those pews are not made to just come in there and sit and sit and go back out and do the same as you've been doing in street; going home and serving yourself. You're supposed to serve people, serve humanity, and be a working human being in that community. Not only in that community, wherever you are needed. You're supposed to get the training out of those pews. You're not supposed to just sit there and be taught about just what you want to learn about. Some of the things that you are being taught, perhaps you don't even want to know it. But you have a responsibility to learn it because you have an obligation to your fellow man. The church is one place to get that type of teaching. If you minister is not giving you that type of teaching then I think you need to have a tremendous debate about that.

EDUCATION

I received my primary and secondary education from the public schools of Brooklyn, Amityville, Queens and Manhattan, New York.

I remember the Morning Prayer and the moment of silence, the pledge of Allegiance, the singing of the Star Spangle Banner, and the reciting of scripture.

I remember learning Amazing Grace, Sweet Chariot, and Won't You Sit Down in music class.

I remember that if your behavior took too much of the teachers time he or she would take you to the "board of education" (a foot long six inch wide paddle with holes in it). I also remember that if I told my parents. That I had met the board, before bed I met the belt that evening.

I remember getting into trouble for, cutting classes, sneaking into the girl's locker room, and saying "beep" when a friend was operating the film projector.

I remember when the older brother of a friend impregnated a classmate, she disappeared. While the official word from the teacher was she had moved to be with a sick relative, I, we knew better.

I believe I can safely say that when I went to school there was an unspoken cooperation, if you will, between the parents, teachers and schools.

We were paddled by our teachers, chaperoned by our teachers, and counseled by them. They talked to us about girls, sex, drinking and drugs. They coached us, brought us lunch, encouraged us concerning our futures, and directed us into careers they believed were best suited for us.

To Mr. Izzi, Mr. Reese, Mr., Williamson, The Brock Twins, Mr. Burns, Mrs. King, Mrs. Fraction, the uncle and nephew team, and all the others whose faces and voices are vivid and clear, thank you!

This article is not about my experience in the New York State Public School System. This article is about Christian Education and why I believe it is important and needed today.

Four and five year olds reading and comprehending, writing in cursive, quoting scripture, and grasping not only yes and no, but right and wrong. Students in grades first through fifth are reading above grade level.

Grades in English, math and science that are above the state average. Students not only learning, but developing a love for learning. Teachers who see teaching as ministry. Investing in and making a difference in the lives of God's future army and America's future citizens.

Each student being prayed for, nurtured, loved, disciplined and supported. Parents encouraging the interaction between teacher and student.

Smaller classes so that there is enough time for teachers to teach, instruct, and reinforce with each individual student, How about this no guns! No knives, drugs, or cursing. Yes we do see the occasional name calling, silly disagreements, tattle telling and talking without raising hands.

Public school teachers would say "If this is heaven, let me die now". If the only problems they dealt with daily were those I just mentioned.

Yet I am personally aware of the recruitment of teenage male and female escorts (prostitutes) on the campus of one of the city high schools in which I reside.

In the corridors of our middle schools and high schools children are involved in heavy petting in the view of their peers and teachers. Young people have no problem discussing sex in schools today. In some of our schools it's not unusual to hear a 12, 13, 14 or 15- year-old discussing sexual activities openly.

Provocative dressers, gang bangers, sex, drugs, and cell phones. That which goes on in our public schools today would have been material for a steamy adult paper back thirty-five years ago.

As a parent one of my greatest challenges and fears came from the unknown and the uncontrollable. As long as my sons were home I could control what they were told, what they saw, were taught, and what they did or didn't do.

However, once they left home the only control I had was the parental influence of the love, nurturing, discipline and training I had given them, I could not control the moral values of the other children they went to school with or even played with in our neighborhood. I had no control over what they saw at a friend's house or might see or hear that came from a friend's house.

In fifty-two years of living and learning, I've found that most people treat other people's children kindly. They say nice things to them, offer them cookies and don't hit them. They treat them like one of their own.

So if their child watches "R" movies, guess what? So, does yours. If their child hears the "F"' or "S" word or any other word, that's right, so does yours. The list goes on and on.

It is said that there are only six people separating us from other people. You and I have never met. But each of us knows someone, who knows someone, who knows someone, who knows someone, who knows both of us. So, there is a strong possibility that you and I will meet.

So how large is the public school your child attends? It doesn't matter large or small, someone at that school knows someone, who knows someone, who knows someone who, knows someone who is a dope smoking, gang banging, beer drinking, card playing, masturbating, cigarette smoking, gun toting, lying student at the school, who knows someone, who knows your child. It's just a matter of time. Someone will make the introduction and you won't have control.

My son's didn't see their first "R" movie at home. We didn't allow it. If their first" R" movie was seen at a friends house. Drinking and smoking were not learned or seen at home; it was seen and learned outside of the home.

Profanity and pornography were not used in our home. The first nudity book found by my wife was not one I had brought home, but one my son got from a friend.

The gun pointed in my son's face, at point blank range, wasn't done at a place I'd taken him or told him about. It happened at a place where all in attendance were from his school.

If you ascribe to the Tooth Fairy, Easter Bunny, Santa or Mother Goose, before you can come clean, someone else or your child's friend will.

Take a moment, consider what outside influences are in contact with your child. What questions are they asking, that aren't from the foundation and training that you've given them. This will give you some idea of how much control you may or may not have, or could have, or be in danger of losing.

Mom, Dad, if you don't already know it, you'll soon find out there is a period of time when it appears that everyone else in your child's life has more influence over the choices they make than you.

Face it! Once our children leave our sight, there is no way of knowing who they will come in contact with and what new information, good, bad, or indifferent, they will come in contact with.

Raising children isn't easy. Someone said "It takes a village". If it does you definitely need a like minded village. What appears to be dysfunctional to one individual, may well be in the norm for another.

The larger the sea, the greater variety of fish in it. Any novice fisherman will tell you. Every pretty fish isn't an eatable fish. Try telling that to your children.

I believe the most important and challenging job you and I face in our life time is raising our children.

One day Cain left his father's house and came in contact with the spirit of the world outside his home. Even though he could hear the words of his father ringing in his ear," Cain do good, do what's right and God will honor and accept you". For one moment the spirit of the world around Cain, became greater than the love, nurturing, discipline, and training his parents had worked so hard to instill in him. Cain killed his brother Abel.

So, what if you were able to have more control over those eight hours your children are away from you in that sea we call PUBLIC EDUCATION!

The scriptures teach that God fashioned every man's heart the same. Think about that! The doctor, the lawyer, the butcher and the baker all began life the same. The most hardened criminal, and the individual who guards them. Each began life the same. The optimists and the pessimists, both began life the same. An empty slate open and waiting not only to be nurtured and loved, but written upon and poured into to.

By the time children are five years old, the age when the foundation has been laid, that determines how they will learn, reason and behave, it is possible for them to have spent some fourteen thousand plus hours in environments where their parents have little or no control. The more public the environment the less control you and I have.

That which has cost nothing, public education, could well cost us and our child plenty; their spiritual and intellectual well being.

Scripture also teaches us that we are to teach, train, and raise our children in the way they should live and conduct their lives. If one does this the counsel and promise of scripture are two fold. First what you instill in your child, will remain in your child. The teaching, training, love, nurturing, advice and example, you put in your child, stays with them. Second, that which is in your child is what your child will come back to. He or she has to. It's their foundation, their basics. The teaching and training won't leave them and they can't leave it. No matter how far our children stray from our teaching, training, love, nurturing and example, God promises that they will return to it.

It has been said, (especially in the black community) "We have lost our children, to the streets". I don't agree with that, but if we have lost our children, it's our fault. We have delegated our parental responsibility of raising our children to, daycare, head start, public schools, after school centers, television, and their friend's house.

Remember, God entrusted you with an empty slate, open and ready to be written upon and poured into. What about those sixteen thousand plus hours of your child's first five years? What about those eight hours or more each day your child is away from you?

Do you pray with your child? How much prayer is being conducted in the environment your child is in right now? We sat by while they took prayer out of public school. Do you discipline your child? How much and what type of discipline is being conducted in the environment your child is in now. Do you monitor and sensor what your child, watches, reads or listens to. How much of that is being done in the environment that your child is in now. Surely you set examples for your child. What type of example is being set for your child in the environment he or she is now in?

So the question is what your child is absorbing from the television, friend's house, after school center, school house or other environment that you would disapprove of.

If you are unable to have your beliefs and values, reinforced during those hours your children are away from you. Then what they are seeing, hearing and doing daily in these environments are doing more to shape them than you realize.

They are helping to build a second belief and value system within your child. Another foundation if you will. One that will call into question what you are instructing, teaching, and living before them. Abraham Lincoln may have made it famous, but Jesus said it first. "A house divided cannot stand". Our prosperity are failing and failing as children and adults because they were and are being raised in houses divided. We are allowing them to spend too much time in environments that are out of our control too soon.

They are hearing us pray, and then sent to a place where they can't pray or are told pray to yourself. We tell them what's right and wrong, and then we send them to a place where there is no right and wrong. We tell them to work hard, it will pay off, and then we will send them to a place where they must be politically correct. Children are funny; they think everyone is going to bed at 8:00 pm, until someone tells them I stay up till 10:00. The days of college will come soon enough when they will be out of sight as well at out of your control. Make a decision today. Exercise more control in the life of your children. You only get to raise them once, and then you have a life time to see the results of your efforts.

Godly principles and godly living will get our children far in life. How can a child learn and practice godly principles and living in a place where they aren't allowed to call on God's name.

I said earlier this article wasn't about my being educated in the New York State School System. But my belief in Christian Education, I've seen it change lives, I believe there are only two places where God can be called upon, His advice and counsel sought and His help asked for and no one can stop you- your home and your church.

The home is the first place we begin learning. God made it that way. We learn to obey authority, right and wrong, to share with and how to get along with others. If it's a godly home we learn to pray, read and practice the scripture and worship God.

It is when we leave the home we are open to new views and ideas. Teaching and instruction without reinforcement, isn't teaching and instruction, it is the sharing of ideas. If your beliefs and values are not being reinforced you aren't doing all you can to help your children. What's needed then is an extension of the home.

The church sponsored school is where you will find this extension. This is where you will find the avenue you need to have your beliefs and values reinforced and your children taught, not only academics, but God's rules for life.

I once read a t-shirt that said, "Life is hard so pray harder". I agree, but nothing will replace laying the right foundation in the lives of our children. Not only is life hard, you also must live it.

Reflecting back over my life, remembering the lives of people, men and women I knew; those that were successful and those that were not. I observed the difference in their lives was the foundation that was laid. Those that went to prison and those that did not, the difference in their lives was the foundation that was laid. Of those that went to prison some were related and others were friends. Without fail I observed that getting away from what they were taught and trained got them there. Contact with home, praying, and Bible reading, sustained them there and getting back to their upbringing kept them from returning there.

Then there were those who couldn't break the prison or street habit. I observed these were the ones whose foundation had not been well laid.

God gave man three institutions. They are marriage and the family, human government and the church. At some point man should stop doing what he wants, the way he wants, when he wants and start obeying God.

I figure if God gave us these institutions, if we would follow His instructions our lives would be, if not problem free, worry free.

By Bishop Daniel J. Boone

TRUE GOSPEL MINISTRIES CHRISTIAN ACADEMY
1331 Carolina Highway, Suffolk, VA 23434

"Building tomorrow's leaders through academic excellence using Godly principles"

ALL ARE WELCOME HERE

We have been admonished in scripture to love. Therefore, TGMCA does not discriminate with regards to race, sex or national origin. Please call the TGMCA office to make an appointment for a school tour. Registration and financial details are available upon request.

Founder: Bishop Daniel W. Boone & Mrs. Deidre Hester

LOVE LIFE

Ladies and gentlemen, boys and girls, how are you doing? I hope this day will find you excited about life in a Godly and loving way. Before I say all the things that you may agree or disagree with, I think you need to know why I'm saying this. Right off the bat, the reason I'm saying this is because I'm a person that loves human beings. I don't always like some of the things that they do that are not nice to humanity. I don't always like an individual ideas and thoughts. I might think that they are twisted and out of line with my ideas and thoughts. If I'm thinking about the way you are acting and that allows me to not have an open mind to try to understand you're environment and your philosophy, if you have one, or just your ideas and thoughts; I need to have an open mind to that. That's the only way that we can try to have a relationship with each other. When I say a relationship with each other – we live on this earth together and to agree or disagree we've got to make it so that we can live and compliment each other from some direction. We can't have a society that is viable and constructive based on fighting and fussing and trying to 'I'm going to win over you and you're going to win over me'. No.

That word that you hear thrown around so loosely in this day and time, called love, has a power structure in it. It has something else that nothing else on the face of God's green earth has been able to survive through the millions of years; ever since God there has been love because God is love. What I'm trying to do is draw you a picture the way I see life and the way I have understood it up until this point.

Most of the things I will tell you, I never did them myself. That's the reason I know so much about wrong-doing and things that don't work, things that can tear your character down, and things that can destroy your foundation to build great things. Greatness is not something that is lying around some place on a junk pile, rusting out. Greatness is within our being. It is inside of us. It's the essence of who we are. If we can open up our hearts and reach down into the essence of who we are, and ask God to activate the love that is in us, I can listen to you even though I may not like what you are saying to me.

This thing "I", "just me", "I", "me and mine", doesn't carry us through life running smoothly. But if you have love in your life and you have love that is active; love that's been activated and it's on the move, it will show through your life. A lot of us think we don't have love and some of us think that love is based on affection. They think that love is that thing that is in two individuals that have a personal encounter; that it may a have a sexual orientation. It may be joined together with just your family and you use love just in that family unit. If that's the kind of love that you have, you may be heading out in the wrong direction.

There is nothing on this earth that is more important than the family unit. That's important. We have allowed it to disintegrate. Now, when I say 'we', I've allowed that to happen. I don't mean every family in United States. There is one thing that I admire about yesterday, back in the times when I was a young man, we had a strong – most people – had a strong family unit. For a while I thought that I didn't have a family unit because of the way that some members of family acted. It gave me the wrong impression about my family tree at the ground roots. When that happens, you're going to have a struggle throughout your lifetime because you don't have a foundation that can carry you through the things that you need to go through. You're going to spin your wheels a lot. But we can't allow that to give us a selfish motive today. I allowed it to be. I thought about no one but myself most of my life after that. I felt I had to make a way for myself and I lost a lot of traction by doing that.

The community was family orientated. A person who was drifting or floating around the country – all we needed to know was that he needed somebody, he was alone and we'd take him in and adopt him into our family. It was people that came up in our family that no one knew that they weren't blood related to us. We adopted him and people throughout our lifetime. We allow too much independence to come into the family and destroy the family structure, the foundation of the family, the moral value of a family. I want you to know that I'm not one of those that feel that morals of one man and the morals of another are not the same. They are not valued the same. My moral standard could be one thing and yours could be another; and both are right. No, I don't believe that. I don't believe it because I haven't always been up to what I call family morals. I think a Godly person, believing in God Almighty; I believe that type of person will have the right kind of morals. I don't believe that you can be a believer in God Almighty and in the way He set up the standards on this earth for you to live by and have different morals, one from another.

You can have different ways and different habits and that's different. That's what I call independent; things that you might do one way and I may do another but we are all reaching for the same goal. I have no problem with that. You may eat chicken and I may eat fish, or you may be a vegetarian; I have no problem with that. You may decide to go to church on Sunday, Saturday, Friday or you don't go at all; I have no problem with that. You may decide to serve your God at home by yourself; I really don't have a problem with that. If you truly believe in God and you are satisfied with that and it shows through your actions and in the way you live your life; I have no problem with that.

But love is basic. Love is all of you. You have to give what you need to give. God will give you intelligence, principles, and standards, and you will be able to judge for yourself where you need to be if God is in your life. He's already told you and you're close enough to Him to understand what He means now. If you don't understand it, He'll make you understand it. Not only that, the way I live my life in the front of you, and the way I live my life in my community, people will see the love in me. You can't have a blind love and people not know it. You can't possess love in your community and in your home and no one not know it. It is so powerful. It has so much essence in it and it will just make itself known.

The person you are talking to may not accept but they will know that you love them. The child that you bring up in your home, they may not understand love right now. They may not know that love sometimes will hurt the person that you are using it towards. When I say 'hurt' them, I mean their feelings. You may insult them and they may insult you, but that's not your business. That's God's business. You will not minister love to someone out of God's care. No, you will not minister love out of God's care. Because if you have love in you, the kind of love that is a Godly love, people will not misunderstand it. It will make itself known. It is ministered by the Holy Spirit, by the Holy Ghost and it has such a power structure that you can't possibly misunderstand it. You would have to be completely out of God's care to not understand that kind of love.

Everyone may not accept your love. Some people may reject it even though they know its love, they are not ready for it or they don't know they're ready for it. What I am trying to say is when you love someone, really love them, you may not always tell them what they want to hear. You may tell them what they need to hear. That may not sit so well with them but that's not your business, that's God's business. When you are dealing with people who haven't accepted Christ in their lives yet and you're dealing with their personalities, and sometimes their frustration, you have to remember when God dealt with you. You have to remember those times when you were so frustrated.

You have to deal with man on God's standard not the human standard. You have to talk men with God's principles. When you do that you did it with God's supervision. You don't go out on your own because if you do that, you're going to be at a lonely place. You're not going to be able to administer the needs of your fellow man.

I want to talk about some controversial things that I believe few people have talked about in so many years. I mean boldly come out and recognize and understand the seriousness of this. If we understood it, we have been walking around in the dark. If we understood it, we haven't wanted anybody to know we understood it or we just stuck our head in the sand and walked away from this thing.

Ever since the slaves were freed in the nation, the white people that were prejudiced and the ones that held us under suspicion from their teaching during the Jim Crowe days. I'm speaking about black people and people of different races that have been discriminated against and had problems being able to get on equal footing or an equal standard; or try to dominate the discrimination that we fought against so hard. Something is happening in this nation today that is portraying us, as a black people. This is hard to talk about. I walk through the streets of these cities, week in and week out. I've seen our country being destroyed, our communities being condemned and literally buildings being condemned because of our neglect. Communities are being destroyed because of our neglect. Young men and women are being destroyed because of our neglect. Drugs, prostitutes, gangsters and everything are roaming the streets of our cities. Theft and robbery and every imaginable kind of crime are going on out there. I walked through the streets trembling, scared to death. Then there is the worry about my automobile and the attempt to have it stolen. Every place I saw and walked by, gas stations, they are all locked up and the people are looking out of little peep holes. People are afraid to talk to you. These communities are mostly black people. I've seen communities that black people have moved into that were wonderful, lovely communities. Then you go back in 10 years and they have destroyed it. I saw a restaurant that I was afraid to go in. Five or six years before that, it was decent and beautiful. Now people where laying around in there sleeping. It was filthy and dirty – a flophouse. The owners are even scared to say anything to them about it.

We are allowing our generation of people to become contaminated with chaos. It's a statement of our society. We just keep moving away from it and not trying to deal with the problems that are going on there. The police officers; they are almost afraid to do anything about it. Free speech, free movement, and free to die as a bum. Drug addicts dying in the streets; nobody is making a move to do anything about it. The churches have walked away from it. The ministers throughout our country are refusing to touch this thing. We threw up our hands and walked away from it – just keep moving from one to community to the other.

I can no longer say that I'm not worried because they are allowing us to live in a way that almost all of our young people are going to be in prison. If a young man joins a gang and the excitement of unknown; once they get in it, they can't get out without help. We as a society are allowing this to happen in our nation. If there is someone out in your community selling drugs; we allow them to be out there. If there is someone that's running a gang in your community, it's because we allow that to happen. The police can't do anything about it if the community doesn't come together and back them up.

There is a way to stop this. We must come together as a community. It doesn't make a difference whether you belong to a church, whether you are a Christian, or whether you're a sinner. If you're intelligent and have decent morals, we all need to come together so we can come to some consensus to be able to handle the situation. We can't lock ourselves up behind the church doors and talk about how good we are or talk about how much we love each other. If your love doesn't go any further than the church door, I doubt very seriously if you love anybody. A Godly love is not hung up behind some church doors that don't go any further. A Godly love comes out in our communities and we work together as a team and do something other than just talk. I haven't done anything in my life other than just talk.

I'm going to do everything for the rest of these few years that I have left here on this earth to make the public aware and get them to stop sticking their heads in the sand. We as a Godly people, those of us standing behind the church doors and think that we can just stay inside of the church, keep our people in the church, and not allow them to go out in the streets and talk and share their lives with somebody; we've got to put our lives on the line or we're going to be destroyed. All our moral standards, everything that Martin Luther King, Jr. fought for is going down the drain. They are going to have a reason to not want us in their places.

They're tearing down our communities. They are taking those little huts that we used to live in and they're putting $200,000 and $300,000 homes there. They are putting businesses there. They are condemning our communities and making them commercial because there are not enough of us that live in the community that will sign a petition to not allow them do it because the ones that have money have moved away from those communities and they keep moving away. I don't care how far you go; it's going to follow you until you do something about it. You can't keep moving from communities then condemning them and moving and then condemning them. There is a certain segment of our society that wants us to do that. They want to get us out of the downtown areas and the business areas of the city, and they've got a good reason when they come down there and look at us and the way we are living our lives.

I'm a human being and said 'we'. The reason I said 'we' is because there is not a single soul down there; I don't care how low and how rotten and how terrible he has let his life disintegrate, he's still part of me as a human being. If he's a part of me then I love him. I don't care how rotten he is, how bad he smells, how ugly he looks, how much vulgarity he uses, or how many times he curses and swears at me, I still love him. I don't want him to pull me down there with him; not my race.

The time has come that I must speak up because my race is at stake. When I walk through the streets at night I don't see very many whites out there. I see mostly black people. There are people loitering around in the front of businesses and businesses have to put locks on and board their places up. People are afraid to go to the store because there might be a person out there begging and looking just like he's ready to tear you to pieces or jump on you at that minute. I was frightened. I've never been so frightened in my life and I'm not a scared kind of guy. I've been through some pretty rough times. I walked through the streets in Newark, New Jersey. I drove around there for 6 or 7 hours up in Orange, New Jersey. I drove around 10 or 12 hours and I was frightened to death.

A lot of our cities are getting like that throughout the nation. We need to draw it in because it's gone far enough. That's not called freedom to me. You don't have a right to infringe on other people's rights. That is not right. That is captivity.

There is going to come a time when our race is going to feel this pain. They are going to be pointing their fingers. Our jobs are being replaced all over this nation with foreign labor. I don't blame them for doing it because they've got nobody else to do it. They are willing to do it. The jobs the African Americans used to have, they gave them up. I say they gave them up because they've decided that they don't want to do cheap labor any more. They are being replaced. We think those jobs are beneath our integrity. Rather than work for $5, $6, or $7 an hour, a lot of us are turning in the wrong direction. I don't mean all black people are like that, just a few. But a very few sometimes can add up to a lot when they are doing crime rather than working.

The people that are on the lower end of the spectrum; and I don't believe they're doing it just because they want to; they're doing it because they didn't get the guidance back when they are younger. We have too many children raising children. We've got too many one parent families. We've got too many people that don't take their marriage oath seriously enough. We're buying what we want instead of what we need. We're buying the things that make us look good instead of us being good.

We're losing our toehold on life. We're becoming desensitized. We're becoming frightened and we're running from our shadows. It's soaking in all over this nation. We can't just talk about change. When we look at our communities and our cities, we don't see anything to draw on. We don't see any reason to put any money in the cities.

I understand why you hear people talking about private schools. I wouldn't want my son or daughter to go to the average public school in certain areas of the big city today. I never thought that I would ever make that statement. We can't afford to lose our public schools. If we lose our public schools, there is a certain segment of our society that is not going to be able to send their children to school.

We can give a person a choice. You get on a work program somewhere and allow your labor to mean something to you and the community that you live in or you're going to have to answer to labor laws. We don't need people loitering around in the streets and standing in front of people's businesses because they don't have a job and they're hungry. We need a program where they can go to help themselves and help others. That's not impossible. We need a program that will put clothes on them instead of the ones that they have that are so filthy that no one would dare hire you and let you come in your place of business. They need a dress code, those that work on these jobs. Let them know that they have a standard to live up to if they want to change their lives. If they don't want to change their lives, we cannot allow that to stop us from cleaning up our communities.

Sometimes what you want is not always what you need. We're going to have to start giving people some of the things that they need instead of so much of what they want; what they need to bring them back into the cycle. I'm tired of hearing people say what they want. We want a lot of things. I want stuff myself. I've wanted all my life, but me wanting didn't get it. When we start thinking more about what we wear than what we eat. When we start thinking more about our trendy clothes more than where and how we live and how we eat and how my children are getting along. We're getting too selfish. The people in the street are getting too selfish. The people that don't have a place to live are being too selfish. We're all allowing ourselves to be selfish. We're taking our labor force out of the cycle of producing and being productive. When people let themselves go and don't do anything for themselves and let their health and morals decay, they're pulling the nation down with it.

When a race of people start to allow themselves to become contaminated with the mess of this earth; the drugs, liquor, crimes, and all of the things that mess our lives up, you're not just messing up your own life. That's not just your business and your business alone; what you do in this nation, what you do in my community, what you do in my home. It is my business as well as it is yours when you start to contaminate the things that take for me to live on. I've got just as must of a right to feel free to walk down the street as you have to feel free to walk down the street, regardless of what part of society you are in or what you doing with life. I can't let your freedom infringe on mine. If I have a daughter, I don't want to see her raped or beaten up or her pocketbook snatched because she didn't act like you wanted her to act.

These streets have got to be cleaned up. This is not the way that we need to live. We can't allow one segment of our society to go down like that. If people in this nation can't afford to pay for all these prisons that are going up all over the nation – that's going to be the slave market of tomorrow. That is going to be the labor force of tomorrow.

I believe that you need to know about something even bigger. This is what I want to allow you to think about. I want to mess with your mind here, right now. I want to give you a brain storm. I want to set up a scenario that will make you think. Think about the things that are going on in these inner cities that we are allowing to happen. Do we have a segment of our society somewhere in this nation that wants our inner city schools to fail? Do we have a segment of our society that wants to condemn these lower standard houses; the houses that are being misused and the property is being abused? Do they have an environment that decent people and people of high integrity and high morals that don't want to be around them; that there are things going on that the inner city people are wanting to move out to the suburbs? If they move out, there won't be anything left in the city for poor people and the elderly people to look forward to.

Have you ever thought about that, just maybe, the corporations or the money-grabbing people maybe want this to happen so they can re-build a city with $150,000, $200,000, and $300,000 homes, and manufacturing plants and things that will be more convenient for them? Have you ever thought about those schools that you have now, that are public, that one day may be corporate schools; schools that are manufacturers? These schools might have presidents and supervisors and foremen that are operating them. If you have Fortune 500 companies running these schools are you going to see skyscrapers come up and you're only going to be able to go to certain classes of schools. There might be certain things that you're not going to be able to do anymore because you're not going to have the money to afford that occupation. Have you ever thought about that this nation is being put on the level of class standards and you're only going to be able to live in certain sections? It doesn't matter how black you are or how white you are, if you don't have the money. If you haven't been to certain schools and you don't have certain diplomas that you're not even going to be able to apply at that school. You see, the schools that you've been going to you were unable to learn that specific trade or occupation that you wanted to take up.

I believe personally, that the city wants to get rid of all the low rent housing. I don't mean all cities. I don't mean all states would tolerate it. I don't mean all people would tolerate it. But, I'm saying that it looks like that could be something that could happen. That's what it looks like to me. It looks like if that happens, the rich millionaires and billionaires would make a lot of money. I can see forced labor. I can see you being forced to work for a certain amount of money. All of the jobs are leaving this nation to keep from paying high salaries. There is no way on this earth that you can make a living if you don't have a job, or that you can support sending your kid to a school that can give him a decent education if you don't have a job. These jobs are leaving this country for one reason and one reason only, and that is to get cheap labor. The people that are asked to come in this country are coming in this country to work for cheap labor. They're not going to get paid very much. You are either going to work for the same thing they are working for or you're not going to have a job.

Many people to be imported to this country because they say that they can't find people in this country that will do those jobs. Yet, we've got thousands and thousands of young people that are on the streets today and they don't have a job. The reason they don't have a job is because they don't want to think about being a shoeshine boy. They don't want to think about being a dishwasher. They don't want to think about scrubbing floors and cleaning toilets. If you don't have any other opportunities and you don't have any other alternative, then there is one thing you're going to have to do and that's scrub floors, dig ditches or you're going to go to prison or you're going to get your brains blown out by somebody. You'll wind up being a drug addict and die in the street.

Elderly people are being housed. The reason they are being housed like that is because we don't have the family unit anymore. There are people 60, 70 and 80 years old, like me, living in a house with two people and plenty of room. But the young people don't want to live by the elderly people's rules these days. So we separate because we can't put up with each other anymore.

Love is not strong enough to pull us together. Love is not strong enough to do something about our standards, our integrity. Love in our life, the kind that we know about, is not strong enough to bring us under submission. The reason is because we haven't had God magnified in our lives the way we need Him. We've thought too much of the dollar. We took everyone out of our homes and sent our kids to the nursery. We don't have a mother that takes care of the family unit anymore. She doesn't have enough time to raise her children. Things and things are setting our standard.

This country is not broke or in debt because it has to be. It's in debt and it's going to be almost broke if we don't get our people back to work and we don't come back together as a family unit, and realize what is going on around us. There must be somebody on this earth that understands what is going on. We're allowing the cities to fall apart. We want them to fall apart. When I say 'we', I mean the power structure of this nation. We want to put a new thing in the city. We've got so much technology until technology has us. We don't have technology. Technology has taken us prisoner.

Between money and technology, we don't have anybody thinking about Godly principles that make us what we need to be. It looks like history is repeating itself. We're going to have a slave market here and we volunteered to be slaves because when you allow a country to fall apart, allowing its people to fall apart like this, you have no choice but to be an outcast. Only God can handle this now. Only your faith in God and begging Him to prepare your life so you can do the job on this earth that needs to be done, and we're not hopeless if that happens. It's not hopeless. We all can come up. We all can be strong again. We all can have life abundantly. But we are going to have to come together as a Godly nation and as a Godly people. Those of us that claim that we love Jesus Christ, God Almighty, our families, our children, and our mothers and fathers, are going to have to stop allowing the families to be torn apart. There are too many people in the nursing homes. There are too many elderly people struggling and it's not because there can't be hope. It's because we've allowed government assistance to take over our lives and when that happens they are in control of us. When you take over and start handing out money and we start taking a free handout, you are in control of us. We have volunteered to be under your supervision.

We've got to take back our families. We've got to come back into the cycle of love and really have the type of teaching that shows us, not just tells us, but shows us what love really means and how it works to make us grow and to make us thrive. We've got to plant more seeds of love and integrity. We've got to make people understand what that word means.

Oh, God. Help us to be what we need to be and not always what we want to be.

MAN'S ESCAPE CLAUSE

If I were to give this a title it would be Man's Escape Clause. I once said God's escape clause, but that's wrong. He doesn't need an escape clause but man sometimes thinks he needs an escape clause. That's what a lawyer will put in a contract sometimes. The person who has the contract, his lawyer will put it in small print or he will have a hidden situation where he can ease his client out of the contract because of something that he didn't put in or something he put in; that he can kind of ease around and get out of the contract and not live out the contract for the life of the contract.

We humans try to play that game with God. I think some of our religious leaders are sometimes fearful of giving us all of the facts. They have a unique way of framing something. They won't give us the full impact of a given situation. They'll give us a way to get around doing what God said to do. I hear the minister say that there's nothing wrong with smoking; in other words, it's not a sin to smoke. I'm not sure it's not a sin to smoke. As a matter of fact I believe it is after you have accepted Christ in your life. I'm not so sure that's it's not a sin before. I believe that it is a sin to smoke because you contaminate your body and your body is the temple of God. Not only do you contaminate it by destroying the physical part of it, but in many cases, you destroy it by destroying some of your mental capacity.

What I mean by this is in later years you might be wrestling with your conscience because of something you did in your life to destroy your health where you are unable to take care of your family as you should have or to be able to make a living for yourself to create the type of finances for yourself that you need in order to be self-sufficient. I believe those things are contaminating to a Christian. Not only to that, but I believe they are contaminating to a sinner. It's not up to me to know who a sinner is or to point out a sinner or to label them a sinner. But I do know those things that contaminate, that make your body unable to function as an instrument for God, I believe after you accept Christ in your life, that those things are a sin. I believe it and I know it is if God's word is true. The funny thing about it is that I know God's word is true. He says your body is a temple. When you destroy your body, you destroy the temple.

You may have an escape clause. You may be living quite well, doing quit alright, worked hard all your life, saved your money, sent your kids to college, and you were a good husband or a good wife. You did all that you thought you were supposed to do for your family. If you have a personal friend and he asks you for something, you're going to share with him. What about the people that you don't know personally? What about the people that you see that are troubled, that are having problems that life deals all of us? Some of us are not as well equipped to face the hard knocks that life has to offer us sometimes. Some of us can weather the storm a lot better than others. Some of us get knocked out by the first sign of something ugly coming on in our lives. The trials and tribulations burden us down. We're not able to carry the load by ourselves.

Should we be concerned about that type of citizen even though he may not be a member of the church, or he might be a member of the church? Do we bother to introduce ourselves in our community? Are we troubled when we look back over our lives and find out that we haven't shared our wisdom and knowledge with those who are less fortunate than we are? Can we look back over our lifestyle and our life and see that we have not done all we should have done? I'm sure all of us can do that.

If we now see what we possibly could have done in the past and we're still in a position to do it, maybe not quite as well as we could have done it if we would have started out earlier, and we can't catch up, most likely, in the things that were left undone. But now we have learned about what we should have done, should we do anything about it now? Should we try to mend a few fences that we've left undone? Should people have to come and fall in our doorway before we are willing to do something that might help them over the next hill that they have to climb? Is it possible that we climbed that same hill 10 years ago, 15 years ago, 20 years ago? We might be able to help them over it. Should we share our experiences and downfalls, as well as our climb up the tall mountain?

You know some of us feel mighty proud about what we have accomplished for our families and ourselves. We feel that we have given and given and worked since we were very young; some of us since we were a child. And now we are able to lounge around a little bit. We think we have it coming and we think we deserve it. Suppose God decided that He has been dealing with the world ever since the beginning of it and man has let him down on almost every single thing that has happened, and He is tired and sick of giving and since He has everything that He needs, that He's going to let us make it for ourselves from now on. That time may come. It hasn't come yet.

God has never taken his hand off any Christian man and let him die because He didn't care for him or He didn't like him. He's let a lot of men die because He loved mankind. He has let men die in order that other men would learn a lesson from that; He's done that.

I'm troubled about what's happening in our churches. I'm worried about the rules and regulations that they are forcing on God's word. I'm worried about the deep concern of the officials of our nation being concerned where we put the 10 Commandments at. I'm worried about people being concerned how much prayer will influence the school system. I'm worried and troubled that the believing communities, the people who believe in God and what He stands for, that have backed off of this. They have chosen to let the government and the state rule and regulate, men from all statures of life, different segments of our society have come against God's word being put in a position to influence our children in the public educational system. I'm troubled about that because that is the most important place in the world other than our homes.

Those of us over the age of 50 have had that influence in our lives whether we wanted it or not. Now we're so concerned about embarrassing somebody else's religion or religious beliefs. Religious belief has to do with God Almighty and the same God serves all men regardless of where they come from, regardless of what denomination they are. He's the same God or else somebody's lying. Just put it that way.

Jesus Christ. He expects man to obey Him. He doesn't expect man to set his own agenda. He asks us and tells us and demands us that if we want to be in this church, we're going to have to live by these rules. This is the way we want it. This is the way it's going to be set up. God wants the ministers and the religious leaders of our nation to empower the people in the church. My personal belief is the reason that Christianity hasn't reached its full capacity is because man, meaning the leaders of our religious organizations; and that's what most of them are – organizations - want to run everything themselves. They want to be in charge and do not allow God to set their agenda. They do not want the people in the congregation to be empowered.

What I mean by empowered is that you are there to teach and to lead the congregation. You are not to do everything in the church. You are supposed to be able to have men and women in that church that you can delegate certain jobs to, certain responsibilities. Nobody in the church that has accepted Christ and signed their name at the foot of the cross – when you sign your name at the foot of the cross and accept Jesus Christ as your personal Savior, that says to me that you have promised to live His lifestyle and to teach others to live His lifestyle to the best of your ability. You are supposed to search out and seek out men and women in your congregation that you can give responsibility to. Make them bring you a report card about their lifestyle and the way they are living in God's presence.

You see, when people in the church, your congregation, have been empowered by the minister they know that he is not the only one in the church that can lead. He needs followers that are following Jesus Christ's lifestyle. When you teach men and women about the way that Jesus led his people, then you will get the church moving outside of the church building. You can't lock up the people in the church house and expect them to be what God meant them to be. You can't expect men to be leaders of men when you're not leading them at all. You're telling them. You can't stand behind the pulpit every Sunday and shake people's hands on the way out the door and do a few hospital visits and say you know the members of the church. You should know the members of the church as well as you know your family. The members of the church are your family. They are your children. They are your loved ones. They are your neighbors. You need them empowering you as a pastor. You need your members backing you up with their deeds not just their money. You need to see your members in your church making God visible in their lifestyles before other people, other sinners of this world.

When you bring forth that type of gospel, you will have results because people will get the gratification and the feeling that you get most of the time. You see, if you're only looking for gratification, you may not get that in your whole lifetime. You may live a whole lifetime and die and never see what you want to see. You may never see men and women moving the way you want them to move. If you show your lifestyle and show your leadership, and let them know that you don't have a selfish motive but you love them and you want them to love others, you can encourage them to bring out the love that is available to them. They don't have to go anywhere to get it. They have it right there in their own personal life.

God didn't just put love in the hearts of people he liked a lot. We shoved so much ugliness down people's hearts and minds and souls that they have a problem bringing out love. They have to see love working in us in a way they can recognize it before they will share their love with us. They have to see God visible. We can serve an invisible God maybe, those of us who have been saved and have accepted Christ in our lives. But you cannot ask a person who has never lived the lifestyle that Christ set an example for. You can't ask that individual to serve an invisible God unless he sees it visibly in you. Then that builds his faith and you'll find that you will see it orchestrated in him. You'll see it moving. You'll see the growth within him, when you make it available in yourself.

I feel that a lot of our religious leaders have gotten captured by the luxuries of this world. We've been taken up in the dress code. We've been captured with all of the jewelry and the fine cars. If a minister doesn't have a nice, beautiful, fine automobile, he feels that he hasn't arrived yet. He feels that he deserves a beautiful and exciting car whether you have one or not; it doesn't matter, as long as you get it for him. Don't you know if you do God's work in the way that He wants it done that you will receive everything you need abundantly? None of us has everything we want and we never will. I don't care how many millions you have, you'll never have everything you want. Why don't we concentrate on getting the things that we need, not only for ourselves, but for our people in the community and nation?

Religion that was brought here from England many years ago, it was meant to be built on Christian principles. It didn't take long before we turned it around. This nation was not built on Christian principles. It is not living on Christian principles today. The forefathers never meant for this nation to be discriminating against Christian literature being placed in all of our government buildings, being placed publicly and exposed publicly. When they said separate the church and the state, they meant that the government was not to interfere in the lifestyle of the Christian principles. It was meant to be that Christian people, a Christian nation, would have Godly principles and they would see that the government would operate under those principles.

But no, in later years, those rules and regulations were changed. It was because men and women didn't want to live up to the Godly principles standing before them every day of their lives. They didn't want to see those principles in which they signed for when they signed on to do the job they were supposed to do. They don't want to be reminded every day of their lives that their supposed to live by the 10 Commandments, that they are suppose to live by certain moral principles, by certain Godly principles. They swear on the Bible. They use it in the courts all through this nation. They swear on them in the White House. Very few people live up to that standard.

I'm going to tell you right now, they intimidate me. The 10 Commandments intimidate me. It puts me to shame. All the time, every day of my life, somewhere I suspect I've broken one of the Commandments. Those are the 10 Commandments. Those are the only ones that are demanded. But I've broken so many more. But it doesn't mean that I'm not to be reminded about it.

In The United States, we ask churches and religious groups of people that believe in God; at least we say we do, have not stood up for the principles that we say we believe in. We back down all the way. We're scared of the government. We're scared they'll take our tax deduction privileges away from us. I believe with all my heart. I know I'm going to get a whole lot of slack for this but I don't know of any other reason why you should back down other than that.

This nation changed the Constitution 25 years after it was written and decided that they were going to change the laws separating church and state. It wasn't done in the original Constitution. It was changed 25 years after that. It wasn't put in the original Constitution and what they were talking about when they made the statement, was to keep the government from trying to control religion. Now they are actually blackmailing religious beliefs because when they come out of the courtroom and they see the 10 Commandments someplace, you can bet your life that it's condemning. How would I want my little boy to learn about the true Godly beliefs and what Jesus Christ and the Almighty God taught us as Disciples of Christ and disciples of God Almighty that are on this earth? That little boy may call your attention to what his teacher taught him today and the government is blackmailing the religious beliefs in this nation. I don't care who contradicts me. I know that I am right.

THE UNITY OF THREE BROTHERS AND SISTERS: Guy, Claude, and Mary

I feel like praying this morning. I feel like talking to my father. Sis, I want to pray for me and you. God has blessed us and I want to pray for my brother. We three have never, since we've been born, had a falling out where we disliked each other or disrespected each other. God has mended our minds and hearts together and given us that lasting love that very few families maintain. We can seriously say over the years – I'm 76 years old and I know you are so very young you don't want your age told. My brother is probably 65 or 66. God has blessed us so wonderfully. Maybe we don't always feel like we need, and know that our brother is very sick, but God has blessed him to still survive and have the opportunity to accept Christ in his life. I really believe he is a saved person. I believe that he has accepted Christ in his life and it toned him down as well as we all have been toned down by the Holy Spirit of Almighty God.

Isn't this wonderful that we live in a country that we have the opportunity, at least amongst ourselves, is to talk about God, to preach about God, debate about God, and all those wonderful things? The only thing that hurts me so bad and I pray to God that I will be blessed to see, and that is that prayer gets back into the schools that need it so badly. I can't imagine Sis, how on earth anyone could possibly think about taking the prayer out of school. This is a place of learning. This is where you get your roots of knowledge and wisdom. If God is not considered One who is worthy enough for your knowledge to learn about and about His place in your life and His place in the world, and about the things that He has done - I think, Sis, that's the reason that a lot of our children today are having such a rough time climbing the hill of life.

Lots of them don't get the prayer at home and they don't get the prayer in school. They don't get it anywhere. Some of us send our children to Sunday school and Bible study, but they certainly can't get the teaching that they need just in the church. Some of them don't have the opportunity to go to church. And, Sis you know the reason I think that some of our teenagers, especially when they get to the age of accountability and they get to age where they begin to understand and know what's going on around them; I think that maybe some of the parents don't send them because they feel that the child will condemn them and convict them about the type of life that they live in front of the child.

The child has been taught about Jesus Christ and about God Almighty and about the way that we're supposed to live on this earth if we expect to live as Christian men and women. I think to have a child like that in a home that is going on with sin and all the turmoil that goes on in a home, I think that child would probably be the one that would have to speak to the parents. If parents stay in fear of that - I know I would. I'd pray to God that something can happen.

That's the reason, Sis that I'm trying to get this book in print so badly. I believe it has a lot to say to me and you. I believe that God has spoken to me and is trying to allow me to amplify the good and the bad in my life in order that someone may see where I went wrong, and how I've changed and how I've come up. Just because I can't read and just because a lot of people don't know how to read and write, doesn't mean that they are stupid and it doesn't mean that they don't have something to offer this country and its people and this nation.

You know, the world is looking for people that don't think of themselves all the time. That's what I did in my past life, is thought of myself and my personal and intimate friend but there is a thing called God and man's relationship to humanity that can't be taken out of our life. We've got to realize that we are more responsible. In other words, we're responsible for more people other than just us and our families. We've got to realize that. That's our survival kit.

I hope I haven't bored you again Sis. I'll talk to you later baby.

INTUITION

I was asked by my neighbor, Guy Darden, what God and humanity meant to me. He asked me to think about it and write it down in one word or a short brief description.

First I think before I write what I feel I think, I should first tell you of my neighbor, Guy, and how we've become friends.

In March of 2003, Linda and I bought this 1927 colonial house on the edge of town, a fix-me-up. Over the past two years we have worked on it steadily in our spare time and are almost finished. In doing yard work, Guy came over and introduced himself to Linda and me. Guy is an elder man with a smile and gleam in his eyes. A neighbor that always has a wave and a smile I've notice over the years.

One evening we noticed ambulance lights reflecting on the walls as we were watching TV. I got up to see where they were coming from as it pulled out of Guy's driveway. The following day I walked over to see if everything was okay. Guy's wife said that he had fallen down the stairs and would be okay but banged up pretty bad. I think after that, every time I come home I look to see if everything looks quiet.

During our first winter here, I purchased a used snow blower. It takes about 20 minutes to clean my drive. The snow here on Lake Erie – we're in the Snow Belt here – can build quickly, especially on the drive apron after the snow plows go down the street. To my left I have a disabled man and family, Guy is on the across the street, and an elderly women straight across the street. In an hour I can at least get their driveway apron's cleared out so they can get in and out.

It makes Linda and I feel comfortable to have such neighbors. We're not the come over and have coffee neighbors, but if we can help we will talk when we see each other in passing or just a hello.

Just this past week Linda wanted to go home to Boston for four days as this would be here last visit until after baseball season. She was concerned about a package coming in the mail for her mother's birthday present. It had not come and we had to leave. It had rained while we were gone and when we returned, Guy brought the packer over to us and said it had come the day we left. It makes us feel good to have such a neighbor. I could go on with little stories about Guy – all good, but back to his question; God and humanity.

The American College Dictionary defines God as "the one supreme being, the creator and ruler of the universe. 1. God or goddess. 2. Divine character or nature. 3. The estate or rank of a go., 4. The character or nature of the supreme being."

God and Man's Relationship to Humanity

Linda and I, being both raised as Christians which we neither attend mass regularly except on Christmas or when my mother comes to visit, but we still have faith.

At an early age in a large family I was taught we were made in God's image and maybe through this saying is how I came up with, I am my own god while on earth. I have the choice to do what I do. Treat people how you want to be treated. What goes around comes around. Live by the 10 Commandments. Reap what you sow, etc.

And from this, the next question; humanity: "1. The human race, mankind. 2. The condition or quality of being human; human nature. 3. The quality of being humane; kindness; benevolence. 4. Polite learning in its various branches as grammar, rhetoric, poetry, etc."

This is what God preaches – humanities. In the world we live in today it is frightening if you keep up with the current events. It is also easy to see why many don't believe in God or say He is a cruel god. When hard times hit I think what my parent taught me. We're only passing through and we will be judged on our actions and deeds at the end.

This past fall, Linda and I took a two-week trip to the Dakotas, visiting Mount Rushmore, the Battle of the Big Horn and the Crazy Horse Monument under construction. At the Crazy Horse Monument I learned of the Hopi prophecy which was written by Dr. A. Ross Ehanamani, who was raised on a reservation in the Dakotas, in his book entitled "Crazy Horse"; the real reason for the Battle of the Little Big Horn told by the Indians of the error. Humanity is definitely felt while reading this. There god tells them of the three shakings of earth and the only man can survive.

If we continue thinking with our head only (rational), we will eventually destroy ourselves. If we take the road of thinking with our heart (intuition), we will eventually return to respect for nature and our survival.

With this I will close and take a second to thank Guy and his wife for being our neighbor. This is maybe our last season here which was on a three-year contract. Our next place, I hope there is another Guy.

By John and Linda

The reason I asked John to put down what he thought the meaning of love was because he seemed to demonstrate it all the time; what I call love. I wanted to know even if he demonstrated it and did it every day of his life, did he know the meaning of the word. It may sound contradictory but what I am trying to say is that some of us do things every day that we're supposed to do but yet we don't know that we're doing it or it becomes a part of our lives. I believe it is something different that when it becomes a part of your life and your lifestyle and it motivates you from the heart; just to do something because that is what you have been doing all your life. That is your motive for doing it.

What makes you say grace? Well, I've been saying it all my life. I got to thinking about the words that I say when I sit down at the table: Dear Lord, make us joyful and thankful for all these blessings that we are about to receive, for our heavenly Father's sake, amen. Those are strong words but so help me God, until a few months ago I just really understood what I was saying. I said the right things but I said them because I'd always been saying them. I say the Lord's Prayer because I've always been saying it. The meaning of the words has a bearing on us. I'm not so sure that I know every single meaning that the Lord's Prayer means. I certainly hope I do and if I do, good, and if I don't, I pray each day that the Lord makes me understand the meaning of the His Prayer. I've never been to Heaven and I don't know what they do up there but I do know this, if God's up there, they're doing what we supposed to do. He's already told us what we're supposed to do even though every day of our lives somebody's trying to remove Jesus Christ and God Almighty from the Bible and from this earth. They want to have more freedom in their own way. Who are they? Those who work against God; whoever they may be. I don't care where Christ was born. I don't care who had Him. I don't care what is in Heaven. I don't care what's in Hell. All I care about is that I know from the way that He has treated since I have been on this earth that God Almighty is in charge. God Almighty! God Almighty! Those are powerful words. It means that He is the strength of everything that exists. I want you, Almighty God, to exist in my heart and through my actions. I haven't had you in my heart for a long time. Now I have you in my heart. I want to represent you wherever I go throughout my living and the way I handle myself.

Yes, John, I believe deeply now after I have examined your life and the way you have lived it, I believe John that you know what love is. Yes, John, I hope I'm going to live a long time but I want to live the kind of life that people like you express through their actions not just through their words. May God bless this nation and its' people. Hallelujah!

By Guy P. Darden, Sr.

THE BUMPER OF DESTRUCTION

We ask You to bless this nation today. Dear God, we ask you to take this walk with us today. Holy Father, let us walk along with You today as You lead us through the garden of life. Dear Lord, put a bumper of some kind on us so that it will knock away the hate. Take away the resentment that some of us have, Lord, for each other. Holy Father, give us the strength to endure the things that we may encounter today that may not be pleasant to us. Give us the opportunity, Lord, to realize and understand the freedom that we have by praying with You.

Oh, God, give us the knowledge and the good sense to kneel down by the bedside before we leave home this morning and pray with our families. Lord, allow us to look our children dead in the eye, embrace them in our arms and tell them about God. If we have accepted Christ in our lives, talk about it with our children. Tell them and explain to them how important it is to them. Tell them how much God means to them at this particular moment. Tell them how much they need God to walk the journey with them this day. Let them know Father that this day is the only day that they can count on. This moment is the only moment that they can count on because they know not when You come back to gather them up.

Lord, lead them through this rugged world today that is so troubled with the hate and so troubled with all of the sins and sex acts and things that are moving through this country. Lord, protect the children at school today. Inspire in their parents' heart to pray with their children every single morning. Make that the most important thing in their lives. Let them know that prayer is the only thing that we can hold on to and use it as a weapon towards Satan.

We ask you Lord, to bless all the members of our families. Bless this government that governs our nation. Bless this State Lord, and the State officials and the police officers, Lord. Unite their hearts with Jesus Christ. Let them see the good in men instead of so much hate. Lord, keep their hearts from becoming so desensitized. Lord, let them accept the love in their hearts. Let the love hide the hate that tries to get out. Give them compassion towards all mankind.

We ask this in the name of the Father, and The Son, and The Holy Spirit. May the Holy Spirit travel with us this day and give us the strength to do what we need to do. We ask this in Your name Father. Amen.

GOD IS NOT COMPLICATE

I think some time that we're not satisfied with things when they are simple and plain; when they are not complicated. It's too easy to do what we want to do when it is very easy; it seems like it doesn't have a value. Unless it is complicated, it must not be real, it doesn't have the strength. If we hear someone talking and we hardly understand what they are saying and the words kind of bounce over us a little bit and we pick up something here and there, we say that person is very smart. He is very educated. When someone is up for election and their big words that kind of bounce over us, we don't make any comments very much except that he is very educated. He is a nice speaker. What I call good English speaking is someone that takes all the complications out of it, that it's simple, plain old down-to-earth, common sense conversation. They kind of make parables as they go along to make you get the picture. I've never been that good. I try to be myself and that tells you right there that I'm not that good. But I think when you are truly educated and if you are a real intellectual, that you can understand most conversation if it's in your language.

I don't think God is a complicated or an I-don't-understand type of god. I believe God is - when you really understand the structure and power of God – I don't think He's complicated. But some of our leaders have always got to make it complicated. They don't think they have impressed you if those big, fancy words don't come out. But I notice when I really listen to someone who has truly been educated and feels confident that he's got what you need, and the words are not complicated. If you've been to the first, second, or third grade, you'll understand every word. You may not be able to read and write but you'll understand every word he has to say. Because he doesn't try to bounce things over you where you've got to reach and try to analyze and understand what it means.

God is the same way. When God tells you something He speaks in your spirit. You don't have a lot of problems understanding what He's saying. Sometimes we don't want to do what God says. We don't want to get involved and hurt people's feelings sometimes. We don't want to say things to people that may not make them want to pat us on the back. We don't mind insulting someone or saying something to someone as long as it's compliments us in some way. As long as it makes us seem like we are above their standards. I think we sometimes try to reach above ourselves. I want to talk to people who have been on that level of where they feel that the education process has moved away from them. They've got all the fancy words and they'd don't understand English anymore. I hear people talk about speaking good English. What is good English? What I call good English is when you understand what a person is saying without having to look it up in the dictionary. And if you are like me, you can't look it up in the dictionary. I want it so plain that it just lands on me. And even if I don't want to hear it, I know what it means. I understand it thoroughly. I understand it because I feel it. And even when I was a sinner, I felt truth, honesty, and integrity; I respect it, even when it hurt.

But I respected men that have been were I would like to go, that have been where I am at now. When men used tell a story, or testify, or tell about their lives and how they used to be alcoholics, drunks or on dope. When they used to talk about how they misused people; how they robbed and stole. You don't have to tell about a specific crime, you just say, "I used to steal and rob, and I used to be a drunk, and I used to be a womanizer." And it didn't matter whose wife it was, it didn't matter whose daughter it was because there had been a time in my life when I didn't respect people's standards and their morals; when I was behind their back. I did what you would call the "closet stuff". I was very careful to hide and sneak in and out of windows. People always respected me. But the funny thing about, I disrespected a lot of people behind their backs. For what you do in the dark, sooner or later, comes to the light. If it doesn't come to the light where it is publicly known, it will catch up with you and you will go through some of the same thing that you carried other people through. What we do in committing sins against people, even though they don't know about it, is damaging to our nation. It's damaging to our community. Because somebody sees you somewhere, if no one else, God does, and you're going to reap the penalty of doing the things that are wrong.

We don't have to be so complicated when we talk about God. All you have to do is talk about sin and talk about the things that we do to each other. You see, there is nobody on this earth to harm but human beings and our environment. When we talk about doing wrong and doing right, we're talking about each other. You don't just do wrong out there to yourself. When you mess up, you don't just mess up your life, you mess up somebody else's life too. It may be your family, maybe a daughter, a son, or it might be your neighbor. You say, "I got drunk and lost all my money. That's my business." No, because when you take your economical base out of the society and squander it on something that doesn't do you or anybody else any good except maybe the bar owner or the drug dealer, you've taken something out of the cycle of life that could have been positive. And when you do like I have done most of my life, be irresponsible with your economical base, the things that you have to do to make you develop into a prosperous person as far as the financial part of the cycle of life is concerned, you can't be what you need to be in your community and in your family.

If you are a young man that is wasteful in your young life and now you've met Miss So-N-So. You married her and she married you because she loved you and you married her because you love her, both of you want to give your best to each other. But what you have done is wasted your best behind you and unless you can pick up some knowledge and utilize it through wisdom and understand that the boo-boo that you made back there; it taught you a lesson and you're going to try to do better from now on. You are going to live a different life and you do it at a young and early age, where you don't have to go through the hell that I went through and that you have learned in time enough to recycle, so to speak, some of your life; not let it all go down the drain. But you learn enough from some old guy like me that is telling you about processing and re-processing your life until you've got it to where you are doing the things that are right; not just for yourself, but for those that are around you and that you are responsible for. And that you have learned enough about life that you know right from wrong.

Now, some of us don't know right from wrong. Some of us don't know we're messing up. I think most of the times when I messed up, I knew. I knew what I was doing. But I felt like if I wasn't saved and I hadn't accepted Christ in my life that I wasn't doing anything more than a lot of other people were doing. I was calling the people in the church that I saw out there, at the night clubs and the after hour clubs, after they had left the church on Sunday afternoon and went to some club and were goofing off and messing up; I saw myself as a much better person than they were. I saw them as hypocrites and I didn't think they were real. I thought I was being honest with my life. I felt that I was sinning and I admitted I was sinner, and was living a simple life and everybody knew I was living a simple life. When I went to church, I went to church because I thought every once in a while I ought to go because God had protected me all my life, through all the hell I went through. But I didn't go to church because I was saved and felt like I was not a hypocrite because I hadn't accepted Christ in my life.

But I was a liar. I was telling myself a lie. When I was 12 years old, I did join the church but joining the church and allowing Christ to take your life and giving Him the freedom to mold you into what it needs to be, is a lot different than being a member of a church. When you are a member of God's army and you truly, really and truly, have given your life to the Lord and accepted Him as your Savior and Leader; and I put emphasis on the Leader part. He is leading you through this land and through this world. Don't wait until you get old and you're shaking all over because you're scared you're going to Hell, and you're only repenting because you know you messed up all your life and you don't have much time, like me. Don't wait like that. Make your change in the early part of your life where you'll have some type of life that you can enjoy being with Christ. You can enjoy the Glory of God Almighty. You can enjoy Christianity. You can be proud and happy when you are serving people and you see the results of it. That's a great thing when you accept Christ in your life at a younger age and you've led people to Christ, and you see the results in their lives. Nothing, nothing, could be more exciting than that.

I've had that experience in life. I was in my tailor shop one day and this young man came by and I looked outside and there were two or three dump trucks, a couple of front-loaders, a big Caterpillar earth mover, a big truck, a trailer and all this contract equipment. He came in my shop and he said to me, "How are you doin' Mr. Darden?" I said, "Fine, thank you. How are you?" He said, "You don't know who I am, do you?" I said, "No, but your face looks familiar." He said, "I used to live in Kinston Court. I lived across the street from you." I said, "Oh, my God. I do know you. How are you doing?" And I asked him how his mother and father; I couldn't remember their names. He said they were doing beautiful. He said, "Come to the door. I want to show you something." I had already seen it but I didn't know who it was. I went to the door and I looked outside and he said, "You see that equipment there?" I said, "Yes". He said, "You're the cause of me having that." I said, "I am?" He said, "Yes". He told me, "When I used to be sitting on the curb and you'd run up behind us and we'd try to take off and run, and you would call us back. You would sit down there with us and talk about life and tell me how I could be anything on earth I wanted and you told me how the drugs and pot that we were smoking, how it could goof up our lives and ruin our lives. And that there was another side of life and that we could actually enjoy going to church and enjoy being with Christian men and women and young Christian men and I got to thinking about that. You told us about you not being able to read and write and noticed how much business you had and how well you were doing in your business. You always would sit down and talk with us. You never scolded us or put us down. You always told us that there was another route in life, and that we could be anything on this earth that we wanted to be. I remember your nephew came down from Virginia and he used to play with us and talk with us. I remember the time that we were stealing a man's apples and you came out there and told him not to take them. That if we wanted some apples, the best thing to do would be to go and ask the man and if he didn't give us any apples and we wanted it that bad, that you'd buy us some apples. I remember you coming out there the next day and Billy wasn't taken any apples, but we were and you punished him for it. You tore his butt up. He said, "Uncle Guy, I wasn't stealing any apples", and you told him that he was with the crowd; it was the same thing. Because tomorrow, if somebody saw him coming up the street with a bunch of guys that stole those apples, they weren't going to call him Billy. They were going to say there comes one of those boys that stole those apples. I always remembered that and I remember you kept telling us that there is nothing on this earth that we wanted that was right, and we put forth an effort, that we couldn't get. The little things that I wanted, I noticed that when I worked hard and tried to get it that I was able to get it."

And as he was talking the tears started to run down my cheek. Like right now, I'm very emotional about that because it tells me that somewhere in life out of all the turmoil that I went through, I learned something and I was able to pass it on.

In later years, Billy wrote me a letter. He was at the University of Virginia. During that time, he was some of the first black people to graduate from there, and he told me, he said, "Uncle Guy, me remembering something you told me many years ago, you told me I could be anything I wanted to be if I put forth my best effort and tried hard that I would be successful. And Uncle Guy, you are the cause of me this day being in one of the most prestigious universities in the United States. I am so proud that you are my Uncle." Later on, Billy went to the University of Texas. He studied law at that University. He became a linguist, a lawyer, and he became a minister. He worked awful hard and one of the most greatest thing that I feel, that I am the most proud of, and that's the letter he wrote me telling me how much he appreciated me being there for him from time to time. I told Billy, it was his mother that was the cause of him being the young man that he was because she gave him the guidance and she was there for him. She followed up on everything I'd ever told him because she's one of the greatest mom's that I've every known, my sister, Mary.

But I want you to know that when you see the results of things that you might have had a little something to do with, bloom and prosper. He later on preached a sermon and he mentioned about the apples that he stole. It was part of his first text when he had his trial sermon, he mentioned that time. You see, there's a whole lot in life to be proud of but I think the greatest thing to happen to you is to have God to bless you for those things that you've done. But most off all, to accept Him in your life as your personal Savior. Any he'll do the teaching if you'll ask the questions.

LOVE IS AN ANCHOR, THE REVELATION OF HOPE

Love. Love is a gift. Love is a gift that God gave us to filter out the ugliness and meanness that are torturing us throughout out lives. Love is an anchor. It's a revelation of hope. It's a beginning of understanding life's cycle in man's heart. It is a belief. It let's us know what we need to be. It's freedom of understanding the hopes and the dreams. Love is a passport to hopes and dreams of all of us. It makes us believe in something more than what we can see. It is a dream that's hidden in all of our hearts. It can't be defined by one single word. It's a generator that keeps us above water. It keeps us struggling and fighting for hope. It is a motivation to look for things that are greater than what we are. It is God's communication cycle. It's what the Holy Ghost...I would say the Holy Ghost is a power pack. It's that strength that gives love hope; that thing that we feel inside of us, that grounds the hate and it destroys the ugliness and meanness that comes up in our minds. Its things that bring people up when they think they're down. It is that thing that makes you look straight out and give people your love and kindness and you draw people to you instead of pushing them away from you. You consider the feelings of others and you magnify your obligation. Because you know love is a lasting thing and it not only gives other people hope, it gives you hope when you see other people being drawn in. It magnifies the Holy Spirit in your life. It makes you realize the needs of others. It gives you a hope, it gives you an everlasting strength that if God is in your life, you've got something to look forward for. Hallelujah.

REPENT

When I took on this assignment to do this book, there were quite a few things that I was concerned about. I want to talk about some of them here. I try with all my being to be truthful in every way I can. I will tell you this; I felt that my years of experience on this earth must have some type of value some place. I felt like there had to be something in there that might help somebody. I have traveled over this nation, year after year and I've seen a lot of things happen. I've seen a lot of negative things going on and I've seen a lot of positive things going on.

So I accepted the Lord in my life. I've been able to look at both sides of the fence. I look at my life and remember back over it how many wrong things I did; how I had goofed up my life over the years, and then how I survived a lot of things. I was able to do rather well in some things. I remember one time in my life I thought about God and how I thought about the church and church people. I've seen Christians do a lot of things that they shouldn't have done. I've seen sinners do a lot of things that they shouldn't have done. I've seen sinners do a lot of beautiful, wonderful, and fantastic things. I've seen them succeed in life as far as material things are concerned. I've seen people that hadn't accepted Christ in their lives and they were wonderful ladies and gentlemen; they were wonderful people. They respected themselves and they respected others. They did a lot of wonderful things for this nation and they would do anything they could for you. Many of them had done so much for me. As a matter of fact, most of the people that have done something for me were sinners, people that had not accepted Christ in their lives. I have seen men and women that give and share, worked and done volunteer work all over this nation that never accepted God in their lives.

So, when we talk about people sharing their lives with each other we need to know the essence of what we're talking about. We need to know those things that motivate us into doing things that God wants. But most of all, those of us that have accepted God in our lives and He is the leader in our lives. In other words, we joined His army. What we want to do for ourselves doesn't really count a lot unless we want to do the things that God wants us to do. Now having said that, I've seen bad people that say that they don't particularly care for people, they don't trust people, and they don't respect people. I've seen the same person that said that, after seeing somebody giving and sharing, turn around and be completely reversed from what they were. I've seen godly people; people who say that they have accepted Christ in their lives, from the pulpit to the pews, do exactly the opposite from what God had asked them to do. They would gamble, drink, date women that were married or single or whatever, and they were men and women of the cross. I've seen those men and women turn their lives around and come back to God and repent. So the word repent is all through our lives. Now I have a controversial scene here that if you have done all those things that I just talked about and lived in the world and goofed off and messed up and just been a man that did the things of the world. Now your life has been saved by Christ and you have repented. Regardless of what you see people doing, what's happening in this world that you don't like, they can't condemn you. You condemn yourself.

In this book I speak about the things in life that I feel will motivate somebody. You hear these people say that "you're not going to give me a guilt trip. I'm not going to allow you to do that." Or sometimes you hear people say, "I don't want to give you a guilt trip." Well, I'm different. I want to give you a guilt trip. I want to say some things and talk about some things that will make you feel guilty; that will make your conscience kick you around and talk to you. I don't answer very many questions. But I try to tell you to re-evaluate your life. If you have blown it somewhere I don't want to say anything that's going to get you down but I want to say something that will allow you to take a second look at your life. Don't get hung up on your past. Learn from it and move on.

That's what this book is about. It's about looking at your brother not just walking around and pointing your finger at him, but try to say something that will turn both his and your life around. You see, just because I'm not without sin doesn't mean that I can't talk about sin and I can't talk about the things that we do that we need to take a second look at. Because I stumbled through life most of my life, even when I thought I was doing well, I wasn't doing well. The foundation that we build under our own lives and the foundation we build under our children's lives will decide the future for tomorrow. We can no longer walk away and talk about "I gotta' live my life and I gotta' have some fun" when our families are in need in our lives or when we keep talking about what we want for ourselves unless the lifestyle is based on Godly principles, we're not going to have what we want. I know this is extremely controversial, but who better to talk about overcoming wrong than someone who has been there?

I'll say this to you, there is so much joy in life. There is so much happiness even when you're hurting and sick and things are not going your way today. Don't let that bother you because as long as you keep your hand in God's hand, He's going to fix it. I know that for a fact. It's going to be alright.

WHAT IT ALL MEANS TO ME

A long time ago, I had decided that I didn't want to bring a child into this world. It seemed such an unkind place. What could they possibly have to look forward to? People have turned their backs on one another. No one wants to get involved. Crime is so out of hand. The family unit is not what I remember it to be. People are fighting all over the globe. Why aren't we all working together as a people to help ourselves and our fellow man to make the entire world a better place to live for everyone? No one is supposed to be better than anybody else. Everyone is created equal. When did that change? Who changed it? Why did it change?

I was at my niece's wedding and I remember the minister talking about when they have children, they should raise them in a Christian way. Then it hit me – who was I to decide whether or not to bring a child into the world? God wants us to be fruitful and multiply. Maybe my child will make a difference in the world someday, somehow. If God did not want me to have a child, he would not have allowed me to get pregnant. Well guess what, I have a daughter now and she is almost grown and on her own. I hope she does make a difference someday, somehow. We have to try and we have to start somewhere.

God and man's relationship seems to be so one-sided. God does all the giving and man seems to do most of the taking. I truly believe if you put your hand into God's hand and walk with Him, you can not go wrong. He will guide you to do what is good and what is right. But not many people seem to want to get involved and that means to me that they don't want to hold God's hand. What a shame. Have they decided to walk with the devil or just walk alone?

Now the humanity part – we have got to get it together. Humanity is "all mankind". If everyone is going in different directions and segregating themselves into classes, groups, religions, ages, and so on, how can we come together as a human race? God and man's relationship to humanity is a trinity; not unlike the Holy Trinity. God + Man + Humanity = Eternal Life with the Holy Trinity; Father, Son & Holy Ghost. What more could you ultimately strive for than that?

In order to earn that eternal life you must live your life according to God's rules and commandments. They are in place for a reason. If every single person followed every single Commandment can you imagine what a wonderful place the world would be? It is only then that God and man's relationship to humanity will be as it should be.

Time is running out but there still is time. Make a difference to someone who is near you. Reach out and connect with that person and if they need something, help them. If they can give you advice, take it.

We all need to be there for each other. We have to stop turning our backs on the problems around us and do something.

Of all the things that I learned from working on this book with Guy; these are the most important to me.

By Nancy A. Dennis

I met Nancy through a company that assisted me in finishing up this book. The lady that assisted me that owned the company, Jackie, told me about a lady that did a lot of work for her and she loved the Lord. So she thought we ought to meet face to face and get to know one another. I found that her intelligence is beyond comprehension. I have the opportunity to meet her and her husband. We have become very close friends. My wife's name is also Nancy.

She is a God-fearing lady that loves the Lord. She believes in what I am trying to do. She is extremely serious in her actions but she doesn't take herself too serious and jump up on a pedestal. She is one of the most intelligent people that I know. My family and I love her very dearly. She has removed a lot of mountains from the front of this book. May God bless her and her family. She is truly a great lady.

By Guy P. Darden, Sr.

SET AN EXAMPLE

I've been thinking about the handicapped; those of us who handicap ourselves. We put a blockade in our way. When we first start out in life and even when we learn best. In other words, when we get some wisdom and we change our lives and decide to go the right way. It is when we really know the right way; especially those of us who have gotten acquainted with the Bible and understand the philosophy and the lifestyle of Jesus Christ and some of his followers. In other words, we know which way to go. We've lived long enough to have some wisdom and understanding about life. We've learned the value of having sensitivity towards our brothers and sisters. We really have set up our lives in a positive way but yet we are handicapped. Especially those of us who haven't gotten our knowledge from the books or we haven't been to school or learned all of the fine words or the beautiful way to say things. In other words, we don't have an oratory where we can make our words look beautiful and speak all the beautiful and wonderful languages. We kind of stumble through our English and we stumble over ourselves sometimes. Especially those of us who have not lived a real good and wholesome life; we haven't been a Christian all our life. We've messed up along the way. Our friends know we've messed up. Not only just our friends, our society knows that we've blown it. We live the kind of life that didn't compliment us. Maybe we haven't robbed banks or done all the ugly, nasty things but some of our lifestyle was not a model for the generation today.

As a matter of fact, when you're as old as I am and you're a Senior Citizen, they don't see very much that you have to offer; especially those who haven't had a foundation in their lives. What I mean by a foundation; those children and those young people who were brought up in a home where they weren't taught about integrity or that they didn't have an example. You know, a lot of us were taught about integrity and we were shown in the books and our preachers told us about integrity. Sometimes our parents took us to church but we didn't have an example. They didn't live the type of life in the front of us that made us what we needed to be. When you build a foundation you take time, and not only that, you will bring your family in and show them the type of ground that you need to cultivate in order to make life what it needs to be. In other words, you have discipline in your family. Not just the kind of discipline that you buy and give your family to buy your way into but you let people know about the hardships of life and about the ladders that they are going to have to climb and the mountains that are going to be in front of them. You show them that type of life and not just tell them to do what I say; don't do like I do, do what I say, they don't have a good foundation. You tell them to go out there and do what you say to do but you're not setting an example. When we say "come on and let's go" and you lead them and show them a lifestyle that they need to live, and then they'll have something to hold on to.

If someone hasn't seen that and they haven't had a mentor that showed them that, then they're going to have a problem finding something to hold on to; their wheels are going to spin.

REPAIR SHOP

We're supposed to talk about each other. And when I say talk about each other I'm not talking about putting you down. I'm not talking about telling you that you're no good and you're trifling and sorry, we're not talking about that. You know some people think we're not supposed to correct each other because we all are sinners or we all have sinned and come short of God's word and God's teaching. I don't know anybody that hasn't done that, it may be a few, but Jesus Christ made this statement when a young man, a rich young man I understand, came to Him and called Him "Good Master." And Christ asked him why did he call Him good? He said, "No one is good but my Father which is in Heaven." Now, I want you to know if the only people that are good could teach you, you wouldn't have any teachers.

That's what I tried to do in this book. I don't give many people many answers. I tried to make me and you think. Everything I talk about I have to run it through me first. And in putting this book together I've taught myself a lot of things, not nearly enough, but I want to say enough about me and you, to make us think and make us back track and activate the love that is in us and amplify the goodness and mercy that we claim that we demonstrate now. I'm not one of them that's going to go around just keeping my mouth shut because I've even done what I see you doing, because I even done worse than what I saw you do. I'm not going to keep my mouth shut about the church.

Now, I want you to know that I have never said anything against the church. People say I attack the church. That is a lie. I do not attack the church. I want you to know that that building, that prayer house, that repair shop, that we go to on Sunday morning, where we go to get the broken pieces put back together, where we go to congregate and meditate and talk to God in unison, and exchange ideas and thoughts; that place is not a church. That is a building that we go to; it's a house of God, a prayer building. That's where we go to get knowledge and to be analyzed. That's where we go and fall on our knees in unison to God Almighty; that's what it is. It's where we try to get the people that are sitting in those pews activated so they do more than just read a Bible or pick up a Sunday school book.

Now I'm going to talk about life and I'm going to say things about me and you that we don't want to hear. I've blown it all my life, I've messed up, and I've been a 'goof-off' all my life. If you don't understand that kind of language, that's your problem. If you're educated, you'll figure it out, you'll ask somebody.

The Church is in your heart. The church is the essence of God Almighty's substance. It's what you go to that building to bring out of you, to make it alive. The church is where you find God and where you allow Him to be alive in you. It is a store house. The church is in the temple of your heart. The church is you; it's not that beating heart, but that spiritual heart that makes you what you are. It's the essence of who you are and that's what I call the church. That's what I believe the church is. That is what God visualized in me. I saw it through God, amplified. I believe that I have to live the type of life that makes it visible for you to become acquainted with me. I believe you could feel it and I think you can understand it somewhat. Whether you are saved or not I believe that it's something in me that will make contact with you. You see, that's how I feel about the church and don't let me tell you that I love you and don't love the church, and that I love you and don't love God. I've got to treat you like I love you, not just say I love you, but I've got to live that kind of life in the front of you.

Now, I'm on the border of something I'm going to talk about right now. You see I don't like everything that I see people do. Now someone told me I couldn't love you without liking you. I don't know about that. I'm going to be honest with you; I've seen some people doing things that I did not like and I didn't want to hang out with them. I didn't want them to be my friends. I stayed away from them because I didn't like what they did but I hoped I loved them. I really hope I loved them, but if I did, I had a problem with it. I think I'm better now. I've learned more about life and dug into the Holy Spirit a lot better. I'm trying to love those people. I love God and I know I love God. Since they put that stipulation in there – God put it in there – and I have to recognize that but I have to fight with that. I really have to fight with liking some people. I want to love them and I'll do anything for them that they would ask me to do. I tell you right now, I'd have no problem telling them that I didn't like them, but I'm going to do this. I really would. I'm just that kind of person. I'm not going to say more I'm going to leave that and move away from it.

I'm saying these things because it gets so complicated when you don't understand love in its true essence. This thing, love, is a power pack. It has so much value and so much strength because it reaches over a lot of problems. It crosses a lot of bridges. The Almighty God said it covers us a Host of sins. We are always telling someone that we love them. We are always saying this one word. We throw it around an awful lot - I love you, you know. Well how am I going to know that you love me unless you act like it, unless you do the things that people do when they love people. That's a touchy thing there. I don't believe that you can really love somebody unless you love God because it doesn't give you that separation from the world. You feel that when you don't love, you have a freedom that doesn't belong to you and you take advantage of it – you can't do that. You see, when you love God, you are his slave. His Son bought you and paid for you with his blood. You're not free to do anything and everything you want to do. You are under His commandment. You don't have that type of freedom to say anything you want to say to anybody; to put anybody down, to curse and swear and do that kind of thing. You have something that covers that area that you live and that you stand in. You have a circle around you. You're kind of fenced in. You have certain values that you have to live up to. You can't say anything to me that you want to say when you love somebody because they tell me that God is in charge of your life.

That's the reason that so much is going on now that they're trying to take the Bible out of this and the Bible out of that and separate it. They said they want to separate government from the religion. They act like the government is a thing; something that they have made and built it out of material or something. The government is made up of people; human beings, individuals. City Hall, other than having a building down there, is made up of people; peoples' opinions, peoples' ideas and peoples' thoughts. When you tell people that you don't want the government in your life, you are saying that you don't want people in my life. In other words, you're telling me to go work today to be governor of this state, and while I'm down there that I can't have anything to do with people; that if the government does so-and-so, it doesn't make any difference if it's wrong or right, if that's what the government says. I'm supposed to ignore my feelings and my principles and do what the government says. That's not real. That's phony.

We know what we're trying to do; we're trying to give ourselves the freedom to do what we want to do. We want to use people. We're talking about how we don't want to exercise the integrity that we're supposed to have towards each other. I don't want to do things that we know maintain order and decency. If I want to get buck naked in the middle of the street, that's my right to do so. If I want to curse or swear to anybody or by myself – in other words, I'm free to do what I want to do and I'm not supposed to have any order in my life if I don't want to. In other words, you can't hold me to certain principles.

Anybody that is a human being and knows anything about God's principles at all knows that you can't do that and be real, and be honest, and have integrity. I don't care who you are. You can't separate God and use Him when you want to use Him. You either believe in God or you don't believe in God. Are you telling a lie when you say this nation was built on Godly principles and yet you throw Him out when you get ready to do Godly things in the government? You don't believe anything can be done in the government that's Godly?

The government is not a thing – it is people!

A FEW MORE THOUGHTS ABOUT...

VOLUNTEERS

I know some of you may disagree with me here but I believe the volunteer help, those people who are not asking for money but they volunteer their time and effort in the hospitals are usually not paid the attention they are worth. They work on answering the phones and switchboards and things or transporting clients from one area of the hospital to another. They don't ask for any funds. They do it as a volunteer effort. I want to mention them first because they are working out of love and care for humanity. I believe that is our foundation for humanity. I believe that is what we all need to think about. We all cannot do that. The young and old people who dedicate their time and effort throughout this nation – I don't believe we pay enough attention to those lovely and wonderful people.

We want them to be respected and honored because most of all they are the ones that demonstrate love rather than just talk about it. May God bless you.

MEDICAL COMMUNITY WORKERS

What I would like to discuss is what some people would probably call the lower echelon of the medical community. I don't believe it is the lower echelon. I believe it is almost the foundation and perhaps is the foundation. That foundation is the hard core labor workers of the medical community, such as chamber maids (we don't call them that anymore) who do the dirty cleaning and sweeping and nursing the patients. They do the work that the doctors don't do anymore. In other words, those nurses and medical assistants, the people that do the hard core labor work in the hospitals, doctors' offices, and clinics throughout this nation.

I became acquainted with the medical community, including the doctors, because something happened a while back. It caused me to become extremely concerned about that area of our society. I had some very particular surgery done to me and there was an error made during that time. It concerned me deeply. It was not negligent I don't believe but it might have been or it might not have been. I'm not sure but I'll tell you this, two wrongs do not make anything right. You can't take two rights and make it wrong and you can't take two wrongs and make it right. So the medical community was a little nervous; the one that I was acquainted with at that time. I think they thought that I might sue them. But the doctors were very skeptical of me. They stayed away from me for a few days and let the nurses wait on me and serve me. They would come to the door and ask questions but they would not bother to touch me much. I understand because there are some greedy people on this earth.

However, it made me become concerned and see how interested that the nurses and nurses' aides were and how much love they had for that community, how interested they were in their jobs, how much love and care they give the patients, and how neglected that community would be if they were to walk away from it. They don't get the respect and honor they need to get. They don't get that credit that the doctors get in that community but they do a great deal of the work. They are the foundation of the medical community, in my opinion. If it wasn't for them the doctors could not perform and they certainly wouldn't be able to perform in the way that they do if it were not for the nurses and nurses' aides. They wouldn't have the strength that they have if it weren't for them. They get paid such small fees compared to doctors that it has to be more than just a job for a person to ask for that kind of work knowing the salaries that they are going to draw. They have to love what they do. I don't mean every single person that works there loves what they do or that they are even dedicated to it but I find most that I have met were. They cared about what they did.

I wish that their job would be lit up more in the community. When I say lit up, I mean that they should get more recognition and attention than what they do get. The doctors should be more concerned perhaps than what they are. I know some wonderful and fantastic doctors in this city that I live in, especially in this community, Lake County. There are wonderful doctors and nurses. Sometimes we feel that if we give a certain segment of our society more credit then they will demand more out of us. I don't think that they should demand more out of it because we give them more credit but they should demand more out of us because they deserve more.

I love the medical community. The doctors and nurses have been kind and wonderful to me. I've been let down a few times but I think we all have in whatever profession we start out in. The medical communities, especially those that I call the foundation of the doctors of this nation in the medical community – it is something like the farmers. They don't know the strength that they have. I don't believe in all these unions but I believe in Godly principles and working together as a community regardless if it's the medical community or whatever community it is. I believe we owe humanity more than just what we get out of it in the financial area. I think we owe it our commitment and our loyalty. I definitely believe that the nurses and aides that serve the doctors and clinics in the communities of this nation deserve a lot more credit than what they are getting. I hope that this will push a button somewhere. I hope it will give someone some sensitivity towards theses wonderful workers.

I want to also mention the fire departments, the rescue squads that work in the fire departments, and the police departments. We deserve to talk more about their nitty-gritty, hard labor work that they don't get paid enough for. They give it out of their heart. I think our communities owe our medical community; our police and fire departments that take so many chances each day of their lives fighting for the people of this nation especially here in Painesville where I live. I know a few of the policemen. I know a few of the people that work on the emergency squads and in the fire departments. They are dedicated men and women. They love their job and they love what they do. They give everything they have in their hearts to it. They need the support of their communities. They also need the support from their supervisors, from the leaders, from the government, the governors, all the way from the President down to the lowest level. I salute you with all I have. I dedicate these comments to the medical community, the fire the police department in the emergency areas, and not only to the city that I live in but to America. God bless you. Thank you so much and I thank God that I have not had the tough breaks in life that a lot of us have had where we point our fingers at the police department and put them down. I hope that we will try to assist them in every way we possible can from this day forward. God bless you and thank you that I live in a country that I can state my opinion.

MY SIS - VERA MITCHELL
This is a wonderful day, especially when you wake up and the sun is shining and everything is bright outside. I feel like this is a magnificent time for me and you to accept

God has blessed us in a mighty way. If we could take heed to all the huge work that He does for us and sometimes ask Him what He wants us to do for Him. As a matter of fact, I don't think it should be just sometimes, I think when you do what God wants you to do then you're working for Him all the time. Foremost, you are working for yourself. I believe we are putting in a few dividends in our bank account of love and kindness. I know a lady like that. She was born and bred in the hills of Georgia. She has learned the meaning of neighbor. She has captured the holiness that allows you to meditate on those things that we need to do in life for ourselves and others. Most of all, she has understood the meaning of love.

I get the feeling sometimes that, I certainly hope I'm wrong, but I get the feeling that people feel if they express their love by telling you "I love you, you know" – that is a familiar phrase throughout the United States. It is especially true on the telephone. You hear people use that phrase continuously almost. As a matter of fact, I have had friends and relationships that call me back and say to excuse them because they didn't say they love me, you know I love you. I believe most of them that said that did love me. You've got to show more to life and mankind and the Almighty God than just words.

This lady does not show just words. As a matter of fact she has very few words to say. She is not a great talker when it comes to that type of thing. She doesn't talk about what she does. She does it rather than talks about it. I think she believes that God is her greatest source on this earth. I believe she realizes it and she certainly shows it in her actions. The elderly and the youth in her area – she works almost continuously trying to do something for them. She tries to show them the meaning of love by giving and sharing. Not long ago the church and members of her family in the community where she lives gave her an appreciation dinner. I was unable to go to that. It truly hurt me a lot. This lady is the daughter of my lady. I feel like she is my own daughter too because she gives me that respect. As matter of fact, all of this lady's children give my lady and me great respect. I honor them for that.

I want you to know that love is more than just saying I love you. This lady travels all over that city and beyond, giving and sharing. She is a great singer and piano player. She is a marvelous and fantastic lady. I wish I could see that in all of the people in this nation because then we would have a different place for our seniors. She is sneaking up on the senor side. She might not want me to say that but it's not that far away. Some day she is going to be a senior. We all are if we live long enough. The senior citizens of this nation should realize that they still owe God and mankind. We still owe humanity everything we have to give. Anything that we can give to humanity that is positive, we should take all the muscle that we have and put it to use. God bless you.

THE SHAW'S

I came here to Painesville, Ohio, in May of 1997. I went to the D&M Dry Cleaners at Painesville Shopping Center and I talked to Mr. and Mrs. Shaw. I told them about my tailoring work. Mrs. Shaw told me she had tailoring from time to time but she didn't have enough to hire an extra person. I told her I would like to work for her and I would take a chance on building up the business. She gave me an opportunity to come to work for her. I worked for her for quite a while. She didn't ask me about my qualifications. I told her that I would like to show her what I did and the kind of work that I did. She told me to go right ahead. Up until now, from time to time, she would give me a piece or two of clothing to do.

The Shaw's became my very best friends. They became like a granddaughter and grandson to me. Their son is like a grandson to me; like part of my family. They never challenged me about my background. I asked her one day why she didn't question me about not being able to read and write. Maybe it was because they were from another country and perhaps where not supposed to know English as good as I did. Once she told me that was in God's hands. He set that standard, not her. Mr. Shaw is one of the most fantastic gentlemen I have ever met. He is kind, quiet, persistent in whatever he does, and does it the very best he can. This is a man, who out of his spirit, he produces integrity and honesty. The truth to him is like a light that shines from above. Mrs. Shaw would pray in her language. I did not ask her to pray in mine. She would pray in my language sometimes and I would pray with her. She respected that. She is the most respectable and honest woman and displays her integrity by actions. Her deeds and everything she does is by action. She is one of the hardest working people I have ever known. I treat her and her husband like I do my own children. I talk to them. I slow them down. I try to tell her not to work so fast and don't push so hard. Her life is so important. Her mother who lives outside this country, from what I have heard, her life is based on that same standard; integrity, honesty and Godly beliefs.

The hopes and the dreams that have a foundation are built on that, whether it is this nation, Korea, China, Germany, France, or anywhere on earth. Hopes and dreams to have endurance and have the essence of purity are built on a foundation that is based on Godly principles. It is based on love and not that thing "I love you, you know". The only way you can know that a person loves you is by the way that they treat you. They are persistent on doing those things that are right. I know I used to go around saying, "I love you, you know". That was my favorite phrase. I think when we were courting many years ago – I think some of you seniors remember - we used to ask people what love was. I never met anybody back then that actually explained to me what love was. It was always a mystery. They would go through so many questions and things that they never came up with the true answer of love. Love is the hopes and the dreams and the power that God shows on your behalf. Love is the care that you give yourself. It is the faith that pushes Godly principles ahead of the things that you need rather than what you want. You see, love will generate the things that you need rather than just the things that you want. It gives you priorities in your life.

That is what I see in Mr. Shaw and Mrs. Shaw; pushing ahead. They have a son that is going to be a doctor pretty soon. That young man has built is hopes and dreams around love. He was able to put love patches on his patients and give them the faith that had been passed down to him through generations. I was in the hospital and he came to see me. He showed the love and expressed it in his feelings and you could see it in his body language. These are the things that we need on this earth to propel us through the rough times and rough spaces. Yes, Mr. and Mrs. Shaw. We don't have a blood relation but we have a Godly relation and they are my granddaughter and grandson through Christ. I love them as much as I love my own blood. There is nothing that they couldn't ask me to do, if I was able to do it and it was right then I would do it. Yes, you gave me and opportunity and a chance and you still pass things on to me. They call me almost daily when I was sick. Recently, when I had a bad fall down the stairs, they called me almost every day. If I don't call them, they call me to see how I am doing. That is love ladies and gentlemen. I hope that I can express it and I hope no one will get fooled like I have about love. Thank you for [listening] to this passion of hope and dreams for you and me.

PHOTOGRAPHS

Guy and his lady

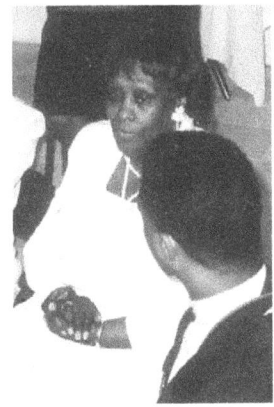
My sister, Mary

My grandson

My son, Guy Jr.

Not a well-built foundation; the house fell down but the chimneys remain

My son, Vernice

My daughter, Lovestar

Guy and his brother, Claude

MEN & WOMEN UNITED FOR HUMANITY

<u>Minutes of Meeting - February 22, 2001</u>

Mr. Darden asked everyone to take a piece of paper and write at the top of it "Time." We should be proud to have the capacity to love. Many of us hold anger inside; we must learn the true meaning of time, because many of us take time for granted. We don't have or control time; it doesn't belong to us. We need to put value on our time. Our organization needs to find the time to help others by taking the time to identify others who need our help and support. Discover a way to reach people.

The soul is the essence of an individual-feelings, pureness, and part of us only God can touch. We know about our souls; others may not. They know only what they see—their opinions, our reputations, our appearance.

We need to mirror fruit bearing trees—be able to communicate with each other, develop positive relationships with our local police, mayors, government and civic leaders. Learn to touch the lives of others. Make them care more about themselves and others. Think about what we can do for others...utilize time to help others.

We need to speak, listen, and learn. Develop our God given inspiration to help people. Use God's wisdom to help others; develop a plan....organize.

Some view the efforts of those offering help as a burden..."not going to put your guilt trip on me!" We need to learn how to touch people, to stir their emotions...bother them into looking inside themselves...self reflection-get their attention. Develop a course of self change; a bank of wisdom and strength.

First step is to give our mission to God in prayer. Be consistent as we go we grow. Trust in God-he will favor us in this we're trying to do. We must be of sound mind and spirit: God honoring-spirit. We need to get out and deliver our message by being a witness of Christ. Like David, we must consult the Lord and study success and failure. We must get together and train ourselves for this mission of God and be prepared to fulfill our duties. Mr. Darden writes his book with this in mind...do it the way the Lord would direct him through prayer. Our group should call once a week and meet every two weeks.

We must begin by working on one thing at a time; work on inside of us-conduct a self-examination; open our eyes to what needs to be done.

Time may not be available; everyday we should write time and concentrate on the meaning of time. Meditate on time. Remember everyday to write down time and examine our priorities. Time, Love, and God - concentration.

Concentrate on getting human banks full of the talents of people. Donation of time needed to cause change. Lifestyles of people today lead to problems and take away from our human abilities. We need to learn how to release our true selves through Christ. Saving sinners in a Christ-like fashion...seeing the invisible God in our daily lives; seeing him through us.

We need to begin our work by developing our ideas. Invite young people in order to talk and relate to them. Possible host a party to reach out to them and cross races. Reach them young people first and hopefully their parents will follow, and maybe we even need to write organizational by-laws. We must work together. Our group needs to be unusual; search for human resources first, money last. Time...be patient so we do it right. Set goals for our next meeting. We may be able to use local community centers and form a non-profit organization. Collect money only for the benefit of the people.

A discussion was held about the organizational name... ideas include Anonymous Men and Women for Humanity; another was Men and Women United for Humanity.

TAILORING

THE TAILORS THOUGHT

BY GUY DARDEN

We are all familiar with the forever changing styles and we are all going up and down with our weight problems.

Mr. Darden has taken a long and careful study of this annoying problem to us as consumers. He has tried to find an economical way to solve this particular problem. Mr. Darden also works with leather and suede. You can now take those old discorted garments and bring them back to the original service by having them changed to the latest styles and fashions by having Mr. Darden come out and analyze your closet.

He can now take ladies or men's one and two button coats and jackets and have them restored to three or four or maybe five buttons.

Mr. Darden has worked for some of the nations finest manufactures. Most any garment can be brought to him and restyled to the day's latest fashions. He also does major and minor alterations with ladies and men's garments.

Therefore if any man be in Christ, he is a new creature: old things are passed away; behold, all things are become new. **II Corinthians 5:17**

Proprietors: *Guy and Nancy Darden*
1059 North St
Painesville, OH 44077
(440) 352-9486

www.ingramcontent.com/pod-product-compliance
Ingram Content Group UK Ltd.
Pitfield, Milton Keynes, MK11 3LW, UK
UKHW051256180426
11947UKWH00020B/1749